Given all of this, one might suppose that we would write off children altogether and leave them to their own devices until they reach the "age of reason." But of course we do not do that, for we must willy-nilly see them as tomorrow's citizens, albeit often with dismay, and we are deeply committed to them, but our commitment all too often has a strange flavor consisting of part scorn because they must be classed with the Great Excluded, and envy because they can violate the joyless principles of the Puritan Ethic and get away with it, a crime we would all dearly love to commit.

—Natalie Babbitt

Publishers' Weekly, July 19, 1971

Cover design "Circle Game"
by Charles F. Bendzans

Children's Literature

Volume 2

Journal of The Modern Language Association Seminar
on Children's Literature and
The Children's Literature Association

Temple University Press
Philadelphia

Editorial correspondence should be addressed to:
Editors, *Children's Literature*
English Department, U–25
University of Connecticut
Storrs, Connecticut 06268

Manuscripts submitted should conform to the second edition of the Modern Language Association *Style Sheet*. An original and one copy are requested. Manuscripts should be accompanied by a stamped, self-addressed envelope.

Temple University Press, Philadelphia 19122
© 1973 by Francelia Butler. All rights reserved

Published 1973
Previously published in Storrs, Connecticut as *The Great Excluded: Children's Literature*
Printed in the United States of America

International Standard Book Number: 0-87722-080-8 cloth; 0-87722-079-4 paper
Library of Congress Catalog Card Number: 75-21550 *mc18-2585*

Second printing, 1975

CONTENTS

Reviews

THE EDITOR'S HIGH CHAIR
Children's Literature and the Humanities

Recently, a young English professor of a large university asked to teach children's literature.

"You're much too bright for that, my dear," the chairman of the department said. "Let me give you a course in modern poetry or Renaissance drama."

To many humanists (including department chairmen) in languages, philosophy, psychology, sociology, anthropology, or history, the most embarrassing literature to study is not autoeroticism or cunnilingus. On such works scholars pride themselves on their broadmindedness. What truly embarrasses them is literature for their own children—"Kiddy lit," they call it.

If a state legislature forces a chairman of an English department to add children's literature to the curriculum, he generally looks about for someone whom he regards as too incompetent to teach any other course. And male chauvinism being what it is, this someone is most often a middle-aged woman ("fair, fat, fifty, female, finished" is the phrase in academia).

Sometimes children's literature carries no credit toward a major. Seldom—virtually never—is it taught seriously on a graduate level. (For the most part it is regarded as a pragmatic teacher-training course to help future elementary school teachers and librarians learn how to deal with the kiddies.) Most colleges of liberal arts in fact refuse proposals for doctoral dissertations in the field or, in a few cases, accept them with great reluctance.

Several doctoral candidates expressed their shock at this situation at the Children's Literature Seminar of the Modern Language Association last year in New York City. One young woman with a bachelor's degree from a large Midwestern university asked the audience of some 80 college teachers of children's literature where she could go for graduate study in the field. Not one participant could honestly recommend a school.

The scorn for children's literature and for those who study it is equivalent to the scorn that black studies and women's literature encounter. The prejudice is oppressive against these three fields, both psychologically and financially, and tends to foster the lower standards that are often then used as condemnation by the established system. In children's literature there has been a tendency for pseudo-experts and commercial interests to dominate the field. Outside of specialized fields, such as library science or education, very few college teachers of children's literature actually have doctoral degrees in children's literature.

Many arguments are advanced to justify this situation. The oft-repeated one is, "Children's literature is so simple and obvious that any fool can understand it. It doesn't need study."

True, children's literature is simple, but simple literature can be often surprisingly deep and rewarding. Scholars who have examined the style and grammar of the "Infancy" stories of Jesus in St. Luke's Gospel suggest that these stories, long considered adult reading, were originally children's stories. The Psalms of David, Christ's Parables and Blake's Songs are for the adult—and for the child. The late C. S. Lewis, religious philosopher at Oxford, recognized the power of simple statement when he wrote, "A children's story is the best art form for something you have to say."

Possibly the reason behind the objection to the simplicity of children's literature is that most scholars don't know how to go about teaching something unless they can lean on intellectual crutches. For literature these crutches abound in the numerous books of exegesis and volumes of criticism of criticism. There are also complicated passages in the works being studied which afford delightful opportunities to display verbal and intellectual prowess—or at the least, excellent memories. A scholar likes to talk. Confronted by a children's book, he can't think of anything to say. The simplicity shocks, leaves him speechless.

A second objection which many academics have against children's literature is that it is not in the established curriculum. When asked why his department did not teach the subject, the chairman of the English department of one of the leading Ivy-League universities replied that it was not "traditional" enough. (He nevertheless deplored the low level at which children's literature is being taught throughout the country.) If such a scholar would get off his ars poetica long enough to think less traditionally he would recognize that children's literature has an ancient tradition in the culture if not in the curriculum, and that scholars have an obligation to study it.

A third argument advanced against teaching children's literature in the liberal arts curriculum is that no standards of criticism exist comparable to those for adult literature. Obviously, scholars who argue this way are blind to their responsibility. They are victims of their prejudice against a literature which they associate with their kindergarten teachers, their mothers, their own childhood. They are behaving like Victorian gentlemen, who, though taught at their mothers' knees, grew up to deny that their mothers were capable of voting. They regard children's literature as something to concern old hens.

Moreover, scholars in the liberal arts justify their reluctance to teach the literature of children by claiming that the job is already being done by those in education and library science. People in these schools have been meeting their responsibilities for decades. Now it's time that those in liberal arts stop dragging their academic security blankets and face the adult realities of children's literature.

Now with lowered enrollments in colleges throughout the country, and the urgent need to pay attention to student interest, scholars who have hitherto stuck their noses up at children's literature are having their noses forcibly stuck into it. One hears less frequently such wisecracks as "I'm afraid I'm not interested

9

in literature with washable covers." Something good, then, may come out of the academic recession.

—Francelia Butler

Book Review, <u>The New York Times</u>, Sunday, May 6, 1973. Reprinted by permission of The New York Times Company.

We wish to express our gratitude to William T. Moynihan, head of the English Department of the University of Connecticut, for his loyal support of the program of children's literature over a period of several years.

Our thanks to the University of Connecticut Research Foundation and its Director, Hugh Clark, whose foresight and support of humanists' study of children's literature have made them international pioneers in the field. We wish also to express our appreciation to Kenneth G. Wilson, Vice President for Academic Programs, for his encouragement.

Finally, we wish to thank Clifford Ewert, Manager of the University of Connecticut Bookstore, for making it possible to publish and disseminate critical volumes in the field.

The Editors

BACK TO POOH CORNER

Alison Lurie

> Help me if you can, I've got to get
> Back to the House at Pooh Corner . . .
> Back to the days of Christopher Robin and Pooh.
>
>   —contemporary rock lyric [1]

I was surprised when I heard these words sung to the accompaniment of elec-
tronic instruments, and also when, in the same week, I saw on the cover of Rolling Stone an advertisement of another rock group called "Edward Bear." But inquiry among my students confirms it—Pooh is still a big culture hero. He
means as much to the Now Generation as he did to us Back When.

My friends and I not only read Milne's books over and over as children; all
through high school and college we went on speaking his language, seeing people
and events in his terms. My husband lived his first term at Middlesex as Piglet,
with friends who were Pooh and Eeyore, and the school grounds and surrounding
country were remapped accordingly; at college, I knew girls who went by the
names of Tigger and Roo. Even today, occasionally, I will go back and reread a
favorite passage.

Writing about the Pooh books, on the other hand, has been awkward (if not impossible) since 1963, when Frederick C. Crews published The Pooh Perplex. It
is not often that a satirical work achieves such success that it effectively de-
stroys its object, but Crews almost managed it. He was not able to laugh into
silence any of the dozen varieties of current literary criticism he so brilliantly
parodied; but he did manage to stifle almost all critical comment on Winnie-the-
Pooh for a decade. [2] No one likes to imitate an imitation, and anyhow Crews had
said most of what could be said about Pooh in one disguise or another; his best
insights occur in the essay by "Harvey C. Window," which appears to be self-
parody. Even now, I begin this piece with some embarrassment, aware that I
am in part only following one of the suggestions for further "responsible criticism" made by Crews' "Smedley Force," a prominent member of the MLA who
was "struck by the paucity of biographical connections between Winnie-the-Pooh
and the [life] of A. A. Milne."

At first glance, Milne appears to be writing about his son, Christopher Robin,
who was six when Winnie-the-Pooh appeared in 1926, and about his son's toys.
But there are indications in the books that Milne was also thinking of his own
childhood, and the people that surrounded him in the past.

Born in 1882, Alan Arthur Milne was the youngest of three sons of John Vine
Milne, the headmaster of a small suburban London school for boys. At Henley

House the three Milne children lived a half-private, half-public life, playing and eating with their father's pupils, and joining the classes as soon as they were old enough. The world of Pooh repeats this in many respects. It is a very old-fashioned, limited society, without economic competition or professional ambition. There are no cars, planes, radios, or telephones; war, crime, and serious violence are unknown. Aggression is limited to the mildest form of practical joke, and even that generally backfires. Except for Kanga and Roo, there are no family relationships. The principal occupations of the inhabitants are eating, exploration, visiting, and sports. The greatest excitement centers around the capture of strange animals or the rescue of friends in danger; but the danger is always from natural causes; accidents, floods, storms. Apart from occasional bad weather, it is a perfectly safe world.

The setting seems to suggest pre-1900 Essex and Kent, where Milne spent his holidays as a child, rather than the milder and more thickly-settled countryside of Sussex where he lived as an adult. The landscape is fairly bare and uncultivated, consisting mostly of heath and woods and marsh. There are many pine trees, and the most common plants seem to be gorse and thistles. Rain, wind, fog, and even snow are common.

Milne claimed in his Autobiography that he did not invent most of the characters in the Pooh books, but merely took over the toys which Christopher Robin happened to possess:

> . . . their owner by constant affection had given them the twist
> in their features which denoted character. . . . They were what
> they are for anyone to see; I described rather than invented.
> Only Rabbit and Owl were my own unaided work.

Nevertheless, there seem to be some echoes from Milne's own past in the dramatis personae. Milne's father, whom he describes in his Autobiography as "the best man I have ever known," was a serious, kindly schoolmaster, devoted to all his sons, as well as to the boys whose temporary guardian he was. Yet everyone recognized that Alan was his favorite child. The same situation occurs in the books, where Winnie-the-Pooh is the undisputed favorite of Christopher Robin. As a child Milne believed that his father "knew everythere there was to know"; but in fact he was pedantic rather than wise. ("Later on . . . I formed the opinion that, even if Father knew everything, he knew most of it wrong"). In this aspect, Milne senior may appear as Owl, the pompous schoolmaster ("If anyone knows anything about anything, it's Owl who knows something about something") who turns out to be nearly illiterate.

Milne's happy childhood centered around his father. As for his mother, he remarks:

> I don't think I ever really knew her . . . I neither experienced,
> nor felt the need of, that mother-love of which one reads so much
> . . . I gave my heart to my father.

He remembers his mother chiefly as a sensible, very efficient housekeeper ("She could do everything better than the people whom so reluctantly she came to employ: cook better than the cook, dust better than the parlour-maid . . ."). Like Rabbit, she lived in a state of preoccupation with small responsibilities and bossy concern for the duties of others. It is interesting that Rabbit, the officious organizer, and Owl, the solemn pedant, the characters most like caricatures of Milne's own parents, are also the only ones he claims to have invented himself, the live animals among the toys.

Next to his father, Milne's greatest attachment as a child was to his brother Ken, sixteen months older. Ken, he writes, was "kinder, . . . more lovable, more tolerant;" but Alan was brighter and quicker, though more timid. Like Pooh and Piglet, they were inseparable, so much so that they had hardly any use for other people:

> We had two day-dreams. The first was of a life on the sea. . . .
> Our other dream . . . was, quite simply, that we should wake up
> one morning and find that everybody else in the world was dead.

Or, as Pooh puts it:

> I could spend a happy morning
>   Seeing Piglet
> And I couldn't spend a happy morning
>   Not seeing Piglet
> And it doesn't seem to matter
> If I don't see Owl or Eeyore (or any of the others)
> And I'm not going to see Owl or Eeyore (or any of the others)

Some of these others may also have real-life prototypes, either in Milne's childhood or that of his son. There is Kanga, the kind, fussy mother or nanny, with her continual "We'll see, dear," and lack of interest in anything except children and counting "how many pieces of soap there were left and the two clean spots in Tigger's feeder." Bouncy Tigger and little Roo are like many younger siblings, always pushing themselves forward in a noisy, simple-minded way, but no use in serious matters. Their arrival in the Forest, like the appearance of a younger brother or sister in early childhood, is sudden and unexplained:

> "Here—we—are—. . . And then, suddenly, we wake up one morning, and what do we find? We find a Strange Animal among us. An animal of whom we had never even heard before!"

Rabbit, Pooh, and Piglet form a plot to get rid of Roo, but as might be expected, it fails—like Tigger in the sequel, he must be accepted into the Forest.

Finally there is Eeyore, the complete pessimist ("I shouldn't be surprised if it hailed a good deal tomorrow") who is depressive with delusions of persecution where Tigger is manic with delusions of grandeur. ("Somebody must have taken it," he remarks when his tail is lost. "How Like Them.") Eeyore may date from a later period of Milne's life, the years 1906-14 when he worked on Punch.

The Editor at that time was Owen Seaman, "a strange, unlucky man," always dissatisfied and suspicious, given to blaming his errors on extraneous circumstances: upon losing a golf match, Milne relates, "he threw down his putter and said 'That settles it. I'll never play in knickerbockers again.'"

Among all these characters seen from a child's viewpoint, Pooh is the child himself. The rest have virtues and faults particular to some adults and some children; Pooh, the hero, has the virtues and faults common to all children. He is simple, natural, and affectionate. But he is also a Bear of Very Little Brain, continually falling into ludicrous errors of judgment and comprehension; he is so greedy that he eats Eeyore's birthday jar of honey on his way to deliver it. But these faults are also endearing; all of us at birth were stupid and greedy, but no less lovable for that. As Milne himself has remarked, children combine endearing natural innocence and grace with a "brutal egotism."

> "Oh, Bear!" said Christopher Robin. "How I do love you!"
> "So do I," said Pooh.

But slow though he is, Pooh always comes through in an emergency. When Roo falls into the river, everyone behaves in a typical way:

> "Look at me swimming," squeaked Roo from the middle of his pool, and was hurried down a waterfall into the next pool. . . . Everybody was doing something to help. Piglet . . . was jumping up and down and making "Oo, I say" noises; Owl was explaining that in a case of Sudden and Temporary Immersion the Important Thing was to keep the Head Above Water; Kanga was jumping along the bank, saying "Are you sure you're all right, Roo dear?" . . . Eeyore had turned round and hung his tail over the first pool into which Roo fell, and with his back to the accident was grumbling quietly to himself. . . . "Get something across the stream lower down, some of you fellows," called Rabbit.

But it is Pooh who rescues Roo, as he later rescues Piglet; it is Pooh who discovers the "North Pole."

If Pooh is the child as hero, Christopher Robin is the child as God. He is also the ideal parent. He is both creator and judge—the two divine functions shared by mortal parents. He does not participate in most of the adventures, but usually appears at the end of the chapter, sometimes descending with a machine (an umbrella, a popgun, etc.) to save the situation. In a way the positions of child and adult have been reversed—the people around Christopher Robin are merely animals and his old toys. (So Alice exclaims "Why, they're only a pack of cards!")

But the ironic view of the adult world and its pretensions is undercut by another sort of irony addressed to adults who might be reading the book aloud. These passages, which appear mostly at the beginning of Winnie-the-Pooh (there are none in the sequel) take the form of condescending conversations between the

14

author and Christopher Robin.

> "Was that me?" said Christopher Robin in an awed voice, hardly daring to believe it.
> "That was you."
> Christopher Robin said nothing, but his eyes got larger and larger, and his face got pinker and pinker.

Behind the godlike child is another and more powerful deity: A. A. Milne, who has created both Christopher Robin and Pooh.

There are other hidden messages from the author to the adult or adolescent reader. The verbal hypocrisies of greed are mocked in Tigger, those of cowardice in Piglet, and those of polite etiquette in Rabbit. The most straightforward anti-establishment remarks, however, are reserved for Eeyore:

> "Clever!" said Eeyore scornfully . . . "Education!" said Eeyore bitterly . . . "What is Learning? . . . A thing Rabbit knows!"

A similar criticism may lie behind the frequent attempts of the characters to elaborate some error or misunderstanding into a system, as with Pooh's and Piglet's hunt for the Woozle. As soon as a real fact or observation is introduced, the system collapses, and the Woozle vanishes.

Milne's language, too, contains hidden messages. He pretends not to understand long words and makes fun of people who use them. He employs a special form of punctuation, capitalizing words usually written with a small letter, as is done now only in theatrical and film publicity. But in the Pooh books the effect is reversed: Milne capitalizes to show that though the character takes something seriously, the reader need not do so. When Pooh remarks "I have been Foolish and Deluded" the words are weakened by the capital letter; to have said that Pooh was foolish and deluded would have been much stronger.

A side effect of this is to weaken words that are conventionally capitalized, and by extension the things they stand for. Milne was aware of this; in an essay on his poem "The King's Breakfast" he makes a suggestion for reading aloud the lines:

> The King asked
> The Queen and
> The Queen asked
> The Dairymaid

> Don't be afraid of saying "and" at the end of the second line; the second and third words have the same value, and you need not be alarmed because one is a royal noun and the other is only a common conjunction.

When he uses a word it means what he tells it to mean; his Bears and Expeditions are of a very special kind. He makes the rules; he determines what things and emotions will be allowed into his books and on what terms.

In the same way, when Milne came to write his Autobiography he tended to remember selectively. His own childhood appears through a kind of golden haze:

> The sun is shining, goodness and mercy are to follow me (it seems)
> for ever, . . . fifty years from now I shall still dream at times
> that I am walking up Priory Road.

As Milne himself once announced, "Art is not life, but an exaggeration of it." And an exaggerated, sentimental—and also sometimes rather condescending— tone sometimes appears in the Autobiography, especially when he speaks of his father. Describing his own departure for boarding school, he writes:

> Farewell, Papa, with your brave, shy heart and your funny little
> ways; with your humour and your wisdom and your never-failing
> goodness; . . . "Well," you will tell yourself, "it lasted until he
> was twelve; they grow up and resent our care for them, they form
> their own ideas, and think ours old-fashioned. It is natural. But
> oh, to have that little boy again, whom I used to throw up to the sky,
> his face laughing down into mine—"

This nostalgic theme recurs in the Pooh books, particularly in the final chapter of The House at Pooh Corner:

> "Pooh, when I'm—you know . . . will you come up here
> sometimes?"
> "Just Me?"
> "Yes, Pooh."
> "Will you be here too?"
> "Yes, Pooh, I will be, really. I promise I will be, Pooh."
> "That's good," said Pooh.

This is also sentimentality, but a sentimentality which rises into pathos, via the pathetic fallacy. In fact, the world of childhood and the past, our discarded toys and landscapes, will not mourn us when we leave; the regret will be felt by our own imprisoned earlier selves. Milne ascribes to his father and to Pooh the passionate regret he feels for his own lost paradise.

It is no wonder that this particular lost paradise, this small, safe, happy place where individuality and privacy are respected, should appeal to people growing up into a world of telegrams, anger, wire-tapping, war, death, and taxes—especially to those who would rather not grow up. Milne's loosely-organized society of unemployed artists and eccentrics, each quietly doing his own thing, might have a special attraction for counter-culture types. For them, Pooh Corner would be both the ideal past and the ideal future—at once the golden rural childhood they probably never knew, and the perfect commune they are always seeking.

1   Sung by Kenny Loggins on "Sittin' In" by Kenny Loggins with Jim Messina,
    Columbia Records. I am grateful to my student, Laurence Bassoff, for
    calling this album to my attention.

2   Roger Sale, with characteristic daring, was the first American to break
    this silence, in "Child Reading and Man Reading: Oz, Babar, and Pooh,"
    Children's Literature, Volume 1, 1972.

BIBLIOGRAPHY

Frederick C. Crews, The Pooh Perplex, a Freshman Casebook (New York,
    1963).

A.A. Milne, Autobiography (New York, 1939).
            Winnie-the-Pooh (New York, 1926).
            The House at Pooh Corner (New York, 1928).

AN UNPUBLISHED CHILDREN'S STORY BY GEORGE MACDONALD

Glenn Edward Sadler

There is hardly a nineteenth-century writer of fairytales and stories for children and adults who has undergone a greater eclipse of popular reputation than has George MacDonald (1824-1905), praised in 1924 by G. K. Chesterton as being "a Saint Francis of Aberdeen" and by his son Dr. Greville MacDonald as having a "spiritual genius whose art was so rare that, had he confined himself to poetry and purely imaginative story-telling, he could not have been almost forgotten." MacDonald's "fairy-tales and allegorical fantasies were epoch-making," claims his son, "in the lives of multitudes, children and parents alike, and still are widely read."[1] For all of this, MacDonald has been neglected but not entirely forgotten. At least half a dozen or so of his stories have gained free entrance into the Palace of Classics: At the Back of the North Wind, 1871 (possibly his most famous); The Princess and the Goblin, 1872, and The Princess and Curdie, 1883, which have assured his fame; The Wise Woman, 1875; and his two adult faerie romances, Phantastes, 1858, and Lilith, 1895, fairytales, parables and fantasies which are currently in print. [2] (A first edition copy of his classic collection, Dealings with the Fairies, Illustrated by Arthur Hughes, 1867, commands an extremely high price, even in worn condition.) In the midst of a revived interest in the ancient art of myth-making, and of symbolic literature, particularly folklore and fairy-tales, there is reason to believe that the general reader will be joining again the literary critic—as C. S. Lewis and W. H. Auden have done—in pursuing more of MacDonald's "working genius," his canny ability to cross successfully over the hazardous modern age barriers into Faerie and to spin wonder out of a night in the woods. "I do not write for children," insisted George MacDonald, "but for the childlike, whether of five, or fifty, or seventy-five."[3] No dictum about the intention of writing (or enjoying) books for children could be more necessary, demanding or rewarding than MacDonald's.

As a lifelong poet and novelist, MacDonald nearly exhausted his genius. Forced by financial stress and a rapidly growing family (eleven plus two adopted) to become a novelist and critic, MacDonald economically published almost everything he wrote, reissuing his stories and poems in varied forms. Meticulously he revised his lyrics and translations of Novalis, at times to the point of literal rigidity. Fairytales like the English Märchen, "The Fairy Fleet" (renamed in its longer form "The Carasoyn") or, for example, the highland romance of Second Sight, The Portent, he altered, unfortunately without an increase in power or structure.

A study of MacDonald's manuscripts, drafts and revisions reveals the painstaking care which he took with details (one can hardly read the text of Sir Gibbie because of corrections), and we see something of his mode of composition. One notes at once how MacDonald's visual and musical senses—faculties not uncommon among Scottish writers—[4] influenced and often activated him verbally, when he wrote poems as a first expression (frequently when confined to his bed during illness), poetic beginnings which later went into longer pieces or were placed in novels when he felt better. An example of this is his use of juvenile verse. Almost every reader of children's verse had read MacDonald's classic couplet "Baby"—

> Where did you come from, baby dear?
> Out of the everywhere into here—

which he embedded in <u>At the Back of the North Wind</u> as a poetic key to its meaning; thus making the tale of Diamond and Mistress North Wind a fanciful adventure into the spiritual maturation of the child or childlikeness (as he called it), rather than simply an instructional story which ends in death. Critics of MacDonald's stories have yet to fully appreciate the relationship of his poetry to his fiction in spite of their repeated comments on his "mythopoeic" imagination.

MacDonald did not ordinarily leave stories unfinished, as he did poems. His manuscripts, scattered widely throughout Britain and the United States, [5] show how frugal he really was. There survive only two short unpublished prose sketches of any consequence, both included in a sort of author's commonplace book compiled by MacDonald's son, of his father's "First-Fruits and Fragments," now at Houghton Library, Harvard. Contained in this large notebook are early poetic drafts, printer's proofs, some unfinished and obscure poems (for instance MacDonald's curious ballad fragment, "The Slave Ship," which was supposedly published in reaction to his views on slavery during his visit to America), and an additional chapter of <u>Robert Falconer</u>, largely in verse. In the notebook, the holograph, are also two stories: "The little girl that had no tongue" and "Robin Redbreast's or The Clergyman's Story," a dialogue of fowls based on the biblical story of the "tax-collector," Zacchaeus.

Of the two stories, "The little girl that had no tongue" is the best and no doubt the earlier, written nearly without revisions, and one should say, probably not intended for publication in its present form. It notably reflects, however, MacDonald's lifelong interest in the existential worth of childhood and his favorite theme, namely, forgetting one's self as the means of achieving the greater gift of knowing one's self and duty better. We find this theme, sometimes in paradoxical form, in almost every fairytale and story which MacDonald wrote: the Light Princess, for example, who has her sense of gravity restored when she surrenders herself for the life of her prince, or the Lost Princess who must learn from the Wise Woman daily submission to the task of tidying up her magical hut in the forest of trials and rewards. Like the story of <u>Sir Gibbie</u> (which is perhaps the end product of "The little girl that had no tongue"), Elsie must go down into the dungeon of self-forgetfulness before she can regain her speech. Throughout Elsie's story we discover MacDonald, the moralist and parable-maker, at work. Even a small child can understand what it means to escape from Old Ironhand, as the children do in MacDonald's well-known tale, "The Giant's

Heart," another parable of retribution, confession, and restoration.

While reading "The little girl that had no tongue," one is reminded of Mac-
Donald's gift of story-telling spontaneity, his fatherly awareness of the child's
responses. It is a tale, in fact, which could have been written for his own children, as so many were; because of its strong treatment of damnation, he may
have decided not to publish it. In type it belongs with his parable "The Castle,"
that strange tale of sibling rivalry and restored brotherhood, and with "Papa's
Story," of the Scottish child-shepherdess Nelly, who is sent on a mission to rescue her wayward brother Willie—another fine example of MacDonald's overwhelming concern for the final triumph of goodness.

But what of the harshness in it? Like most writers of parables MacDonald
wrote in the tradition of Bunyan; ugliness was as <u>real</u> to him as beauty. There
runs throughout MacDonald's (and Bunyan's) stories the allegorical paradox of
choices: encounters which result in instructions which, if obeyed, bring deep
satisfaction. This is not unusual; however, MacDonald's expression of life's
contrasts is cloaked in a reversal of joining parts—the key without a door and the
door without a key, or the little girl without a tongue and the giant without a
heart. The act of Exchange, especially when performed by a child, puts something more than doors and keys or physical organs and bodies together; MacDonald wants us to understand that giving is <u>actually</u> better than receiving. "The
little girl that had no tongue" illustrates, finally, that George MacDonald could
not have written the kind of stories which he did if he had not held strong views on
human nature and relationships. Self-insight comes not by looking for it but, as
Elsie learns, by forgetting one's own afflictions and giving to others: "She did
not know whether anyone else could find a voice as she had done, she only knew it
was when she had forgotten all about it, that it came to her."

---

1 Introduction to <u>George MacDonald and His Wife</u> (London: George Allen &
Unwin, 1924), p. 14; Foreword by Greville MacDonald, p. 1. In a recent
study of <u>George MacDonald</u> (New York: Twayne's English Authors Series,
1972), Richard H. Reis surveys MacDonald's "rediscovery."

2 <u>The Gifts of the Child Christ: Fairytales and Stories for All Ages</u>, ed. Glenn
Edward Sadler, is a centennial, complete edition of MacDonald's fairytales
and stories, in honor of his visit in 1872-73 to America. It is to be published
in two volumes in August, 1973, by W. B. Eerdmans Publishing Company,
Grand Rapids, Michigan.

3 "The Fantastic Imagination," in <u>A Dish of Orts</u>, enlarged edition (London:
Sampson Low, 1893), p. 317; reprinted in the forthcoming edition of Mac-
Donald's stories.

4 For example David Lindsay's <u>A Voyage to Arcturus</u> (1920), which belongs in
the same genre with MacDonald's <u>Phantastes</u> and <u>Lilith</u>.

[5] See the "Index to MSS Located and Consulted," in Glenn Edward Sadler, "The Cosmic Vision: A Study of the Poetry of George MacDonald," Ph. D. thesis, University of Aberdeen, 1966. Recently a correspondence between Mrs. MacDonald, her children, and Lewis Carroll has been discovered which demonstrates how vital the MacDonald-Dodgson friendship was to both writers. The full story of MacDonald's many famous friendships has yet to be told completely. (See George MacDonald and His Wife, pp. 342-346, regarding the origins of the MacDonald-Carroll friendship.)

Hirofumi Takeuchi
Kochi-shi, Japan

The little girl that had no tongue.

There was once a little girl that had no tongue — She could not speak a single word, even the shortest or simplest, — all day long she had to be silent. But she could hear wonderfully well, and she was always listening, — listening to her brothers and sisters, — listening to the winds, the brooks, the bees, the birds and the grasshoppers, and the more she listened, the more she wanted to speak. It seemed as if she was the only one in the whole world that could say nothing at all. At last when the spring days came, she said to herself "I must speak. I must find a tongue somehow". She thought if she could only hear some new grand sound, perhaps it would fill her so full, that she would be obliged to speak — So one fine morning she set out. — She listened to the sea as it plashed on the black stones, but no voice came to her; she listened to the music of the great cathedral organ, but that only made her feel more and more how very dumb she was, and she ran away from it as fast as she could go. She never looked about till she found herself in a great forest, trees were all around, & everything was still and quiet, not a footstep to be heard. She did not know where she was going but still she went on. The paths were narrow, the sky which had been blue, became grey and cloudy, the trees were thicker and instead of oaks and beeches, firs and yews lifted up their dark branches. Stones and weeds ran across the path, once she almost trod on a hare, that slipt into a long tuft of grass, flat toads sometimes crawled into a wet ditch, and blind worms crept under the hollow trees — There were a good many smoothly folded leaves of the deadly night-shade, but no flowers. Thrushes and swallows did not seem to live there, only great black nests were in the fir branches, the sun had gone in, the wind sighed, rooks cawed, and sometimes a raven flew by —

Dark grey walls now came through the bushes, there she saw before her — a long, lofty square building — It had small grated windows, iron doors and broken chimneys. She could not tell a-why, but she felt frightened as she looked at it — She came close, — under the shadow of the moss-grown wall, she saw an iron grating; she looked down; two or three of the rails were broken away, and underneath was a dungeon — a dungeon full of men, women — boys, girls and children. Every one was bound down to the damp vaults with strong ropes or rusty iron chains. She could see what red blood shot eyes they had. What pale hungry faces, and what raw ugly wounds they

THE LITTLE GIRL THAT HAD NO TONGUE *

There was once a little girl that had no tongue—She could not speak a single word, even the shortest or simplest, —all day long she had to be silent. But she could hear wonderfully well, and she was always listening, —listening to her brothers and sisters, —listening to the wind, the brooks, the bees, the birds and the grasshoppers, and the more she listened, the more she wanted to speak. It seemed as if she were the only one in the whole world that could say nothing at all. At last when the spring days came, she said to herself "I <u>must</u> speak, I <u>must</u> find a tongue somehow"—She thought if she could only hear some new grand sound, perhaps it would fill her so full, that she would be obliged to speak—So one fine morning she set out. —She listened to the sea as it plashed on the black stones, but no voice came to her. —She listened to the music of the great cathedral organ, but that only made her feel more and more how very dumb she was, and she ran away from it as fast as she could go. She never looked about, till she found herself in a great forest, trees were all around, everything was still and quiet, not a footstep to be heard. —She did not know where she was going, but still she went on—The path grew narrow, the sky which had been blue, became grey and cloudy. The trees were thicker, and instead of oaks and beeches, firs and yews lifted up their dark branches—Stoats and weasles ran across the path; once, Elsie almost trod on a viper, that slipt into a long tuft of grass, flat toads sometimes crawled into a wet ditch, and blind worms crept under the hollow trees—There were a good many smoothly-folded leaves of the deadly nightshade, but no flowers. Thrushes and swallows did not seem to live there, only great black nests were in the fir-branches, the sun had gone in, the wind sighed, rooks cawed, and sometimes a raven flew by—

Dark grey walls now came through the trees. Elsie saw before her a long, lofty square building—It had small grated windows, iron doors, and broken chimneys. She could not tell why, but she felt frightened as she looked at it— She came closer—under the shadow of the moss-grown wall, she saw an iron grating; she looked down, —two or three of the rails were broken away—and underneath was a dungeon, —a dungeon full of men, women, boys, girls and children. Every one was bound down to the damp earth with strong ropes or rusty iron chains—Elsie could see what red blood shot eyes they had, what pale hungry faces, and what raw ugly wounds the rusty iron had eaten into their flesh. When any one moved hand or foot, how the chains did clack and rattle! —

"What o'clock is it?" asked a hoarse voice.

---

rusty iron had eaten into their sides. When any one moved hand or foot, how the chains did clash and rattle!

"What o'clock is it?" asked a hoarse voice

"It must be the afternoon," answered another; "the shadows are getting longer and longer. It must be nearly three o'clock. Old Scarland has gone away. Oh! if we could only get out;- but we can't, we can't get out" Here so many voices took up the cry. The wind sighed in the trees, and the rooks cawed, and flapped their black wings -

Not get out! thought Elsie, not get out. They must get out. If only there were a strong person, man or woman there, or even if she had a voice. The voice that would not come, she might reach off and tell people to guide and help them out; but this she could not do. Still it was impossible to go away, she must stay there for a little longer. She thought no more now about looking for a voice, but crouched down close by the wall, to watch what would come next, and who the deliverer would be -. Surely, someone would come -. A tall bony woman now rushed through the trees, and stopped before the paling. "Aha! there you are," she cried. "It serves you quite right, and I don't pity you a bit. A nice mess you are in, the chains pinch you finely I daresay, and the ground is damp, and you don't get too much of old Scarland's bread and water. What a set of fools you are not to get out, of course you could, if you tried." She had hardly gone, when a man with a large black book in his hand, and a pale grave face came up -

"Just what I expected," he began "I always said how it would be, - you need n't think Giant Scarland will keep you where you are. He has worse dungeons than these, dungeons where you won't be able to see the sun, and chains that are twice as heavy as these. Get out, poor unhappy creatures, get out, if you can, before you are worse off than you are now -"

And there he too went away. The wind sighed more than ever, and loud the rooks did flap their black wings, and caw among the dark branches, louder and louder came the cry "we can't get out, we can't get out" Elsie could stand it no longer, there was nothing else for it, she must go down into the dungeon herself. The bars were broken, she could easily squeeze through the hole, but first of all she began to hunt about in a heap of dust and rubbish -. She rummaged there, till at last she dragged out an old iron bar, and then she pounced upon a worn out pocket knife, which inwardly must have been there a very long time before, once it had had three or four blades, now it had a leg one, and that was tarnished, jagged and blunt.- Still she thought it a great prize. And now she caught sight

"It must be the afternoon," answered another, "the shadows are getting longer and longer. It must be nearly three o'clock. Old Ironhand has gone away. Oh! if we could only get out;—but we can't, —we can't get out"—Ever so many voices took up the cry, the wind sighed in the trees, and the rooks cawed, and flapped their black wings—

Not get out! thought Elsie, —not get out, —they must get out—If only there was a strong grown-up man or woman there, or even if she had a voice, —the voice that would not come, —she might rush off and tell people to be quick and help them out; but this she couldn't do—Still it was impossible to go away, she must stay there for a little longer—She thought no more now about looking for a voice, but crouched down close by the wall, to watch what would come next, and who the deliverer would be—Surely, someone would come—A tall bony woman now rushed through the trees, and stopped before the grating. "Aha! there you are," she cried. "It serves you quite right, and I don't pity you a bit. A nice way you are in, the chains pinch you firmly I daresay, and the ground is damp, and you don't get too much of Old Ironhand's bread and water. What a set of fools you are not to get out, of course you could, if you tried"—She had hardly gone, when a man with a large black book in his hand, and a pale grave face came up—

"Just what I expected," he began—"I always said how it would be, —You needn't think Giant Ironhand will keep you where you are. He has worse dungeons than these, dungeons where you won't be able to see the sun, and chains that are twice as heavy as these. Get out, poor unhappy creatures, get out, if you can, before you are worse off than you are now"—

And then he too went away. The wind sighed more than ever, and how these rooks did flap their black wings, and caw among the dark branches. Louder and louder came the cry. "We can't get out, we can't get out"—

Elsie could stand it no longer. [There was nothing else for it, —] she must go down into the dungeon herself—The bars were broken, she could easily squeeze through the hole, but first of all she began to hunt about in a heap of dust and rubbish—She rummaged there, till at last she dragged out an old iron bar, and then she pounced upon a worn out pocket knife, which somebody must have thrown away long before. Once it had had three or four blades, now it had only one, and that was tarnished jagged and blunt. . Still she thought it a great prize. And now she caught tight hold of the grating, squeezed through, and let herself drop—She slipped on the wet ground, —in the long narrow dungeon the air felt damp, mouldy and close, and then how dark it was! she could just see, and that was all—Here, close by, was somebody doubled up into a heap, groaning terribly; there was another with tangled dark hair, and deep red scars on both arms—"Oh! dear, Oh! dear, oh! dear," cried one, "will it ever be night?"—"What good will night do?" answered a gruff voice, and then the chains clanked again.

Elsie felt ever so many blood-shot eyes fixed on her, and hoarse voices called out, "What is she here for?"—She could not answer, her heart now beat fast, she stumbled over a bruised ankle, she nearly fell over a bit of rusty chain—Just

hold of the grating, squeezed through, and let herself drop. She slipped on the wet ground
in the long narrow dungeon the air felt damp, mouldy and close, and how black it
was! she could just see, and that was all — Here, close by, was somebody doubled up in to
a heap, groaning terribly. There was another with tangled dark hair, and deep red
scars on both cheeks. "Oh! dear, Oh! dear, Oh! dear" cried one, "will it soon be night?"
"What good will night do?" answered a gruff voice, and then the chains clanked again.
Elsie felt so many bloodshot eyes fixed on her, and hoarse voices called out, "What
is she here for?" She could not answer, her heart was beating fast. she stumbled over a
bruised ankle. she nearly fell over a bit of rusty chain — just then, she heard some one say
"I would it be such a fool as to go on rubbing any more, Peter, it's no use" — "I know it
isn't" was the answer — These voices came from the end of the dungeon, Peter must be
he that boy in the corner, with light hair just like Elsie's brother Ralph's, he had
let the chain fall, and his head was resting on his hands — She took courage, went over to him
tied herself down; some link in the chain was worn very thin, and she began to hammer away
with her iron bar, still she found there were too strong for her, they wouldn't break. First
sorry second link had to join, and of the least was there, and the joins open, it might be just
possible to slip it through — Peter began to help, they pulled till their hands were sore
they pulled till they were covered with sweat, they pulled till their hands were sore
and tingling but still they pulled on — The sun was going towards the west, the owls
would begin to screech if evening came — and what if the giant should come home? —
As the rocks grew fainter and fainter, in another hour or two, the owls
one — two — three — There! There! at last it hardens that jerk had done it, Peter was free
was free indeed! —
"I'm out! I'm out!" he screamed. He jumped up, stretched his numbed arms and legs
caught hold of Elsie, iron bar and all, and squeezed her, till she cried with pain and
joy — a bit of rusty chain was still dangling at one of her feet, but that was nothing
The groaning had all stopped, every one turned round to look on, and the bruised and
the forwards, the cry went "only think, Peter is actually out—" if Elsie had to days after the
would have succeeded as well, it would have seemed quite enough. but now, she began
to think she must have another out, only any more. Presently a voice behind her said
"little girl, little girl" she turned about. there was a white hollow face with wild
staring eyes. He looked a boy a good deal older than Peter, and Elsie
"I saw it all" he said. "sorry but. dark here, very square to Peter, and I've tried
with ropes — I've been hard at work trying to undo the knots. but I think they
meant to some charm in them, they won't come undone — so for the ropes
I really it's as tough as a cable — if I only had a knife I should cut it. but there
is not such a thing in the place —
let the word knife Elsie pointed into her pocket, and drew out her prize.
Peter's eyes glistened. but no sooner had he tried it in his threads. than his
face fell again — "to the blunted old thing. I wouldn't," he grumbled. "it wouldn't
cut anything, there, take it back." But Elsie wouldn't take it back, she was trying it on the ropes already

then, she heard some one say "I wouldn't be such a fool as to go on rubbing any more, Peter it's no use"—"I know it isn't," was the answer—These voices came from the end of the dungeon. Peter must be that boy in the corner with light hair, just like Elsie's brother Ralph's, he had let the chain fall, and his head was resting on his hands—She took courage, went over to him and knelt down: some links in the chain were worn very thin, and she began to hammer away with her iron bar, —still she found them much too strong for her, they would never break. But every second link had a join, and if the link was thin, and the join open, it might be just possible to slip it through—Peter began to help, they pulled till they were red in the face, they pulled till they were covered with rust, they pulled till their hands were sore and bleeding, but still they pulled on—The sun was going towards the west, the cawing of the rooks grew fainter and fainter, in another hour or two, the owls would begin to think of coming out, —and what if the giant should come home?—On they pulled in good earnest, —one more—two—three—four—five—six—seven—eight—nine—ten—eleven—There! there! at last it had come, —that jerk had done it. Peter was free, was free indeed!—

"I'm out! I'm out!" he screamed. He jumped up, stretched his numbed arms and legs, caught hold of Elsie, iron bar and all, and squeezed her, till she cried with pain and joy—A bit of rusty chain was still dangling at one of his feet, but that was nothing—The groaning had all stopped, every one turned round to look on; and backwards and forwards, the cry went, "Only think, Peter is actually out."—If Elsie had had any idea she would have succeeded as well, it would have seemed quite enough, but now she began to think she must have another out, only one more. Presently a voice behind her said, "Little girl, little girl"—she turned about; [and] there was a white hollow face, with wild staring eyes—It be-longed to [was] a boy a good deal older than Peter who spoke—"I saw it all," he said, "every bit. Look here:—my name is Robert, and I'm tied with ropes—I've been hard at work trying to undo the knots, but I think there must be some charm in them, they won't come undone. As for the rope itself, it's as thick as a cable—if I only had a knife I could cut it, but there isn't such a thing in the place"—

At the word "knife" Elsie fumbled in her pocket, and drew out her prize—Robert's eyes glistened, but no sooner had he tried it w [against] his thumb, than his face fell again—"It's the bluntest old thing I ever saw," he grumbled, "it wouldn't cut anything. Here, take it back." But Elsie wouldn't take it back, she was trying it on the rope already. Now After great sawing, the tiniest bit in the world gave way, then They bit it with their teeth, they tore it open with their nails, and again the old blunt blade came in, and sawed it a little more. Slowly —very slowly it was beginning to loosen. You might have heard a pin drop in the dungeon, all strained their necks to look on, and there was nothing but [now the] whispers on every side [were] "Will it ever give way?" Another cut, —it was giving, —certainly it was giving. —it was giving more, —it was giving still more . . . It had given! Down fell Robert, but up he was in a trice—He shook him-self out from the broken cord, and shouted till the dungeon rang again—As for

Soon after great sawing, the tiniest bit in the world gave way, ~~and~~ They did it with their teeth, they tore it open with their nails, and again the old blunt blade ~~crackin cord~~ sawed it a little more. Slowly, very slowly it was beginning to loosen. You might have heard a pin drop in the dungeon, all strained their necks to look on, and ~~there was no~~ now the ~~word~~ a whisper on every side. "Will it soon give way!" Restless cry—it was giving,—certainly it was giving,—it was giving more,—it was giving still more...... It had given! down fell Robert—but up he got in a trice—he shook himself out from the broken cord, and shouted till the dungeon rang again—As for Peter, he capered about like a wild thing—

"Come, come." said he catching hold of Stas, "there are two of us now. let us be off while we can, or old Ironhand will be coming home, and then there will be a row"—"And you are going to leave me behind." said a miserable little voice in the corner. But the creature that it came from, was even more miserable than the voice—He was all wizened and shrivelled up just like an old, old man, and this was little Johnny, the youngest in the whole place—It would be impossible not to try and take him—So the hammering and filing began again, his chains were not strong and they were eaten with rust, they would soon give way—Before the last red gleam had faded out of the sky, they did fall rattling to the ground, while Johnny crept out trembling from head to foot; for he could hardly believe such a good thing could be true—

And now they must go indeed. Hark! there is the great watch-dog. Giant Ironhand is on his way home, and will be at the door in no time—Robert the tallest, must stand up, and let the others mount on his shoulders. there they must catch hold of the bars, and squeeze themselves through as best they can—up, Peter, up, Stas, up, little Johnny, and now Robert himself who bent his pin a tremendous pump, and they must hold out their hands and help to drag him through. A tight squeeze. A good many bruises, and it is done ~~And~~ Once out of the dungeon, there is nothing to be thought of but running soon, not through the thick part of the forest, they would only get entangled in trees, and perhaps fall into gins and traps. but out into the open country, through the fir plantation, that must be their way—There! listen to the hoofs of the giant's black horse. Old Ironhand is riding up to the castle door. he is getting down, his spurs clank on the stone steps! and how sharp the crack of his great whip sounds! He will be after them in a minute, soon the tread of the heavy boots that can take ten-league-seven steps at their one, will be heard coming closer and closer. Their hearts beat quick, hand in hand they dart along the thick pass, and scramble over the deep ditch. Peter bit of rusty chain dragging all the time in the damp earth, and how

Peter, he capered about like a wild thing—

"Come, come," said he, catching hold of Elsie, "there are two of us now—let us be off while we can, or old Ironhand will be coming home, and then there will be a row"—

"And you are going to leave us behind," said a miserable little voice in the corner. But the creature that it came from, was even more miserable than the voice—He was all wizened and shrivelled up just like an old, old man, and this was little Johnny, the youngest in the whole place—It would be impossible not to try and take him—So the hammering and filing began again, his chains were not strong, and they were eaten with rust, they would soon give way—Before the last red gleam had faded out of the sky, they did fall rattling to the ground, while Johnny crept out, trembling from head to foot; for he could hardly believe such a good thing could be true—

And now they must go indeed. Hark! there is the great watch-dog. Giant Ironhand is on his way home, and will be at the door in no time—Robert, the tallest, must stand up, and let the others mount on his shoulders, then they must catch hold of the bars, and squeeze themselves through as best they can—Up, Peter, up Elsie, up, little Johnny, and now Robert himself must give a tremendous jump, and they must hold out their hands and help to drag him through. A tight squeeze, a good many bruises, and it is done— ~~And now~~, Once out of the dungeon, there is nothing to be thought of but running—not through the thick part of the forest, they would only get entangled in trees and perhaps fall into gins and traps, but out into the open country, through the fir plantation, that must be their way—There! listen to the hoofs of the giant's black horse. Old Ironhand is riding up to the castle door, he is getting down, his spurs clank on the stone steps, and how sharp the crack of his great whip sounds!—He will be after them in a minute, soon the tread of his heavy boots that can take twenty-seven steps to their one, will be heard coming closer and closer. Their hearts beat quick, hand in hand they dart along the thick grass, and scramble over the deep ditch, Peter's bit of rusty chain dragging all the time in the damp earth, and now and then rattling against a sharp stone. On, on, on, —over roots of trees—over briars—over brambles, —over yellow gorse, —over ant hills—over bracken fern, —over tangled heath, over great rabbit holes—Hark! the castle door has shut with a loud bang, the giant smacks his whip, he scolds his servants, he whistles to his fierce wolf-dogs, he stamps on the ground, he is after them indeed. On, on, on, up the hill, out of the plantation, over the ploughed field. There! Peter is down, ~~he has caught~~ his rusty chain [has caught] on one of the deep furrows. Up, again, Peter, run for your life, ~~catch~~ [take] hold of Elsie's hand, never mind the rusty iron, never mind your trembling knees or your panting breath. If you stop for an instant, the giant will have his grip on you. He is coming nearer, and how the wolf-dogs bark! Over the hedge, jump the ditch the thorns are sharp, but once beyond the dip of the hill, once through the sparkling water, and you are safe, and can snap your fingers at any giant. How the great boughs crash, as Ironhand knocks his head against them! What a heavy tread he plants on the damp earth, and then rattling against a sharp stone. On, on, on, over roots of trees, over briars, over brambles, over yellow gorse; over ant hills, over bracken ferns, over tangled heath, over great rabbit holes — Hark! the castle door has shut with a loud bang, the giant smacks his whip, he scolds his servants, he whistles to his fierce wolf-dogs, he stamps on the ground, he is after them indeed. On, on, on, up the hill, out of the plantation, over the ploughed field. There! Peter is down, he has caught his rusty chain in one of the deep furrows. Up again, Peter, run for your life, catch hold of Blair's hand, never mind the rusty iron, never mind your trembling knees, or your panting breath. If you stop for an instant, the giant will have his prisoner, you. He is coming nearer, and how the wolf-dogs bark! Over the hedge jumps the children, the stones are sharp, but see beyond the dip of the hill, see through the sparkling water, and you are safe, and can snap fingers fingers at any giant.

Hark the great boughs crash, as Ironhand breaks his head against them. What a heavy tread he plants on the damp earth, and now it is coming nearer and nearer, the ground shakes under it, they feel his breath blow like a cold wind on their cheeks — it stirs their hair — his big head almost clutches their shoulders, but they are screaming down the bank, they are in the water, it is nearly up to their necks, they have enough to do to keep little Johnny's chin above it, but the middle is reached at last, the worst is over, they are getting near the opposite bank, they clutch hold of great branches of willow wood, and up with them the slippery bank is climbed, they are safe! — Giant Ironhand must go home without them. He shakes his big head with its long matted red hair, he doubles up his great fist as much as to say "I would if I could," and then he stamps frowning away. They don't care a straw for him now. They are panting, they are ragged, they are muddy, they are bleeding, but they are free. — Hurrah! — and Pete Robert, and little Johnny throw up their tattered caps and cry Hurrah! with all their might —

Now it was very strange that whoever went through those waters, which were known in that country by the name of Peace, always had a wish to sing. It was more perhaps than a wish, people felt that sing they must and should. So the three boys all began to think of singing. They had known many songs once, but some they had forgotten, and since they did at last and now it is coming nearer. And nearer, the ground shakes under it, they feel his breath blow like a cold wind on their cheeks, —it stirs their hair, —his big hand almost clutches their shoulders, but, —[they are too quick for him,] they are scrambling down the bank, they are in the water [he can't touch them there]— It is nearly up to their necks, they have enough to do to keep little Johnny's chin above it, but the middle is reached at last, the worst is over, they are getting near the opposite bank, they clutch hold of great bunches of willow-weed, and up with them. The slippery bank is climbed, —they are safe!—Giant Ironhand must go home without them. He shakes his big head with its long matted red hair, he doubles up his giant fist as much as to say "I would if I could," and then he stamps frowning away. They don't care a straw for him now—They are panting, they are ragged, they are muddy, they are bleeding, but they are free, —Hurrah! —and Peter, Robert, and little Johnny throw up their tattered caps, and cry Hurrah! with all their might—

Now it was very strange that whoever went through those waters, which were known in that country by the name of Peace, always had a wish to sing. It was more perhaps than a wish, people felt that sing they must and should. So the three boys all began to think of singing. They had known many songs once, but some they had forgotten, and some they did not care for just then. What, at last, they did remember was a verse, they had heard long before on Sunday afternoons, when the sun shone warm and bright and the bells rang out for church—I daresay you all know it very well—

> "Rejoice, the Lord is King
> Your God and King adore
> Children, give thanks and sing
> And praise him Evermore.
> Lift up your hearts, lift up your Voice
> Rejoice! again I say Rejoice!"—

Whether it was gladness made their voices sweet, I can't tell, but in the silent evening air, they sounded as fresh and bright as a thrush's song—Tears of quiet joy came into Elsie's clear blue eyes—Just then, soft, and very close to her, something said "Rejoice!" It was not one of the three boys, for they were singing on in front, it was not a little tomtit that had forgotten to go to bed, or a starling that was out late at night, —no—the word was said far too plainly for that. Neither was it someone hidden behind the hedge, it was much too near and close —There it was again! "Rejoice! rejoice! rejoice!"—What could it be? and how very near it was to Elsie, it almost seemed to be in her—Why, it was in her —it was her!—

"It's me! it's me!" she cried. "I said Rejoice, —Peter, Robert, Johnny, —Listen, listen, —I said Rejoice—Elsie can speak, Elsie has found a tongue" —They turned round, —Johnny's eyes grew wider and wider—What was this about speaking and finding tongues?—They certainly had never heard the little girl say anything before, but then they [had] all thought ~~that~~ she was not quite 'canny': —not exactly like themselves. But, when they heard how she [had] gone

31

for just then. What at last, they did remember was a verse, they had heard, long before on Sunday afternoon, when the sun shone warm and bright, and the bells rang out for church — I daresay you all know it very well :—

"Rejoice, the Lord is King

Your God and King adore

Children, give thanks and sing

And praise him evermore.

Lift up your hearts, lift up your voice

Rejoice! again I say Rejoice!"—

Whether it was gladness made their voices sweet, I can't tell, but in the silent evening air, they sounded so fresh and bright, as a thrush's song — Tears of quiet joy came into Elsie's clear blue eyes — Just then, soft, and very close to her, something said "Rejoice!" It was not one of the three boys, for they were singing in front, it was not a little one till that had forgotten to go to bed, or a starling that was out late at night, — no — the word was said far too plainly for that. Neither was it some one hidden behind the hedge, it was much too near and close. Then it was again — "Rejoice! rejoice! rejoice!"— What could it be? and how very near it was to Elsie, it almost seemed to ... in her — why, it was in her — it was her!—

"It's me! it's me!" she cried. "I said Rejoice, Peter, Robert, Johnny, Elsie, listen, I said Rejoice. Elsie can speak. Elsie has found a tongue —" What was this about speaking and finding tongues? They certainly had never heard the little girl say anything before, but then they all thought that she was not quite ... — not exactly like themselves. But, when they heard how she had gone to look for a voice, and had found none, and that now, listening to Elsie singing in the quiet night air, it had come to her, they were surely as glad as she was, and all began to shout. "Elsie can speak Elsie has found a tongue —" The echo went over the still dewy fields, over the hedges where the glow worms glistened, over the leafy woods where the wind was at rest, and over the silvery waters of the river of Peace. And some of the birds raised their heads from under their wings, and gave a sleepy twitter in their dreams —

Past the city, and by the rushing seas,

to look for a voice, and had found none, and that now, listening to their singing in the quiet night air, it had come to her, they were nearly as glad as she was, and all began to shout. "Elsie can speak, Elsie has found a tongue!"—The echo went over the still dewy fields, over the hedges where the glow worms glistened, over the leafy woods where the winds were at rest, and over the silvery waters of the river of Peace. And some of the birds raised their heads from under their wings, and gave a sleepy twitter in their dreams—

Past the city, and by the rushing sea, they went, and now they came in sight of the little cottage where Elsie lived—Through the trees, the rushlights gleamed in the upstairs windows, —Everyone was going to bed—

"Who's there?" cried a voice in answer to the loud knocking.

"It's me, it's Elsie!—Father, mother, everybody, get up and come down. Only think, I can speak   I have found a tongue"—

What a great cry of joy there was then!—The bolts were unfastened, the doors were unbarred. Elsie had been given up as lost, and now that she had come back with a voice, they could not be half glad enough—Of course there was a great deal of kissing and hugging, and you may be sure the boys came in for a share—A fire was lighted, the kettle was put on, tea was laid out—Peter, Robert and little Johnny were famishing, and looked on with delight. Soon, great bunches of bread and butter began to disappear, one after another, like lightning, but that night no one ever once thought of the baker's bill—

Elsie had to tell her story a great many times—over and over again she had to say how she had stumbled on the forest, and what old Ironhand's castle was like—she did not know whether any one else could find a voice as she had done; she only knew it was when she had forgotten all about it, that it came to her.

they went, and now they came in sight of the little cottage where Elsie
lived — Through the trees, the rush-lights gleamed in the up-stairs windows, —
every one was going to bed —

"Who's there?" cried a voice in answer to her loud knocking
"It's me, it's Elsie's Father, mother, every body, get up and come down.
only think, I can speak I have found a tongue —
"What a great cry of joy there was then!. The bolts were unfastened, the
doors were unbarred. Elsie had been given up as lost, and now that she
had come back with a voice, they could not be half glad enough — Of
course there was a great deal of kissing and hugging, and you may
be sure the boys came in for a share — The fire was lighted, the kettle
was put on, tea was laid out — Peter Robert and little Johnny
were fascinating and looked on with delight. Soon great tumblers
of bread and butter began to disappear, one after another, like lightning,
but that night no one ever once thought of the baker's bill —
Elsie had to tell her story a great many times, one and one again
She had to say how she had stumbled in the forest, and what old
Ironhand's castle was like. She did not know whether any one
else could find a voice as she had done, she only knew it was
when she had forgotten all about it, that it came to her

SOPHISTICATED READING FOR CHILDREN:
THE EXPERIENCE OF THE CLASSICAL JEWISH ACADEMY

Leonard R. Mendelsohn

The boom in publishing books for children might prompt the conclusion that there is substantial and healthy interest in childhood. More likely, this abundance is but another symptom of future shock, which having invaded the nursery now threatens to lay waste the whole domain of childhood. True, there has never been a greater legion of writers catering to children, and it is also a fact that virtually any discipline, whether it be oceanography, x-ray technology, or aerodynamics, has produced its simplified summaries for introduction into the children's hour. Far from being geared to the mind of the child, as one would naturally assume, these tomes for tots are often part of a misconceived effort to speed his entrance into an adult world in which the child is presumed to be alien. Books now provide veritable primer introductions not only to technological marvels but also to social problems such as drug abuse and unwed motherhood. The appearance of such subjects in toyland is presumably supported by the rationale that early exposure to social dilemmas will facilitate a transition from childish fantasy to adult reality.

Behind these reflections of a push towards a more readily accessible maturity lies the assumption, however unconscious or concealed, that childhood is a state of incapacity. Though Chukovsky and Piaget among others have convincingly demonstrated the rigorous logic underlying the child's view of the world, and although the creative work of children has furnished numerous examples of considerable insight and understanding, the notion persists that childhood is little more than a fanciful pause prior to the serious pursuit of later years. Thus books designed for children are implicitly directed to the goal of gradually sophisticating the toddler, hopefully weaning him from his intellectual invalidity to a premature footing among matters astute.

The concern for graduated doses of sophistication in children's literature is at best unnecessary and wasteful of energies, and at worst it is acutely detrimental to children whose diet is childish books. Much adult reading material, or, more properly, reading matter principally directed to adults, is far more accommodating to the child's world than many juvenile adaptations. Children, after all, are co-occupants of the same world as the adult. Though they view the world with a different outlook, they nonetheless see it with cunning and creativity. For an author to attempt to duplicate this perspective is often as foolish as it is presumptuous. Furthermore, it is not at all necessary. The child has his own set of eyes, and he doesn't need Dr. Seuss or anyone else to induce imaginative observation. What is needed is material which might be productive to his intellect, material capable of delighting him in his present state of mind, expanding with his growth and facilitating his moods and desires. More likely than not such material is to be found in reading matter directed primarily towards adults.

Using sophisticated reading material as children's literature approximates roughly the method used by classical Jewish academies for several millennia. In these academies, every effort is made to bring together the child and the text, but there is no desire to transplant the brain of the adult into the mind of the child. On the other hand, the teacher, ideally a competent scholar in his own right, does not presume to adopt the outlook of the child. His task, simply stated, is to introduce to a child a body of essential material. The material itself is seen as possessing elasticity which will apply to his present world and which will also extend to the world of his parents and teachers. Thus with no fear of traumas brought on by sabotaged childhoods, classical Jewish academies from Babylon to Brooklyn have almost uniformly adopted as their primary texts the Pentateuch, the Prophetic writings, the Mishna and Gemora (Talmud), the Siddur (prayer book) and the <u>Shulchan Aruch</u> (Code of Jewish Law)—all works of considerable subtlety and sophistication, all unabridged, and all presented in their original languages.

These works are used both as primers and as post-Rabbinic texts, with no alteration in diction or syntax. There are no special editions for children. The text itself is the same unabridged, unselected copy whether it is to be used by beginners or savants. In the first grade of a typical yeshiva, as the classical academy is called, students begin translating passages of the Pentateuch from the Hebrew into the vernacular. They are taught to proceed word by word, without skipping difficult passages or avoiding complexities of grammar. The teacher is always present to expedite matters. The young child is encouraged to repeat the translation in his own words. Precise rendering of the words and suggestive paraphrase are both used to assure that the student grasps the meaning. The state of childhood remains intact, but the teacher has established for the child a bridge between his world and a work which will now be a prominent structure in this realm, as well as one which will serve his intellect and life style as he matures.

By the fourth grade a student has encountered, at least to some degree, all of the texts mentioned above, even some complex sections of the Gemora. He learns, for example, problems of ownership and acquisition, and the distinction between objects which have been lost and those deliberately abandoned. He discovers the necessity of definition, as in the word "scattered," which refers to a certain minimum quantity of produce strewn over a minimum area. These problems have virtually no parallel either in kind or in complexity to anything in an elementary or a high school curriculum, as they are rarely dealt with outside of law school. But the study has numerous practical applications, even for the young child. How, for example, does one decide ownership of a quarter found on the playground? Would it matter if this coin had been discovered instead in the chapel? How does someone acquire ownership of an object? How is possession legally transferred? These questions are discussed in the text of the Gemora, and they certainly have obvious relevance to the everyday world of the young student.

The same Talmudic text which presents these sophisticated legal problems will contain equally instructive and delightful tales to illustrate these important principles. All of the study is in the Aramaic original in a text which has not been simplified, adapted or abridged. Furthermore, none of the texts presented to young children are expurgated or bowdlerized. It is in fact forbidden by Jewish Law to abridge, expurgate or for that matter, even to skip over what might be considered controversial passages. Thus children even in the early primary years read unabashedly about the attempt of Potifer's wife to seduce Joseph, of the twins fathered by Judah upon a woman he thought to be a prostitute, and of the rape of Dinah by Shechem. No teacher qualified to teach in a yeshiva would ever presume to act as censor of a holy work. He must therefore address himself solely to the task of bridging whatever gaps may exist between the student's understanding and the text itself. As considerable as the pedagogical demands might be, success has long been a hallmark of yeshiva training. Jewish Law requires that all boys follow this or a similar and equally rigorous program of studies. (The training for girls is also demanding, though the curriculum differs from the course of study prescribed for boys.) But the Law makes such unilateral requirements only when the objectives are plausible. A tour of a modern yeshiva will readily suggest that the learning capacity of most children has been sorely underestimated.

Once when I wanted to demonstrate a young child's ability to deal with sophisticated material, I asked one of my sons, then six years of age, to translate from the book of Genesis for a visitor in our home. The guest would call out chapter and verse, and after a pause to locate the passage, the young boy would provide a quite accurate translation in his own words. Our amazed visitor asked if by chance he were not dealing with a bilingual edition, and if he were not stealing an occasional glance at the English. To my embarrassment, I found that I had indeed given him a volume replete with a literal English rendition of each line. I began offering assurance that the boy was not using any crutch, but was in fact reading only the Hebrew original. Groping for a quick proof of my contention, I asked Steven to look at the English text and read it to me. Obediently, he focused his attention on the other side of the page, stumbled pathetically over the phonics, and with a grimace exclaimed, "I can't."

Here is a situation which is not at all uncommon among yeshiva students: children who can paraphrase the book of Genesis, provide an account of creation ex nihilo, detail properties of seed bearing plants and grasp such concepts as a vacuum, yet cannot understand the same material in their mother tongue. These same children are pursuing the secular curriculum required by state law, and standardized tests show that their achievement is at the very least equal to their counterparts in the public school system. Unless there is something radically unfair about the comparison I have made, the implications are clear. Secular programs, even those of the more enlightened school districts, such as the one I live in, are not keeping pace either with the concepts or the language skills which are being taught in the Jewish academies, taught it may be added in a foreign tongue. Part of the cause for this lag could be the fact that the secular curriculum deals with literature adapted for children. The public school system employs various elementary reading series which for all their claims to linguistic and literary advancement really amount to little more than updated Dick and Jane. Reading programs which progress from one adaptation to another are seriously restricting if not retarding the intellectual growth of school children, and, quite ironically, for all their basic simplicity, they consign a child to precisely the category that the author has determined he should be in. Instead of meeting the young child on his level, whatever that may imply, such readers in fact impose a level as they try to hustle the student on his way to adult concerns.

An adaptation for children is the pedagogical equivalent of planned obsolescence. In a series of readers a child soon learns that his goal is to outgrow what he is reading. Every moment he lingers over his present volume is evidence of retardation. If he were proficient would he not be finished and addressing himself to a more difficult task? In a yeshiva a first grader learns that the lines he is studying always have new possibilities. He need not dispense with his present assignment, as the mere fact that he is reciting any part of the text is merit enough. Intellectual progress is of course applauded and encouraged, but it is quite secondary to the feat of busying oneself with a work which will ever expand with the individual.

While it would be misleading to imply that every first grader could grasp the meaning of every line of Genesis even in a superficial sense, every student does learn that each line has extended possibilities. He has heard his teacher explain the verses in a simple manner. He has heard him derive significant concepts from these verses. He has heard him elucidate a line with intriguing tales from the Midrash. He sees the commentary of Rashi prominently displayed at the bottom of the page of the very text he is reading.. Even though the student is not yet capable of referring to Rashi (this study generally begins in the second grade), he sees the commentary with his own eyes and he knows that it explains what he is reading. He knows that his teacher frequently consults this commentary and incorporates it in his explanation to the class. "Zugt Rashi," i. e. Rashi says, is perhaps the most familiar phrase in yeshiva terminology. The mere presence of this commentary is visual evidence that there is more to be learned, even on the same page he has continually studied. Instead of learning becoming a perpetual exercise in replacement, relegating used-up readings to a scrap heap of outgrown garments, as is so often the case in the public school system, yeshiva students acquire a reverence for the text which is in front of them, and also for the learning process which has joined them to it.

It is of immeasurable benefit to be dealing with a text which will yield further fruits with additional endeavours. Certainly it is less likely that a bright child will be misled into thinking that he has thoroughly mastered material when he sees that his teachers are still continually pouring over the identical lines which he is learning. No such claim to universal applicability could be made for even the best of first grade reading matter now available in the secular curricula. The readers are of only pedagogical interest to adults. I know of no parent who would open a primer today with any intention other than to discover what his child is reading or to gauge the direction of contemporary education. The texts of the first grader in the yeshiva, on the other hand, are the identical readings explored daily by his parents and teachers. As a result of this perpetual and subtle set of reminders of the infinite depth and potential of the subject matter he is pursuing, the phrases "I have read" or "I have already learned" are never used, since finality is neither possible nor desirable.

Study is an ongoing process. The objective is to be continually involved with the text, not to outgrow it, because the material can never be fully mastered. Development of skills means what the student will be able to comprehend more of the levels of the text, but he will do so with the same volume in front of him as the one he began with.

There is perhaps no more impressive ceremony than that of the mandatory feast which transpires when a class (or an individual) reaches the last page of any book of the Talmud. On this occasion the students recite a prayer formulated many centuries ago. It is called after its first word, "Hadran," which simply translated would read "we'll be back." The Pentateuch does not require even this assurance, as a section of it, with Rashi's commentary, is necessary reading for each day of the week, not only for the inquiring youth, but for the centenarian as well. It is to be completed each year and then repeated. A first grader cannot of course maintain this pace, but it is soon apparent to him that the purpose of his education is to be able to participate in this cycle. He will be able to do so as soon as he acquires certain basic skills—regardless of the level of his understanding.

Only a work which has not been trimmed of its suggestiveness can grow with the child. Even Dr. Seuss will soon cloy and be seen for what it is, a deadend excursion into a fantasy which actually inhibits rather than incites the imagination.

Despite the fact that the yeshiva is a special environment, there are a number of lessons from the classical Jewish schools which may be applied with profit to the contemporary school system. The first lesson is that the material should be a well chosen classic in its original language or in a faithful translation. This work should of course be one which is within the plausible grasp of the child, i.e. don't try Dubliners or Paradise Lost in the second grade, but the Aeneid might be possible. A second lesson is that every effort should be made to relate to the work itself and not to reduce it to a simplified formula. A third lesson says that a child should experience the suggestiveness of the material. A fourth would state that the student should not be made to feel that he has failed if he does not fully comprehend the material, since the fact of the matter is that good material cannot be fully mastered, neither by the student nor by the teacher.

MEDIEVAL SONGS OF INNOCENCE AND EXPERIENCE:
THE ADULT WRITER AND LITERATURE FOR CHILDREN

Bennett A. Brockman

> "Sing nou, moder," seide that child,
> "Wat me sal be-falle
> Here after wan i cum to eld—
> So don modres alle." [1]

—from a commonplace book of 1372

The medieval no less than the modern age assumes the child's innocence—his lack of experience in the adult world—and attempts to prepare him for entering that world by explaining its modes of operation and the rationale or the myths which underlie or account for them. The adult effort, and the felt need which prompts it, is vividly indicated by one modern child's book which explains that death—perhaps the fact most difficult for the child to come to terms with—is simply a part of the natural scheme of things: "After burial a body, which is composed of nearly three-quarters water, soon changes. The soft tissues break down and disappear first. Within a year only bones are left." [2] Put into its place in the clinical context of a twentieth-century scientific outlook, death is supposed to become comprehensible and hence less terrifying. The medieval poem quoted above reflects the same basic assumption, which all ages have perhaps held: that the adult must initiate the child into an understanding of the world they both must inhabit.

But the striking thing, as students of children's literature have noted before, is that only in relatively recent times has there been a separate literature for children designed to introduce them to their world. Before the seventeenth century adults and children shared the same literature (a condition we are perhaps approaching again, for good or ill, in the television programs which both adults and children watch). Curiously, it may be that medieval children gained from their exposure to "adult" literature what modern children fail to gain from much literature designed exclusively for their use: an account of "the way things are." The modern children's book frequently conceives of its mission in just those terms. But ironically, because modern children's books generally are designed exclusively for children, they can fulfill that mission only in very limited ways.

A central reason for the limited success of the modern children's book is suggested by some of the earliest English and American children's literature, which used the fear of death and damnation to encourage apprentices and other children to attend Sunday school—to get them out of shipyards and factories where they might damage property. Just as crudely manipulative as these relatively modern stories are the fifteenth-century stories which the Knight of La Tour-Landry compiled for the edification of his daughters. It seems in fact that when societies separate children's from adult literature they do so primarily to use the child's book as an instrument to mold his behavior. [3] Twentieth-century children's books are less likely to employ threats to shape behavior (not many tales of fierce bad rabbits are written), but instead hold out rewards for proper conduct. In Nine Rabbits and Another, a fairly typical example, sharing a cramped room with an apparently derelict rabbit yields a handsome profit: the derelict turns out to be the Easter bunny, who leaves his benefactors Easter baskets filled with candy. [4]

The problem is not simply that children's literature, when separated from adult literature, tends to be didactic. The real question concerns the nature of the didacticism—the substance of the educative content of a work. A separate literature for children presents its points so narrowly that it betrays its proper mission. Children's books convey useful information, indulge the imagination, delight the senses, and inculcate socially acceptable behavior. These services are vital parts of the child's maturation. But they fail to provide—in ways satisfying to an adult or to a perceptive child—the deep accounting for human experience which the adolescent especially needs.

Like modern children's literature, the great body of medieval literature is notoriously didactic. There are in fact medieval tales which parallel Nine Rabbits. The Good Samaritans therein usually discover they have entertained angels unaware, or they find treasure laid up for them in heaven because of their charity. Most societies have folk stories which depict rewards bestowed for behavior the society considers meritorious. But the medieval child was not restricted to such fare, since the children's literature of the age was also adult literature. These works are not didactic in quite so simple a way as separate children's literature tends to be.

Unlike so many modern works written for children only, these works were not limited to one simple lesson—or even one difficult lesson—in getting along, in understanding one another, or in knowing what makes things go. The medieval work participates in the vast myth of the Christian Middle Ages, and the reality it tacitly explains to mature reader and novice alike is that reality, in all its complexity. It is educative in this larger, deeper way. The myth underlies the work, inheres in the work, and provides the context in which the work has meaning. But the best of those works, the only ones capable of being held up as models, are not designed simply to prove a point. In this they are similar to much folk literature—which adults and children alike have known, at least until relatively recent times. Modern literature for children has no widely shared, all-explaining myth to draw upon. And it tends to present what truths it has in over-simple ways which a knowing adult—or child—would reject. Precisely because the medieval works cannot be reduced to pat formulas, they have merited continued study. In explaining—as fully as that society could—what it means to be human, they far surpass most modern children's books. Still, the fact remains that as nearly as we can tell these works were accessible to children as well as adults in the Middle Ages.

In spite of the fact that much of the modern world no longer accepts the medieval Christian myth as a sufficient accounting for our experience, we may find a point of contact between our world and that of the Middle Ages in the emphasis both place on the importance of human experience and on the value of being human. The humanistic outlooks of the two ages are especially close in their sentimental reverence for the child's innocence, and the modern and the medieval meet on common ground in works which show the innocent child coming into contact with harsh reality—the archetypal adolescent experience central to much modern literature. From the great number of medieval works dealing with children I have selected but three poems which treat in especially telling ways the theme of innocence encountering the reality of the adult world. We can assume that medieval children heard or read these poems, or others like them in their complexity and unflinching presentation of some brutal aspects of life. The kinds of assumptions which these works thus reflect may in at least some ways be instructive for writers of children's literature today.

It is convenient to begin with the Parzival of Wolfram von Eschenback (c. 1170 - c. 1220), who presents as high comedy the consequences of Parzival's mother's attempt to preserve her son's innocence of the ways of the world. Her husband the great Gahmuret slain in battle, Lady Herzeloyde withdraws to a forest refuge with her infant son and instructs her people "never to utter a word about knights. 'For if my heart's darling should find out what knights' life is, it would pain me deeply. Now use your wits and keep all knighthood from him.'" [5] Wolfram comments, with his customary good-humored irony, "She well knew how to care for her son," and proceeds to describe the comical adventure of the young Parzival when he inevitably discovers knighthood and, untrained in courtoisie, sets out to become a knight.

The didactic point, and the method by which it is presented, is shared by any number of modern books for children: the misadventures of the hero point out the need for certain civil graces. Children will discover the realities their parents would prefer to shield them from; children should thus be taught what to expect, and so enabled to cope more adequately. But the implications of Parzival extend further. A more meaningful point, that courtoisie is not simply a system of rules to be followed, appears in tragic seriousness when Parzival follows some newly learned rules of conduct without understanding the humane reasons underlying them. In naive unconcern he does not notice the suffering of the host of the Grail Castle and thus fails to ask the compassionate question which would have freed the host from his agony (Book V). He had been taught not to ask many questions, so "for courtesy's sake" he remained silent. He adheres to the rule in ignorance of the deeper ethical demands of pity—the compassionate awareness of the frailty of the human state which is basic to modern no less than medieval etiquette.

Parzival goes on to learn humility as well as compassion. His education is finally complete when, with the aid of a hermit, he becomes not only the strong-

est knight but now, understanding religion, the wisest as well. He is then allowed to achieve the Grail, which symbolizes his accomplishment. He has become
the perfect knight by embodying the highest qualities appropriate to the cloister
as well as to the court and the battlefield. "What knights' life is"—what man's
life at best can be—is the theme which Wolfram explores with genius.

In its profound meaning, to which my summary hardly does justice, Parzival
leaves far behind the modern and medieval didactic literature which it otherwise
resembles. The child exposed to Parzival would be in the presence of "the pro-
foundest work of the literature of the German Middle Ages—indeed, with the exception of Faust, of German literature altogether." [6] The plot, a first-rate adventure story, would hardly bore the child. More important, the tale, though
accessible to children, presents an adult reality with rich complexity and deep
meaning. The artist's selectivity necessarily operates to "point" the work, to
give it meaning; and it thus becomes more comprehensible, more educative, than
gross experience unselectively recorded. The artifact does facilitate the child's
entrance into the adult world. But because this work apprehends more fully the
meaning of the adult world—indeed because its meaning is not reducible to a pat
didactic formula, it "explains" the environment the child must come to understand
in a way most modern "children's books" cannot remotely approach.

The works of Chaucer (c. 1340-1400) reveal a tension similar to that of Parzival: the urge for unknowing, for preserving an innocent unawareness, in conflict with the need for a knowledge of evil necessary to combat that defining in-
gredient of the adult world. Chaucer's interest in children is attested by his
Treatise on the Astrolabe, written to instruct "lyte Lowys . . . my litel sone,"
in one adult skill. He designed it to be intelligible "to thy tendir age of ten
yeer," and he wrote it in English since little Lewis had "Latin . . . yit but
small." [7] A long digression in his "Physician's Tale" admonishes parents and
governesses to exercise proper diligence in instructing children in virtue, for
the greatest treachery is to betray innocence (Works, p. 145f). His Prioress's
account of the murder of the "wydwes sone, A lytel clergeon, seven yeer of age"
(Works, p. 161) strikes emphatically the note of childhood innocence betrayed by
an alien corruption. (That tale calls to mind a number of analogous miracles of
the Virgin in which children's innocence plays central roles in dramatic and
symbolic opposition to virulently evil adult realities. [8])

But it is Chaucer's description of the children of Ugolino, Count of Pisa, in
the "Monk's Tale" which brings home forcefully another aspect of the medieval
depiction of childish innocence confronting the corrupt reality of the adult world.
Wolfram (following Chrétien de Troyes) makes his Parzival achingly ignorant as
a result of Herzeloyde's obsessive desire that Parzival be shielded from the
chivalric warfare which took the lives of her husband and other sons. Chaucer
makes Ugolino's sons quite knowledgeable but asserts their childishness in their
incomprehension.

Dante tells the story of Ugolino and his four young sons in canto thirty-three
of the Inferno, where Dante encounters Ugolino gnawing the head of Archbishop

Ruggieri, who had double-crossed Ugolino and starved him and his four sons to death. Chaucer, as he acknowledges, takes this most memorable of the Monk's tales from him. But his changes in Dante's account (presuming that no intermediate source figured in Chaucer's version) interest us presently, for they point out vividly the strange paradox of children in medieval (and indeed, if Shakespeare is any indicator, in Renaissance) literature: these children are knowledgeable beyond their years, but their knowledge is untainted by the recognition that evil exists and is implied by the events befalling them. Theirs is an amoral virtue, a cloistered knowledge, which by its very witlessness puts the considered evil of the adult world in appalling perspective.

It is significant that Chaucer, while changing Dante's four children to three, specifies their ages. Dante implies their tender years (actually two of the youths were Ugolino's grandsons, and all were old enough to be involved in the conspiracy which resulted in their death). [9] But Chaucer reports that the eldest was scarcely five years of age and that another was three (Works, p. 194). Chaucer is honing to a finer point—perhaps making cloyingly sentimental—an emotional appeal that was central but implicit in Dante's account. So it is that in carrying over from Dante the dramatic report of Ugolino's abrupt realization that they were to be starved to death Chaucer alters the reaction of Ugolino and the children to focus upon their unsuspecting innocence and Ugolino's bitter understanding. Dante reports that Ugolino did not weep, but that his expression betrayed him, so that the children wept and the youngest cried, "What ails you, Father, you look so strange?" Chaucer has Ugolino weep, prompting the three-year-old's question:

> His yonge sone, that thre yeer was of age,
> Unto hym seyde, "Fader, why do ye wepe?
> Whanne wol the gayler bryngen oure potage?
> Is ther no morsel breed that ye do kepe?
> I am so hungry that I may nat slepe.
> Now wolde God that I myghte slepen evere!
> Thanne sholde nat hunger in my wombe crepe;
> Ther is no thyng, save breed, that me were levere." [10]

Dante, when he reports the death of the eldest child, crying, "Father, why don't you help me?" echoes like Chaucer the parable of Jesus which demands,

> What man is there of you, whom if his son ask bread will he
> give him a stone? Or if he ask a fish, will he give him a serpent?

> (Matthew 7. 9-10)

But Chaucer characteristically prolongs the moment and heightens its pathos by dwelling on the child's innocent expectation.

More typical, one feels, of the medieval regard for the child's witless knowledge is the account of Ugolino's waxing grief. Except in the complaint against fortune and in making the death of one of the children the specific motive for Ugolino's frantic gesture, Chaucer closely follows Dante:

Thus day by day this child began to crye,
Til in his fadres barm adoun it lay,
And seyde, "Farewel, fader, I moot dye!"
And kiste his fader, and dyde the same day.
And whan the woful fader deed it say,
For wo his armes two he gan to byte,
And seyde, "Allas, Fortune, and weylaway!
Thy false wheel my wo al may I wyte." [11]

The following stanza reveals the medieval tendency to grant the child precocious knowledge but not adult discernment or adult emotions which derive from the understanding, basically, of human mortality:

His children wende that it for hunger was
That he his armes gnow, and nat for wo,
And seyde, "Fader, do nat so, allas!
But rather ete the flessh upon us two.
Oure flessh thou yaf us, take oure flessh us fro,
And ete ynogh,"—right thus they to hym seyde,
And after that, withinne a day or two,
They leyde hem in his lappe adoun and deyde. [12]

No doubt a horrifying story for children; but equally without doubt a graphic indication of the "cruel world." The story is thus instructive, and its lesson is memorable. But here too, just as in the story of Parzival, there is more than one lesson to be learned. Most basically there is the dramatic lesson of man's inhumanity to man. But in its deeper meanings the story, in a characteristically medieval way, relates the fictional experience to the myths which the age understood to provide meaning for its actual experience. Blaming his misery on the capricious turning of Fortune's Wheel, Ugolino adduces a mythic explanation of suffering which some medieval people—including Chaucer's Monk himself—must have found sufficient. Children or adults in the audience could likewise consider that explanation sufficient. But the really admirable aspect of the "Monk's Tale" as children's literature is that, like Parzival, its meaning "grows" with the maturation or the sophistication of the audience. Perceived more deeply, the tale criticizes the Monk's shallow philosophy of capricious Fortune and suggests that human experience is more adequately accounted for by the notion of Providence, as the philosopher Boethius had explained in his Consolation of Philosophy in A.D. 524: what appear to be the accidents of chance or the whims of Fortune must be understood as part of the benevolent Providential design.

We turn now to some lyric poems from which the profound implications of Wolfram and Chaucer are absent. Their lyric beauty aside, they are of present interest partly because they validate the preceding assumptions about the medieval conception of one role of its literature in the education of its children: as the fourteenth-century lyric quoted at the outset of this piece makes clear, mothers sing—or read poems or romances or any non-whimsical, simply entertaining literature—to their children to tell them what is in store for them when they grow up.

45

Describing the Virgin Mary rocking her child to sleep, the poem from which my prefatory stanza is taken moreover puts the innocence-experience theme in a perspective unfamiliar to modern audiences. We expect children to be innocent, and, having read about Ugolino's and Macduff's children, we are not surprised to encounter their precocious knowledge. Nor are we surprised to encounter perfect Innocence in the Christ-child, the man without sin. But as the poem develops it becomes apparent that the knowledge of the infant Jesus is perfect too. He fills his mother in on what is in store for them both: "Mother, I shall sing and teach you what suffering will befall me while I am here."[13] The poem does not become pathetic, however, because it puts the suffering of Christ and Mary explicitly into the framework of the informing Christian myth, explaining Adam's fall and the Resurrection and Last Judgment as well as the Passion and Atonement.

It is not surprising that the Middle Ages saw ordinary children as participants in this perfect innocence of the Christ child. The processional hymn of the nuns of Chester, combining a majestic Latin hymn with an ordinary lullaby—"Qui creavit celum lully lully lu"—is but one example of a host of lullabies which address the divine child in human terms. [14] Such lyrics suggest the possibility of a significant variation—addressing the human child also as Innocence which will be betrayed by the fallen world.

One lullaby of early fourteenth-century England—the earliest recorded lullaby—[15] strikes this note so bitterly that its incongruity of theme and form seems almost absurd to modern readers. The poem begins with a refrain which must have been close to conventional even when the poem was written down for the first time:

> Lollay, lollay, little child, why wepestou so sore?[16]

But instead of comforting the child with a conventional reassurance the poem's speaker immediately informs the child (in Davies' modern English rendering),

> You must needs cry—it was ordained for you of old
> to live for ever in sorrow and to sigh and mourn for ever,
> as your elders did before this, while they were alive.
> Lollay, lollay, little child, child, lollay, lullow,
> you have come into an alien world.

The verbal juxtaposition of the two poles of the familiar abstract theme—of innocence confronting a pernicious world—is startling. The effect is clearer in the Middle English original of this first stanza:

> Lollay, lollay, little child, why wepestou so sore?
> Nedes mostou wepe—it was iyarked thee yore
> Ever to lib in sorow, and sich and mourne evere,
> As thine eldren did er this, whil hi alives were.
> Lollay, lollay, little child, child, lollay, lullow,
> Into uncuth world icommen so ertou.

46

The five additional stanzas are variations on the same theme.

The shock this poem gives modern readers is a measure of the way medieval literature confronts what a modern parent would likely want to shield the child from knowing. Just as in the story of Ugolino, the dramatically educative content of the poem is disturbingly blunt. But once again the poem is more broadly, more deeply educative: the larger myth is present and informs the poem. "Thou art a pilgrim," the poem declares twice; "look ahead"—not only to your death, the consequence of Adam's sin, but also (implied in references to the paradise which Adam forfeited) to the paradise which Christ regained for man. The poem implies its sufficiency for man and child. Davies indeed titles it "An Adult Lullaby."

Thus we see once more the medieval work introducing the child to experience in an unapologetically complete manner. The child, by grappling with the same literature his parents considered, has available to him the explanations his parents would probably have considered as complete as human limitation could fathom. What is left unexplained when the implied myth is apprehended suggests the deficiency of the myth—as the Renaissance and later ages are acutely aware—but not an artificial "educational" conspiracy between poet and parent.

It is probably no accident that C. S. Lewis, one of the greatest writers of children's books, also wrote adult fiction of stature and was one of the great critics of English literature, especially the earlier literature of the Middle Ages and Renaissance. He puts succinctly what I suspect was tacitly understood by the Middle Ages and deserves to be better understood by our own age:

> No book is really worth reading at the age of ten which is not equally (and often far more) worth reading at the age of fifty—except, of course, books of information. . . . The only imaginative works we ought to grow out of are those which it would have been better not to have read at all. [17]

Regrettably, because medieval literature is informed by the Christian myth, a world view which is alien to increasing numbers of modern children, one cannot seriously advocate that today's children read medieval literature to discover the nature of things. They would have to be taught the myth first, and unless the teacher and the pupils conceived of the myth as vital, the literature would remain simply a curiosity. It could not otherwise be read by the modern child as a necessary and sufficient account of the workings of his world. For reasons like these one is compelled to wonder whether a richly educative modern children's literature is even possible. Modern books for children can mirror the perspective of some ideology; they can present empirically verifiable facts. Perhaps the best (or worst) they can do is to present versions (or perversions) of the truths on which post-Renaissance philosophies tend to agree—varieties of humanism. E. B. White's Charlotte's Web, Swift's Gulliver's Travels, Twain's Huckleberry Finn, and Tolkien's Ring trilogy are some widely variant expressions of that basic theme which share with the medieval works an interest for both adults and children. The list could, of course, be expanded.

No one would seriously propose that the fourth-grader be closeted with <u>King Lear</u> or <u>Moby Dick</u>. But one feels—as Leonard Mendelsohn argues elsewhere in this volume—that we underestimate the ability of children to understand the literature we consider most vital to our cultural heritage. The Folger Shakespeare Library's successful involvement of inner-city high school and junior high school students in plays like Shakespeare's <u>Winter Tale</u> and Jonson's <u>Bartholomew Fair</u> has been reported recently.[18] Such reports suggest that it is not only wise but also practicable to imitate the Middle Ages: to introduce our children, even at very tender ages, to our greatest literature, and therein to our best accounts of what being human entails.

---

[1] In modern English: "Sing now, mother," said that child, "what shall befall me hereafter when I grow up—so all mothers do." Philippe Ariès, in <u>Centuries of Childhood</u>, trans. Robert Baldick (New York: Vintage Books, 1962), apparently overlooks poems like this (and the others treated in this essay) when he asserts that "in medieval society the idea of childhood did not exist" (p. 128), and that "medieval civilization failed to perceive . . . a difference and transition between the world of children and that of adults, a transition made by means of an initiation or an education" (p. 411f). His chapter "From Immodesty to Innocence" is similarly misleading because it overlooks the very real medieval notion of childhood innocence by defining innocence solely in terms of sexuality.

[2] Herbert S. Zim and Sonia Bleeker, <u>Life and Death</u> (New York: Wm. Morrow, 1970), p. 46.

[3] See the introductory survey in Bettina Hürliman, <u>Three Centuries of Children's Books in Europe</u>, trans. and ed. Brian W. Alderson (London: Oxford Univ. Press, 1967), pp. xi-xviii. See also A. S. W. Rosenbach, <u>Early American Children's Books</u> (1933; rptd. New York: Dover, 1971), introduction; and Francelia Butler, "Preface" and "Death in Children's Literature," <u>Children's Literature</u>, I(1972), 7-8, 104-124.

[4] Miriam Clark Potter, <u>Nine Rabbits and Another</u> (New York: Wonder Books, 1957).

[5] Wolfram von Eschenbach, <u>Parzival</u>, trans. Helen M. Mustard and Charles E. Passage (New York: Random House, 1961), Book III.

[6] M. O'C. Walshe, <u>Medieval German Literature</u> (Cambridge, Mass.: Harvard Univ. Press, 1962), p. 157.

[7] <u>The Works of Geoffrey Chaucer</u>, ed. F. N. Robinson, 2nd ed. (Boston: Houghton Mifflin, 1957), p. 545.

[8] See the lists s.v. <u>child</u> and <u>miracle</u> in Carleton Brown and Rossell Hope Robbins, <u>The Index of Middle English Verse</u> (New York: Columbia Univ. Press, 1943), and in Rossell Hope Robbins and John L. Cutler, <u>Supplement to the Index</u> . . . (Lexington: Univ. of Kentucky Press, 1965).

9 See the translation and notes of John Ciardi (New York: New American Library, 1954), pp. 274-281.

10 Modern English: "His young son, who was three years old, said to him, 'Father, why are you weeping? When will the jailer bring our food? Do you have any morsel of bread? I am so hungry that I cannot sleep. Would God that I might sleep forever! Then hunger should not creep in my stomach; there is nothing I had rather have, except bread.'"

11 Modern English: "Thus day by day this child began to cry, until it lay down in his father's lap and said, "Farewell, father, I must die!' And kissed his father, and died the same day. And when the woeful father saw it dead, for woe he began to bite his arms and said, 'Allas, Fortune, and weylaway! I may blame your false wheel for all my woe.'"

12 Modern English: "His children thought it was for hunger that he gnawed his arms, and not for woe. They said, 'Father, do not so, allas! But rather eat our flesh. You gave it us, take our flesh from us, and eat enough'—just so they said to him, and after that, within a day or two, they lay down in his lap and died."

13 Religious Lyrics of the Fourteenth Century, ed. Carleton Brown, 2nd ed. (New York: Oxford Univ. Press, 1957), pp. 70-75.

14 See the New Oxford History of Music, III, 117, and s.v. lullay in the Index and Supplement cited in note 6.

15 R. T. Davies, Medieval English Lyrics, A Critical Anthology (Evanston, Ill.: Northwestern Univ. Press, 1964), pp. 106f, 321.

16 Modern English: "Lollay, lollay, little child, why do you weep so sore?"

17 C. S. Lewis, "On Stories," in Essays Presented to Charles Williams (1947; rpt. Freeport, N.Y.: Books for Libraries, 1972), p. 100.

18 Nona Brown, "Learning to Love the Bard," The New York Times, Sunday, May 13, 1973, sect. E, p. 9.

PINOCCHIO AND THE PROBLEM OF CHILDREN'S LITERATURE *

Glauco Cambon

In my naughty moments I'd like to shock some of my colleagues (especially Italian) with the following baited question: Which three books have most tangibly affected the imagination of the Italian people? Leaving the Gospel aside, here is my answer: Dante's Divine Comedy, Manzoni's The Betrothed, [1] and Collodi's Pinocchio. I can see the frowns, the bewildered smiles, the sudden freezing of features, and I can hear the half-repressed outbursts ("I'd always known you for an unscholarly buffoon!" "Who in the world gave you your professorship?" etc.) In some cases, members of the Benevolent Association of Academic Patrolmen might pat me on the shoulder with a "Bravo! that's really funny! But now let's get down to serious business."

It is part of a critic's serious business to challenge hardened views and contribute to revisions of literary perspective, even by unorthodox means if need be. I cannot help reminding myself of it when I confront the still prevalent solemnity of the Italian academic scene. My immediate reason for putting literary underdog Carlo Collodi, saeculo Lorenzini, in the formidable company of his fellow Tuscan Dante Alighieri and of the half-Tuscanized Lombard, Alessandro Manzoni, is the impact he had on idiomatic speech. Just as several pithy lines of the Divine Comedy became bywords; [2] just as The Betrothed contributed proverbs like "La ragione e il torto non si dividono mai con un taglio cosi netto etc. . . " (Right and wrong cannot ever be so sharply divided . . .), class names like la Perpetua for a parson's maid, graphic similes like "i polli di Renzo" (Renzo's chickens, for a tight situation in which constrained people harass each other), just so Pinocchio has enriched the language since its first printing in 1880, as witness the fact that everybody in Italy will understand you right away if you refer to a pair of unsavory schemers with the Collodian label "il Gatto e la Volpe" (the Cat and the Fox). Nor is this the only instant reference to be gleaned from the book which earned the loving attention of a scholar like Paul Hazard. [3] Characters like Master Cherry or Master Geppetto, those lovable craftsmen, Fire-eater the puppeteer, the Talking Cricket and Lamp Wick the naughty boy have escorted Pinocchio himself into the pantheon of popular myths, where, way beyond ethnic boundaries, he enjoys the company of Alice, Red Riding Hood, Gulliver, and the Cowardly Lion.

Granting some difference in literary sophistication between Jonathan Swift, say, and Frank Baum, I see no reason to immune professional authors of children's literature in a subliterary limbo. If the intentional audience contributes

---

* One of a series of addresses on Children's Literature given at the University of Connecticut, November 27, 1972.

to the making of a work of art, and if the work itself—at least when words are its medium—can be seen as an open-ended transaction between author and audience rather than as an exclusively self-contained object, we should consider children's books as valid literature in their own right, provided the requirements of formal function (style and structure) are met. It does not follow that all successful literary works are children's literature (who would ever think of reading The Red and the Black, The Ambassadors, or Nana to an audience of children?) It also does not follow that children's books are always literature; Alice in Wonderland certainly is, and so is Pinocchio, because each handles its language in the neatest way to create a mythical configuration that appeals to imaginative readers of any age, not just to those in their nonage—though the latter were the intentional audience to begin with. By contrast, any of us can think of numberless children's books that stand to those two as the dime novel stands to The Scarlet Letter. Whether the addressee of a book is conceived as child or adult, the problem remains the same as far as enduring value is concerned: many are the called, few the elect. A related problem is the hierarchy of value within the genre; there are "minor" and "major" works, good and better poems, and Shakespeare is obviously greater than Herrick. Alice towers above Peter Pan, The Wizard of Oz probably belongs somewhere between the two, and E. B. White's Charlotte's Web, while even better than Beatrix Potter's charming Jeremiah Fisher, pales by comparison with Pinocchio.

But what about my surreptitious inclusion of Jonathan Swift's Gulliver's Travels in children's literature? The book was not written for an audience of children; on the contrary, it postulated an intentional audience of connoisseurs who could identify the deadly barbs at contemporary mores, ideas and institutions in Swift's satirical fantasy. This would be the same audience to whom The Dunciad was addressed—hardly childlike indeed. And a political and philosophical satire is the opposite of a fairytale. However, problems of literary genre being anything but metaphysical, it may help to rebound for a moment from theoretical considerations to personal experience—the experience of the eleven or twelve year old boy I was when I first read Gulliver's Travels. In utter innocence, I missed all the historical references and reacted to the fabulous surface of the story, which for me was the whole substance. Wonder and terror, vertigo and laughter; Charles Perrault or the brothers Grimm could not have done it better. I was both spellbound and disturbed. I cannot honestly say that my re-reading the book as an adult erased the effects of this first exposure. Leaving aside the complicity of the Italian publishers, translator and illustrator, who conspired to present the book as just a children's story, I feel sure that my case could not have been unique, in fact many are the acquaintances who recall coming across Gulliver's Travels as a fairytale only. And I suspect that this has both social and literary significance; for Swift could hardly have managed to dupe children into believing that he had written for them if he had not also written for them in a way. He could not retain his hold on the child in me if he had not himself become a child in the act of telling his story, namely, if he had not, while playing the satirical game, let himself go to the magic and wonder which were supposed to serve as mere narrative tools and somehow took on a larger and larger function within his verbal universe. Would he be the great writer we know if he hadn't allowed the imagination to outgrow the ancillary task he had planned for it vis-à-vis reason? Good old Enlightenment man that he was, he came to include children in his originally adult intentional audience, and the results justify this transgression of purpose and genre. A reverse transgression, with equally felicitous consequences, was committed by Rev. Dodgson when, under the mask of Lewis Carroll, he wove pointed topical references, many satirical, in the charmed fabric of his Alice books, which he notoriously conceived and wrote for children; we now have The Annotated Alice to prove it. [4] Collodi's deft winks at a growing or grownup audience point the same way, [5] and it may even happen that some sophisticated readers smell social or political allegory in Pinocchio. At the moment, the scent fails to alert my nostrils; I am fascinated, instead, by the spectacle of Carlo Lorenzini becoming Collodi, or Charles Dodgson becoming Carroll, in a ritual of impersonation that sets the stage for their magical act: the recovery of an ancestral mythical mode of communication suitable to the children they purposely chose as privileged audience. If you don't become like children, you will not enter the kingdom of Heaven, namely, free imagination.

In this domain perhaps Alice reigns supreme, even over Pinocchio, having attained the kind of metaphysical shudder that many a surrealist writer was to covet decades later, and yet without ever departing from the tone of effortless simplicity that marks the work as a genuine fairytale, primarily addressed to children. Well, this hierarchy may be negotiable after all, even though Pinocchio, a notoriously chivalrous marionette, would not mind taking a back seat to Alice. Pinocchio's wonderland markedly differs from Alice's, despite some overlapping. Hers is a dreamland where every law of time, space, and logic is or can be put in abeyance; Pinocchio inhabits a concrete world where identity resists metamorphosis, actions have measurable consequences, and reality incorporates magic. Carroll's fable dissolves the known world into phantasmagoria, while Collodi's points the way, via magic, to the reliability of existence. In an ideal series, you could place Pinocchio midway between Alice and Tom Sawyer. If so, my earlier classification should yield to a different one which recognizes Pinocchio and the Alice fables as complementary to each other, and on the same level of artistic dignity.

In trying to vindicate the artistic legitimacy of children's literature, I have also implied that such a genre need not limit its best specimens to a kind of second class citizenship in the realm of literature. I have made this point empirically, by placing certain books in ideal contiguity across genre demarcations, and in fact it would be very hard to erect impassable barriers between the genre we have agreed to define as children's literature and whatever we may accept as serious fiction, for borderline cases like Tom Sawyer, Huckleberry Finn, Alice in Wonderland, Perrault's Contes de ma mere l'oie, the brothers Grimm's fairytales, Andersen's stories, would frustrate the attempt from one side of the divide. From the other, the peculiar case of Gulliver's Travels as discussed above would likewise undermine the barrier—and along with Swift's book, we would have to take into account such diverse works as Twain's The Mysterious Stranger, Homer's Odyssey (which shows all the traits of a great fairytale complete with ogres, witches good and bad, spells and sundry perils to be overcome on the hero's long circuitous way home), Ovid's Metamorphoses, [6] and the Italian Renaissance chivalric epics, especially Ariosto's Orlando Furioso, with Shakespeare's Midsummer Night's Dream closely following. I was forgetting Aesop, who is among Pinocchio's direct ancestors, while Midsummer Night's Dream seems to count more perceptibly in Alice's lineage.

Why, then, define a genre like children's literature if the definition falls short of absoluteness? Does it hold at all? It does, provided we avoid making it a hard-and-fast boundary line. Apparently, what we recognize as good children's literature, while written specifically for children and from a child's point of view, shares with "adult" literature certain vital elements without which no good writing can take place, and both derive these elements from a common source: the mythical fable which arose and thrived long before the invention of writing itself, and before literature became professionalized and compartmentalized along with its audience. The audience we can inferentially reconstruct for the Homeric rhapsodists who roamed preclassical Greece, the audiences of African or Amerindian folktales are both adult and childlike; they cannot be conceived as specialized. The strength of modern fairytales, Kunstmärchen like Dodgson's and Collodi's, is that they draw on the reservoir of living folklore and thereby reintegrate their audience into a lost unity. The brothers Grimm had done it as recorders, by transcribing their priceless treasury of fairytales from the voice of an old woman who did not know she was one of the last survivors of a timeless tradition once central to court and town culture, and now reduced to marginal status within an increasingly technicalized Western society. What anthropologists call folklore, what litterateurs call myth, is the source of all literature, and its pristine universality glimmers again in today's inevitably "specialized" children's literature. We owe this recognition to the Romantics and to their direct forerunner, G. B. Vico. [7]

Collodi's closeness to living folklore stands out particularly in his style, a terse Tuscan that always rings with the tone of a speaking voice. The oral quality identified by scholars in Homer's style is no less prominent (si parva licet componere magnis) in our modern Tuscan storyteller whose addresses to the reader, brief digressions, lively dialogue, and direct, fluent syntax so appropriate to an evocation of the marvelous, all contribute to narrative effectiveness. Storytelling is a folk art in the Tuscan countryside, and has been for centuries; it was the seedbed of much renowned fiction from the Middle Ages down to the ripe Renaissance, for the novella, or short story, first blossomed there with the anonymous Novellino collection of the thirteenth century to become a distinct Tuscan genre with Boccaccio and followers. Pinocchio's relentless variety of narrative incident, its alertness to social types, its tongue-in-cheek wisdom are of a piece with that illustrious tradition—less, of course, the rich erotic fare which spices up the work of Renaissance novellieri and would have been out of place in a modern book addressed to children. Collodi's Aesopian sententiousness comes through all over in the guise of numerous warnings to the reckless marionette from the magical animal friends Pinocchio repeatedly fails to heed, the Talking Cricket above all; and the proverbs the redeemed puppet quotes at his arch enemies, the Cat and the Fox, when they are finally reduced to an amply deserved abjection, are gnomic folklore of peasant extraction, of the kind you would still hear in a Tuscan village around the fireside:

> "Oh, Pinocchio," cried the Fox, "give a little charity to two old people."
> "Two old people," repeated the Cat.
> "Good-by, masqueraders," replied Pinocchio; "you deceived me once and now you are paying for it."
> "Believe us, Pinocchio, we are today truly poor and starving."
> "Truly," repeated the Cat.
> "If you are poor, you deserve it. Remember the proverb that says, 'Stolen money will never bear fruit.' Good-by, deceivers."
> "Have compassion on us."
> "On us," said the Cat.
> "Good-by. Remember the proverb that says, 'Stolen wheat always makes poor bread.'"
> "Do not abandon us."
> "No, no!" said the Cat.
> "Good-by. Remember the proverb, 'Whoever steals the cloak of his neighbor usually dies without a shirt.'"

Pinocchio had indeed been duped, robbed and nearly killed by the Cat and the Fox, and he lives in no goody-goody world. The first of the proverbs he quotes gains additional relevance from the remembered episode in his early adventures when Messrs. Cat and Fox had persuaded him to sow his four pieces of gold in the so-called Field of Wonders so they could steal them while he waited else- where for a plant bearing gold fruit to grow. Pinocchio's foolishness, a natural consequence of his childish naïveté ever ready to fall for the lure of pure wonder, has now been tempered into hard-earned wisdom. The book has to do with the education of a child, both through the traditional humanist instrument of class- room and books (which he rather resents) and through the school of hard knocks— the resistance of reality to the boundless urge for freedom and (however innocent) pleasure that keeps getting the child into trouble. When he learns that there are limits to desire, and that nothing comes for free, Pinocchio becomes an adoles- cent boy in flesh and blood and the story is over; its only conceivable sequel would be Collodi's own autobiography, describing the way he learned to live in a harsh matter-of-fact world by dint of work, wit, and imagination.

But what a delight it had been to follow Pinocchio's vagaries in his unrecon- structed phase, and how poetically providential his transgressions were! Life certainly would have been dull for him and for the readers if he had been tame from the start (not that his final condition upon learning his lesson can be really described as "tame," to be sure). How exciting it is to see him get out of scrape after scrape, whether by his own devices (there is a Huck Finn in him) or through magical assistance from the Blue-Haired Fairy, his sister and mother figure, or again thanks to the gratefulness of an animal friend (Aladdin the Dog, the Tunny Fish), or to the kind feelings of formidable Mangiafuoco, Fire-eater the puppeteer. The mixture of naïveté and shrewdness in Pinocchio's character makes him a significant type, for he has something of the waif who, though not utterly unprotected, often has to fend for himself. Waif and child of poor workers, and withal, elf-child, the changeling. He loves the sheltered life a family can provide, for he has a warm heart, yet he yearns for frequent escape from that shelter, and if he thereby gets in plenty of trouble, he also meets reality in so many forms that this alone will have been a rich education for him and for his young readers by the time he is through. The world of work, the world of crime, the world of entertainment and the world of nature alternate or fuse with the world of magic fantasy with surprising ease, thanks to Collodi's handling of his narrative strings. Pinocchio's world is a microcosm of the adult world as seen through the eyes of an enterprising child. The complexity of actual life dawns on the child's simple mind, and there is nothing wooden in that simplicity. Pinocchio is alive and kicking, and he never impresses us so much as when he recalcitrates (not just in his temporary asinine avatar) against impinging threats—whether the nocturnally disguised Cat and Fox, or the rioting schoolmates in the classroom and on the beach, or the ogre-like Green Fisherman, or the innocent worker who had bought him (when still a donkey) from the circus master for a quarter, to get his skin. Collodi's master stroke in this regard occurs in chapter XXXIV, when the marionette, after regaining his humanoid shape through the not quite selfless help of fishes which had gnawed him bare of his asinine flesh, down to the wooden bone, is swallowed by the huge Dogfish and has the following exchange with a fellow prisoner, the Tunny Fish:

> "Help! Help! Oh, dear me! Is there no one who can save me?"
> "Who wishes to be saved?" asked a voice that sounded in the darkness like a guitar out of tune.
> "Who is it that speaks like that?" asked Pinocchio, feeling himself nearly frozen with fear.
> "It is I. I am a poor Tunny Fish, who was swallowed at the same time you were. What kind of fish are you?"
> "I have nothing to do with fishes. I am a marionette."
> "Then if you are not a fish, why were you swallowed by the monster?"
> "It is all your fault. If you had not been there, I surely should have escaped. And now what can we do in this dark place?"
> "We must resign ourselves to our fate, and wait until we are digested."
> "But I do not wish to be digested," said Pinocchio, beginning to cry.

(pp. 191-192)

The Tunny Fish's philosophical reply, that it is more dignified to die under water than to soak in vinegar and oil, and Pinocchio's immediate rejection of such stoical philosophy, crown the passage with choice Collodian humor, but what I want to emphasize is the marionette's stubborn defense of his own identity and will to live, a defense which attains here comic and epic proportion as a climax to all his escapades. When caught by the Green Fisherman, Pinocchio had likewise objected to being mistaken for a fish and so devoured; when changed into an ass, he had inwardly refused the punitive metamorphosis, and this came through in his recalcitrance onstage as well as, later on, in his recovery of the marionette form through submersion and nibbling by fish. He is so irreducibly himself that, though he repeatedly refuses being eaten, he accepts for once that uncomfortable fate when it's a question of his returning to his original shape. See his description of the procedure to the obtuse and incredulous buyer of donkey-Pinocchio at the outset of Chapter XXXIV.

Pinocchio's waywardness can also take a silly turn, notably in the medicine scene (Chapter XVI), when the good Fairy tries to cure him of his disease (the mania for telling lies) and he thinks up all sorts of tricks to dodge the bitter potion. It is easy to see how vividly this scene must register on the child readership, since it presents a familiar domestic experience in terms of the marvelous. Here too Collodian humor reaches an apogee, with the trio of doctors (the Crow, the Owl, and the Cricket) two of whom utter pompous Lapalissian inanities just to contradict each other while the third one, the Cricket, manages to talk some sense and health into the devious patient by bluntly telling him off. The fun Collodi obviously had in writing this episode, or the one of the Tunny Fish, bears comparison with the fun Lewis Carroll must have had in penning so many of his, and the comparison extends to the results, which make readers share the fun. Here as there, conventional reality is parodied by a playfully logical absurdity; yet in Pinocchio's case we don't leave the shores of common sense, while Alice does. But then Alice is not a humanist fable. Pinocchio never really loses his bearings, no matter how strange and menacing the situation he encounters; Alice instead does, and this is her great dreamlike privilege, for, unlike Pinocchio, she discovers and inhabits an utterly unreliable world. Dodgson pushed his narrative experiment to a fascinating critical limit, while Collodi stuck to his solid Tuscan tradition, and it stood him in good stead. It also made allowance for a lot of imaginative capers which are the delight of any reader. Remember the Gorilla Judge who sentences Pinocchio to jail for having let himself be robbed (Chapter XIX)? And when the incautious marionette and his lazybone friend Lamp Wick, after a prolonged stay in the Country of Playthings (Chapter XXXII), begin to show symptoms of donkeymorphosis and try to conceal it from each other until the transformation becomes irrefutable, the adult reader laughs with Collodi while the very young reader shuttles between fear, wonder and amusement. If the adult has read or seen Ionesco's The Rhinoceros, he may wonder whether the French-Rumanian playwright brought it off any better than his Tuscan predecessor. I personally think Ionesco is more heavy-handed in his comparable metamorphosis scene. [9]

Classical education strengthened, instead of stifling, the vein of peasant folklore that went into the making of Pinocchio, and both account for the growing dose of horse sense with which Pinocchio ultimately confronts reality. As I said before, this is a far cry from Carroll's wonderful penchant for Nonsense. Classical hints are planted throughout the story; for instance, to name just a few salient cases, when the Green Fisherman (Chapter XXVIII) tells the captured Pinocchio that he has the privilege of choosing the way he'll be cooked, out of respect for his rare and so unfishlike gift of articulateness, the incident is a superbly handled variation on a Homeric theme from the Odyssey, where giant ogre Polyphemus grants Odysseus the privilege of being eaten last. At the outset of Chapter XXXVI, when Pinocchio is carrying his old "father" Geppetto to safety through the boundless sea, the latter's anxious scrutinizing of the horizon is conveyed by a graphic simile straight from Dante's Divine Comedy, Inf. XV, 20-21:

> "But where is the shore?" asked the old man, becoming more and
> more uneasy and straining his eyes to see it, just as tailors do when
> they thread a needle.
>
> (p. 201)

The Dantesque lines in question translate thus:

> and they sharpened their eyebrows to descry us as an old tailor does
> at the needle's eye.

Interestingly enough, a father figure in trouble (Brunette Latini) is also involved in this climactic Dantesque episode, and in fact the whole incident of Pinocchio carrying his own father to safety may remind us of Aeneas shouldering father Anchises in his flight from burning Troy (Aeneid, Book II); for in Collodi's case the analogy has overwhelming chances of being deliberate.

A marked Homeric trait in narrative technique is Pinocchio's frequent verbatim repetition of message or incident in his accounts to friends, and that is further proof of the oral tradition which nurtured both authors, distant though they may be in so many obvious respects. The Blue-Haired Fairy's unfailing assistance to Pinocchio in so many tight situations, her very animal metamorphoses or use of animal messengers, her disguises or white lies (the feigned death), are of a piece with Athena Pallas' resourceful closeness to Ulysses and his son Telemachus in the Odyssey. Like Athena Pallas, the Blue-Haired Fairy embodies benevolent wisdom. Pinocchio's decisive peripeteia, his being swallowed by the huge sea monster in whose maw he will find his lost father Geppetto and then start the long trip back to homeland and mended ways, has a Biblical counterpart in the story of prophet Jonah; yet in fairness to Collodi we should not assume here a mere feat of literary imitation, for Collodi has a truly inventive imagination that can delve into archetypes. The Blue-Haired Fairy is a motherly anima figure, Geppetto is a father figure, and the ambivalent attitude of Pinocchio to them completes the archetypal picture. It is part of Collodi's astuteness to have left the Blue-Haired Fairy in her transcendental domain, instead of materializing the happy family reunion on a terrene level at the end, just as it contributes to his poetical success to have conceived of Pinocchio as a man-made creature that becomes self-reborn. Need I refer to the craftman's attitude toward his creation, whether a marble Moses or a piece of furniture? In a place like Italy, the cultural background would insure a deep response to this aspect of Collodi's myth, and guarantee its authenticity.

One final point about Collodi's ingrained affinity for classical tradition: just as in the Iliad nothing less than private devotion to his dead friend Patroclus could have pulled sulking Achilles back into battle, it takes nothing less than love for the Blue-Haired Fairy and Geppetto to make Pinocchio shed his incurable laziness and get him to work and study at the end. While seeming to make light of his literary sources, Collodi somehow revives them.

He certainly drew upon a rich store of available culture, not just the culture of books, and books accordingly became live sources, not deadening pedantry, in his process of literary composition. In having given the world a uniquely imaginative and educative story like Pinocchio, he ranks high among benefactors of children in all lands. Not the least of his benefactions is the resolute plea for, and exemplary use of, articulateness; an articulateness he would have imbibed with his mother's milk in the Tuscan countryside where the common people have always retained an authentic culture of their own. This much remains true even when we register on the debit side the undeniable fact that Collodi tilts the scales against the element of play in his treatment of plot and incident. In his fable, the urge to play can only lead to laziness and degradation; the Country of Playthings (as well as the Circus) provides a deplorable antithesis to the Country of the Busy Bees and to the Classroom. Art and Play have nothing to do with Work and Study; at times one is tempted to take sides with the unredeemed Pinocchio against the latter options. The consequence of such Victorian bourgeois dichotomy is that books (within the framework of the story) can only become fetishes to the rightfully alienated Pinocchio, while the world of school must appear as pure drudgery, implying chores to master for the sake of further advantages, never a fulfilling experience that can include fun. Collodi never shows the delight Pinocchio could get from books as such, or from the process of learning. Conversely, the Country of Playthings is wholly bad, and it never occurs to the author to shed on it a more favorable light. To do this, he should have been a Montessorian, but history handicapped him by placing him one generation earlier than Maria Montessori. I wonder what would have happened to his little masterpiece if he had rewritten it along Montessorian lines by showing that children first learn by playing and from their toys, and that play is the source of both learning and work. Maybe he needed the drastic antitheses of play versus work and play versus study to provide dramatic space for Pinocchio's adventures, and so his fable could not have taken shape if he had surrendered his bourgeois ideology. At any rate, the poet in him knew better than the ideologist, and he made ample room for Homo ludens in his historically conditioned fantasy. Thank God he did. Thank God for the pixy in him.

---

[1] In the estimate of most scholars, Manzoni's novel, dating from the third decade of the nineteenth century, ranks as first and foremost in Italian prose fiction, thus paralleling the position of Dante's epic in the domain of verse.

2 For instance, "Non ragionaim di lor, ma guarda e passa" (Let's not talk of
   them, but just glance and move on, Inf. III, 51: said of wishy-washy souls);
   "Vuolsi cosi cola dove si puote / cio che si vuole, a piu non dimandare"
   (It is willed so up there where power / is attendant on will, so ask no further
   questions, Inf. III, 95-96: from the lines spoken by Virgil to Charon the devil
   ferryman of Acheron who is trying to stop the two visitors from crossing
   over into Hell proper); "Fatti non foste a viver come bruti / ma per seguir
   virtute e conoscenza" (You were not made to live like dumb brutes / but to
   follow the path of virtue and knowledge, Inf. XXVI, 119-120: from Ulysses'
   famous lines, as recounted by him to Virgil and Dante, with which he persuaded his aging shipmates to venture into the unknown sea beyond the Pillars of
   Hercules); "Liberta va cercando, ch'e si cara / some sa chi per lei vita ri-
   fiuta" (He is seeking freedom, which is so precious / as whoever refuses life
   for its sake well knows, Purg. I, 71-72: from the lines spoken by Virgil to
   Cato of Utica, who killed himself rather than surrender to the conquering
   armies of Caesar in Africa.) Despite its high doctrinal level and literary sophistication, Dante's poem has penetrated the popular consciousness in some
   essential aspects; there are unscholarly people who learn it by heart.

3 Paul Hazard, Books, Children and Men, (1933), trans. Marguerite Mitchell
   (Boston: Horn Book, 1944). Hazard, who died in 1944, was a famous scholar,
   a student of modern literature and of the Enlightenment, and an eventual
   member of the Academie Française. He devotes a spirited chapter to Pinocchio, and is one supporting authority for my views on Swift's Gulliver's
   Travels as set forth below.

4 The Annotated Alice, Alice's Adventures in Wonderland & Through the Looking Glass, by Lewis Carroll, with an Introduction and Notes by Martin Gardner (New York: Bramhall House, 1960).

5 One prime example is in Chapter XI, where Pinocchio manages to mollify
   Fire-eater, the manager of the puppet theater, who wanted to use Pinocchio's
   fellow-puppet Harlequin for firewood, by just lavishing a crescendo of honor-
   ific titles on the burly man: Mister, Cavalier, Commander, Excellency.
   The satire on a widespread Italian bourgeois weakness for titles is evident.
   The same chapter also bears out Paul Hazard's remark on Pinochhio's kinship
   to the tradition of Commedia dell-arte masks.

6 The Metamorphoses can be best described as classical fairytales in which
   magical changes are brought about as punishment or reward. The literary
   fortune of this book was immense from the Middle Ages to the late Renaissance, Dante and Shakespeare having extensively drawn on it. Some of the
   figures or episodes have become proverbial, e.g. King Midas, who trans-
   forms whatever he touches into gold. If Ovid wrote primarily for an adult
   audience, his retelling of Greek myths would not alienate an audience of children. As for the Italian Renaissance epics of Roland, they were court poetry
   emerging from a popular tradition, both oral and written, that has come down
   to us in several forms, for instance the Sicilian puppet theater and the Romag-

nol <u>cantastorie</u>. In these art poems, which affected the European mind for centuries and inspired Edmund Spenser as well as Shakespeare, the historical matter of Charlemagne's wars is absorbed into a luxuriating fairytale context. In <u>Pinocchio</u>, the episode of the wicked Serpent who dies of laughter (Chapter XXII) clearly echoes Pulci's <u>Morgante Maggiore</u> (one of the great Roland epics), where the half-giant Margutte dies likewise. In <u>Midsummer Night's Dream</u>, a fairytale nurtured by both classical literature and English folklore, Ariosto's story of the two pairs of lovers charmed into a circular wild goose chase is adapted by Shakespeare to his own context; needless to say, Ariosto's epic poem <u>Orlando Furioso</u> was well known in Renaissance England, particularly thanks to Sir John Harington's translation.

7 In his <u>New Science</u> of 1725, the Neapolitan thinker propounded history as the true field of endeavor for man's knowledge, and he said that poetry (which he equated with collective myth) is the original form of thought and expression, arising from primitive man's childlike tendency to animate reality by projecting his own anthropomorphic imagination into the external world. The Romantics, especially in Germany, favored folk poetry and folk narrative, hence the fairytale (thanks to the Brothers Grimm), which became the model for a conscious art form, the <u>Kunstmärchen</u> or "art fairytale."

8 Carlo Collodi, <u>Pinocchio, the Adventures of a Marionette</u>, trans. Walter S. Cramp (Boston: Ginn and Company, 1904). Xerox-reprinted by University Microfilms Inc., Ann Arbor, Mich., 1966. Chapter XXXVI, pp. 204-205. My references henceforth are to this edition.

9 Not accidentally, Ionesco has also written children's stories. The kinship between absurdist literature (or theater) and children's literature is worth exploring, and so is the fact that stories like Kafka's <u>Metamorphosis</u> borrow their technique from fairytales.

WEBS OF CONCERN:
THE LITTLE PRINCE AND CHARLOTTE'S WEB

Laurence Gagnon

I

Any literary work is susceptible to an indefinite variety of interpretations. In this respect works of literature are like formal systems. Our understanding of the sequences of words in a novel, poem, etc. or the sequences of symbols in a logico-mathematical system is not completely determined by those sequences of words or symbols, still less by any intentions of the author(s). We achieve an understanding of a literary work or a formal system when we associate with it some model of the way things are or, at least, of a way they could be. Sometimes in order to do this we may have to suspend (temporarily) some of our beliefs about what is the case. But such are the demands of imaginative interpretation.

One type of model which can be used with great success in interpreting works of children's literature and adult fantasy is a Heideggerian model. By associating parts of Martin Heidegger's philosophy with certain parts of these literary works, we can achieve a novel, if not profound, understanding of them. Two cases in point are The Little Prince by A. de Saint Exupéry and Charlotte's Web by E. B. White. [1] It has even been reported that Heidegger himself once considered The Little Prince to be "one of the great existentialist books of this century." [2]

Stated as simply and untechnically as possible, the particular Heideggarian model appealed to here is one concerned with persons and their capabilities. [3] Now persons are capable of many things, of flying planes and watering flowers, of eating leftovers and killing insects. Yet these are rather superficial capabilities, not being characteristic of persons as such but rather only of persons as pilots or gardeners, omnivores or killers. Among the more fundamental capabilities are those of being aware of oneself, of being concerned about things in the world, of dreading one's death, and untimately of living authentically. Since each person as such is unique and irreplaceable, this ultimate capability is also the ultimate personal obligation: to live authentically. Under the present interpretation, The Little Prince and Charlotte's Web are about various personal struggles to live authentically. In each of these works there are characters who find themselves thrown into existence, as it were, amidst other beings with whom they end up being concerned, all the while being confronted with the difficult and inescapable task of truly becoming what they alone can be—even unto death. This is precisely the task of living authentically. The ever-present danger here is that of losing one's sense of personal identity by becoming part of the crowd or by becoming overly concerned with other beings. [4]

II

In The Little Prince, neither the stranded pilot nor the prince himself have succumbed to the temptation of becoming a people-self; i.e., a faceless, anonymous part of a crowd. Since he was six years old, the time at which he produced his famous drawings of a boa constrictor digesting an elephant, the stranded pilot has been of the opinion that grown-ups are not only concerned with inconsequential "matters of consequence," such as bridge and golf, politics and neckties, but also terribly dense when it comes to discussing such important matters as boa constrictors, primeval forests and stars. "So," he says, "I have lived my life alone, without anyone that I could really talk to . . . " (p. 5).

The little prince has not been so lonely, having his flower to talk to. However, his opinion of grown ups is much the same as that of the stranded pilot. They are not merely strange, nor even "very, very odd," but rather "altogether extraordinary" in their denseness and their concerns (pp. 47, 50, 52, 57). The king who has no subjects except a rat, the conceited man who has no admirers except himself, the tippler who drinks to forget that he is ashamed of drinking, the businessman who values his accounts but not what they are of, the geographer who knows nothing in particular about geography—none of these receives nor deserves the admiration of the little prince, for none are living authentically. Worse yet there is little hope that they will change, since they neither take care of things nor care for persons. What interest they take in the little visitor is selfish. Living on their respective planets, the little prince would at best be treated as an extension of themselves, not as a distinct individual worthy of their concern. It is not just physically that they lead isolated lives.

Only on asteroid 329 does the little prince find a man whom he could possibly befriend—the lamplighter—who at least takes care of his lamp. "But his planet is indeed too small. There is no room on it for two people . . " (p. 61). On earth there is at least room. Here, of course, the little prince finds friendship. He tames the willing fox. He establishes ties with the not-so-willing, stranded pilot. He becomes forever responsible for them, and they in turn for him.

But there is always a danger here; one can lose oneself to the things one takes care of and the persons one cares for. One can become so concerned with other beings that one identifies with them rather than striving for the unique identity proper to oneself. As long as one does this, one cannot live authentically. Before he began his wanderings, the little prince was too concerned with his rose; in his conscientiousness he had become a slave to her and she in her vanity and pride encouraged his servitude. This was not good for either of them. At that time it was important to both that she be the only flower of her kind in the whole universe. Because of all this, his agony in the garden is inevitable, when he discovers that there are thousands upon thousands of roses like his own. Yet none are his rose. This the tamed fox enables him to see. What makes his rose precious is not its physical appearance but the time he has "wasted" on it. "It is only with the heart that one can see rightly; what is essential is invisible to the eye" (p. 87). This truth, which men have forgotten, sets the little prince free;

while he still has ties with his rose, he is no longer tied down to her.

In this regard the stranded pilot has much to learn. Although his initial concerns are taking care of his damaged plane and caring for himself, he eventually manages to become deeply concerned for his little visitor. But in this new concern, he becomes overly attached to his new friend. He understands that the little prince must leave but he cannot accept it as the fox has done. He asks for comfort and implores his readers to send him word of the little man's return. Yet this is understandable, for the stranded pilot is neither as wise and patient as the fox nor as young and innocent as the little prince. He requires more time.

The wisdom of the fox is not the only wisdom which the little prince discovers on earth. He also learns that while taking care of one's possessions and caring for others are necessary for one to live authentically, they alone are not sufficient, even when done without attachment. One must also recognize that life, especially one's own life, necessarily involves death, not as a termination of these concerns but rather as a culmination of them. This is the wisdom of the snake who always speaks in riddles. With a certain resoluteness, the little prince advances toward his own death, even though he is somewhat afraid and anxious. As the stranded pilot discovers, it was not by chance that little man was "strolling along like that, all alone, a thousand miles from any inhabited region" (p. 98). Death is always a solitary experience.

But since the little prince is a star-child, innocent and true, there is a resurrection. His "was not such a heavy body" after all (p. 109). Yet even with the element of resurrection, the question of what comes after death ought not to arise. For dying is the ultimate individual act of which a person is capable. The stranded pilot cannot quite accept this. He still ponders the mystery of what happens afterwards: "What is happening on his planet?"; "Has the sheep eaten the flower?" (pp. 109, 111).

These questions are not important in themselves, but only in so far as they symbolize the ties which have been established between the little prince and the stranded pilot. What is important is stated by the star-child:

> In one of the stars I shall be living. In one of them I shall be laughing. And so it will be as if all the stars were laughing, when you look at the sky at night . . . You—only you—will have stars that can laugh ! . . . And when your sorrow is comforted (time soothes all sorrows) you will be content that you have known me. You will always be my friend.
>
> (p. 104)

And this would be true, even if there were no resurrection.

III

In Charlotte's Web, a rat, a pig, and a spider find themselves thrown into existence together, inescapably confronted with the task of truly becoming what they can be—even unto death. The rat, Templeton, commits himself to an inauthentic existence. In a miserly fashion he acquires things without thereafter tending to them. Merely storing rotten eggs like banking stars does not involve taking care of one's possessions. Not having developed even this capacity, he cannot develop his capacity of caring for others. He must be enticed to go to the fair and bribed to pick up the egg sac. He could care less whether Wilbur, the pig, died of a broken heart or whether Charlotte, the spider, died of exhaustion and old age (pp. 168-169). Nor does he really confront the possibility of his own death. He lives for the present, especially when it is "full of life" in the form of feasting and carousing (pp. 147, 175). Of course, his death will come sometime. But he sees it as coming in the distant future, as the end of his life, rather than as a distinctive part of his life. "Who wants to live forever?" he sneers (p. 175).

Wilbur, on the other hand, is not committed to inauthentic existence but he is tempted in a variety of ways to live inauthentically. As a young pig, he does not have an especially strong personality. His attitudes and opinions can easily be swayed by outside influences: a few words from the goose, a pail of slops, a rainy day, the bad news from the old sheep, the reassuring promise of Charlotte. As a result he is always in danger of becoming a people-self rather than a distinctive person. If Charlotte's web says that he is "some pig" and people believe it, Wilbur believes it. If it says that he is "terrific" and people believe it, he not only believes it but also really feels terrific. If it's "radiant," then radiant Wilbur is. (Only with the last, prophetic message is there a genuineness in Wilbur's attitude—he has finally become more of himself, a humble pig.)

Wilbur refuses to face the fact that he might be killed next Christmas-time and turned into smoked bacon and ham. "'I don't <u>want</u> to die. . .'" he moans, "'. . . I want to stay alive, right here in my comfortable manure pile with all my friends'" (p. 51). He does not see his dying as an integral part of his life. He sees it as the end of it all.

Left to his own devices, the selfish and insecure Wilbur would remain a people-self. But "out of the darkness, came a small voice he had never heard before. . . . "'Do you want a friend, Wilbur?' it said. 'I'll be a friend to you'" (p. 31). Charlotte tames him. From the ties thus established, Wilbur gradually grows to care for the large grey spider, who lives in the upper part of the barn doorway. Since he naturally tends toward being a people-self, his initial reaction is to identify himself with his new found friend by imitating her. So he tries in vain to spin a web, ignoring Charlotte's profound observation, "'. . . you and I lead different lives'" (p. 56). When Charlotte says she's glad she's a sedentary spider, Wilbur replies, "'Well, I'm sort of sendentary myself, I guess'" (p. 61).

Gradually Wilbur realizes that he and Charlotte are different, even though friends. They are different not merely generically, as pig and spider, but also individually, as distinctive persons. But persons are beings-unto-death. So Wilbur and Charlotte must also differ in their dying.

It is only after the Fair has ended, the crowd dispersed, and Wilbur's hour of

triumph over that he turns his attention away from himself toward his dying
friend. "'Why did you do all this for me? . . . I don't deserve it. I've never
done anything for you'" (p. 169). With her characteristic wisdom, Charlotte
replies, "'You have been my friend . . . That in itself is a tremendous thing'"
(p. 164).

Now more than ever, Wilbur wants to preserve the ties that have been established between him and the lovely grey spider. He throws "himself down in an
agony of pain and sorrow," sobbing " . . . 'I can't stand it . . . I won't leave
you here alone to die'" (p. 165). But Wilbur is being ridiculous. He can't stay
with Charlotte. For if he stayed, he would not be true either to Charlotte or
himself. His call of conscience is to return to the farm with Charlott's egg sac.
With amazing agility (for a pig) Wilbur accepts this call to authenticity. "All
winter Wilbur watched over Charlotte's egg sac as though he were guarding his
own children" (pp. 175-176).

In the spring the young spiders came. But there is sorrow in this resurrection. Being unique themselves, none can live the life Charlotte did. So Charlotte's children sail away. "This is our moment for setting forth" (p. 180).
However, Wilbur is not left totally alone. Three of them stay. To them Wilbur
pledges his friendship, "forever and ever" (p. 183). Yet "Wilbur never forgot
Charlotte. Although he loved her children and grandchildren dearly, none of the
new spiders ever quite took her place in his heart. She was in a class by herself" (p. 184). From the beginning Charlotte had resolutely advanced toward her
own solitary death, all the while taking care of her magnificent web and caring
for her humble friend. She saves Wilbur from an undistinctive death and gives
him both the situation and the time to heed his own call of concern.

> Nobody, of the hundreds of people that had visited the Fair, knew that
> a grey spider had played the most important part of all. No one was
> with her when she died.
>
> (p. 171)

IV

Thus a stranded pilot and a little prince, a young pig, and a grey spider
struggled to live authentically, each necessarily in his own way and time. Because of them, laughing stars illuminate webs of concern in the dead of night.

---

1 All references cited in the text will be to the following editions of these works:

A. de Saint Exupéry, The Little Prince, trans. by K. Woods (New York: Harcourt, Brace & Jovanovich, 1971).

E. B. White, Charlotte's Web (New York: Harper & Row, 1952).

2 C. Cate, Antoine de Saint-Exupéry (New York: G. P. Putnam's Sons, 1970),
p. 465.

3 Some of the passages in M. Heidegger's, Sein und Zeit, which are relevant to the present model are: pp. 12, 42-43, 53-57, 121-130, 142-145, 175-176, 191-196, 231-236, 245-280, 296-310, 325-326, 386, 424-426. These are indicated in the margins of J. Macquarrie and E. Robinson's translation of the work (New York: Harper & Row, 1962). Of course, if other passages are emphasized or other works used, different Heideggerian models will result.

4 The details of the model are worked out in the subsequent interpretations of the two works. For a lucid exposition of the model, see: J. Demske, Being, Man, and Death (Lexington: University of Kentucky, 1970).

MILTON'S COMUS AS CHILDREN'S LITERATURE

Lee A. Jacobus

History and legend erroneously tagged Milton as a fun-spoiling puritan who disliked his own children enough that he made them read to him in ancient tongues they did not themselves understand. But enlightened biographers have dispelled much of this mist. He wrote about children; he taught them and respected them; and they, including his daughters, spoke well of him in later life. In light of this, then, it may be easier for us to consider the question of whether or not Comus can be seriously thought of as an example of children's literature.

The question is made credible first because the leading role and two important supporting roles were actually played by children and written as children's parts. Further, Comus has a very specific didactic quality emphasizing problems of virtue and faith specifically pertinent to an adolescent girl. Then, the ambiguity of the genre, with a melodramatic quality more familiar to the mid-nineteenth century stage than to the Stuart masquing hall, tends to put Comus— with its children threatened by a magician in a mazy wood—generically close to what we usually consider children's literature.

When the masque was performed at Ludlow Castle in 1634, the Lady Alice Egerton was fifteen years old. She played the Lady tempted to abandon her virtue and her chastity by a night-rioter, Comus (son of Circe), when he discovers her lost in a wood on her way home to her father's house. The parts of the Elder Brother and the Younger Brother were played by Lady Alice's brother, Lord Brackley, then eleven years old, and her brother, Thomas, then nine years old. The Attendant Spirit, from the courts of Jove, was played by an old family friend, Henry Lawes, who also wrote the music and managed to get Milton to write the masque itself.

W. R. Parker, the most recent biographer of Milton, suggests that Milton may actually have played the part of Comus, the tempter. However, it is likely that this part and Sabrina's were played by professionals. A villain such as Comus would most decorously be portrayed by someone who was not close to the family for the same reason the adult Attendant Spirit should be a friend, someone like her music-master, whom she could rely upon in life as well as in fiction. The moral function of the music-master is then doubly significant.

The actual occasion for the composition of the masque was the installation of the Earl of Bridgewater, John Egerton, as President of Wales, an honorary position with no responsibilities. The performance was at Ludlow Castle, the Earl's residence near Wales, on Michaelmas night, September 29, 1634. The masque does not directly celebrate this occasion. Critics have suggested that the successful trial of John Egerton's daughter, in the face of the powerful tempter, is praise enough for the occasion. Yet it seems odd that the entire focus of the entertainment should be directed to Lady Alice, and so little (11.35-6) to the father.

Perhaps this would seem less odd if it were not for the existence of Milton's other masque, Arcades. This masque, one-tenth the length of Comus, and much more "normal" for the genre of the masque as Jonson established it, was composed for a celebration we can know little about. Its subject is clearly the Dowager Countess of Derby, the Lady Alice Spencer, the step-mother, by marriage, of John Egerton. The date of this piece may be as early as 1632 or as late as 1634. French Fogle has surmised that it may have been written to celebrate the seventy-fifth birthday of the Countess—thus marking it at May 4, 1634. In any event, it clearly celebrates this grand lady, and with no shifts of attention to her progeny. She is described as providing the "blaze of majesty . . . Too divine to be mistook," which illumines all. Had Milton intended to praise her stepson in the vehicle of a masque, he could easily have done so.

Comus does not have the same intention as Arcades. Instead of being an encomiastic excursion, it is more a didactic romance, with its purpose to instruct —perhaps terrify a bit—and to delight. But it is surely fair to ask who it is designed to instruct, terrify, and delight. Could it be the adults present at the masque? Not exclusively. The situation of the adolescent girl protected by chastity withstanding the urgencies of the lustful Comus would have amused the adults, but its message would be rather late for them. Even if we take chastity to mean what Milton meant, proper and temperate behavior, as well as virginity, the assault in the masque is still that of a lecherous magician on an innocent lady. It is clearly an assault the children, and specifically the female children, will most benefit from observing.

Barbara Breasted, in recent studies (particularly in Milton Studies III), has given us some new insight into the conditions of the Egerton family which might help us understand more clearly the implications of the didactic qualities of the masque. For one thing, the Lady Alice had been in treatment of an ailment that was suspected to have been cast upon her by the curse of a former family servant, one Quicke. Richard Napier, physician and astrologer, "cured" her at the request of Lady Alice's mother, who was convinced she had been put under a spell. Then, there is the Castlehaven affair, a scandal so serious that the privy council ultimately considered the question. John Egerton was at the time a member of the privy council, but he did not sit on the decisions regarding the Earl of Castlehaven because of his connection by marriage with the Earl. The Earl's wife, Anne, was a daughter of the Countess Dowager of Derby. Anne's daughter, Elizabeth, was the Lady Alice's cousin, and only a few years older. She was married to Castlehaven's son, James, by a former marriage.

The scandal was sexual. Castlehaven's servants had raped his wife as he looked on. Moreover, Castlehaven had homosexual relations with a number of his servants, and—most unnatural—he denied his only son his marriage rights with Elizabeth after their marriage. Castlehaven used her sexually himself.

The son risked the scandal and informed the authorities. The fact that Anne Spencer did not do so went badly for her, and the privy council never fully exonerated either Anne or her daughter since it was never clear that they fully deplored the usages to which they were put. Castlehaven was executed privately, and the servants publicly at Tyburn Hill after satisfying an eager crowd with many of the details.

Castlehaven was executed in 1631, by which time the scandal had become known fairly widely. Certainly the audience which watched Comus in 1634 would have not forgotten it. Barbara Breasted feels that some of the cuts made from the playing version (we assume the Bridgewater ms. was the playing version) may have been made to reduce tension which lines about lust and vice might have created. However, the entire situation of the masque clearly would be "touchy" to the audience unless, possibly, one of the intentions of the masque was to provide the kind of positive example of behavior associated with Odysseus and Circe in adult literature and with Little Red Riding Hood, Hansel and Gretel, and all the other instances in children's literature of the straying of innocents into the woods of danger. The specificity of Milton's masque, with its emphasis on sexuality and an assault on chastity, can be seen as made possible by the Castlehaven scandal. Perhaps it may be more reasonable to suggest that it is not made possible, but made essential because of it.

Comus is not indirect in his assault on the Lady. He disguises himself and conceals his frightening visage, but his arguments with her are clear enough. He accuses her of hoarding the beauty which she must spend in fruitfulness—or else, like such a wasteful nature, she might be "strangl'd with her waste fertility" (729). He then springs upon her his "economic theory of virtue":

> Beauty is nature's coin, must not be hoarded,
> But must be current, and the good thereof
> Consists in mutual and partak'n bliss,
> Unsavory in th'enjoyment of itself. (739-742)

The lines are reminiscent of the parable of the talents, to be touched upon much later in Milton's poetry. They have the same weakness most analogical reasoning has: even is it were true that coin must be current, it does not then follow that beauty must be current in the same fashion, building in value by virtue of passing from hand to hand. The Lady realizes there is nothing but the semblance of reason to these lines, and she says so only a few lines onward.

Her means of coping with Comus' argument have always attracted attention. Readers have contended that she does not adequately blast his argument, but instead leaves it intact. However, the argument, whether she dismantles it with counter arguments or not, is not at all intact. Her refusal to argue with Comus, other than to vent a bit of spleen against his arrogance, is important to the entire drama. Since he is clearly a practised casuist, and since she is also clearly an innocent, there could be little purpose to arguing with him. To begin with, she could not regenerate him:

> Thou hast nor Ear nor Soul to apprehend
> The sublime notion and high mystery
> That must be utter'd to unfold the sage
> And serious doctrine of Virginity,
> And thou art worthy that thou shouldst not know
> More happiness than this thy present lot.   (784-789)

Since he is not capable or deserving of regeneration, the Lady has no obligation to argue him out of his position. Moreover, if he is unregenerate, then he is very likely demonic—which in fact, he is—and therefore has greater powers than the Lady. For the same reason a good Christian would not argue with the devil, she should not argue with Comus. His powers are greater to confound, no matter how right her reason might be. So, ultimately, she chooses correctly in abjuring argument entirely.

The Lady, then, takes something of a passive position in the drama. When the lines above are spoken, the Lady is "immanacl'd" in an "enchanted Chair." Yet it is only her body which is held here, "this corporal rind"; she knows that "Thou canst not touch the freedom of my mind." Her passivity is essential because she must rely on heavenly intervention for her rescue. Such a point is easier to accept if one keeps in mind the fact that Comus is non-human, as is Sabrina. Angus Fletcher, in The Transcendental Masque, discusses extensively the implications of a contest between magicians. Our interest is in the Lady and her role while such a contest is continuing. Clearly she must rely on what virtues she has: chastity is a virtue in the sense of being a power linking her to the forces of good bending down from Jove's court. Without that clear center of chastity the Lady would cease to be the responsibility of the Attendant Spirit.

The parallel with the Lady Alice's cousin, Elizabeth, may be clearly enough drawn. Both she and her mother, it might be argued, were in the halls of a magician of sorts—Castlehaven must have seemed inhuman to more than a few contemporary Englishmen. Their silence as they suffered their injuries could well have been similar to the silence of the Lady in Comus: a holding firm while outside intervention made its slow progress forward.

The facts of the actual case are clouded enough so that we do not know if they would have supported such an interpretation, but we can be reasonably sure that this interpretation would be acceptable to those present at Ludlow Castle. Otherwise the silence of Castlehaven's women would be most difficult to explain except in the fashion the courts chose. As Comus would have it, their innocence is what merited their release and the realization of ultimate justice.

In this sense, then, the masque can be seen as a warning and possibly even as a justification. As a justification, it explains the silence of Anne and Elizabeth, while also explaining that the uses to which they were put sexually were not uses that involved the freedom of the mind. As a warning, the masque can be seen as an example for the Lady Alice to stand firm, as she has done, and keep the clear center of her faith in her chastity.

The emphasis on chastity—instead of simply on virginity—has annoyed critics for some time. Even recent critics have held to the view that Milton prefers faith, hope and chastity to faith, hope and charity in the masque. Clearly, if the shadow of the Castlehaven scandal still fell across the family, chastity would be the logical virtue to celebrate. Virginity may protect the unmarried Lady Alice, but only chastity could protect her in marriage. The most recent danger had come not out of, but in wedlock.

The traditional forms of the masque tend to be dominated by the god Hymen, and the masques themselves, like that in The Tempest, tend to celebrate marriage. Because the Lady Alice was at a marrigeable age when Comus was produced, one of Milton's problems was to find a chance to celebrate her beauty and her promise, while celebrating her capacity to withstand temptation. Milton's problems are delicate in this regard, though he surmounts them. The questions of marriage which lie behind the masque may well explain why the god Hymen is not at the center of things in Comus.

Editors and commentators point to Thomas Carew's masque Coelum Britannicum when discussing the question of whether Comus is a "normal" masque. It was performed in February, 1634, at Whitehall, with Lady Alice's two brothers as masquers. But the comparisons between the two masques are none too useful. Carew's masque resembles Milton's in insignificant ways. The Lawes who did the music for Carew was probably not the Henry Lawes of Comus, and any comparison does Carew's masque no good. It is an overblown, static piece which resembles the Jonsonian masque in many ways—with plenty of dumb-show figures and abstractions, and with the machinery of the redoubtable Inigo Jones. But it is the overblown end of the tradition, a masque smothered by its own weight. Clearly, if Carew and Milton were struggling in 1634 to find a new direction for the masque, it was Milton who solved the problem. Whether we think of Comus as children's literature or not, the masque is—in comparison with Coelum Britannicum—a distinct breath of fresh air. With its moral center, its uncluttered plot, and its relatively thorough characterization, Comus is indeed something of a novelty as a masque; its novelty is what makes it worth looking at.

The plot is reminiscent of melodrama. A young Lady is on her way home to her father's house for a celebration from an unknown whereabouts after an unknown length of time. These unknowns, as in most children's literature, pose no problem; they are not germane, so not developed. She is by some means separated from her brothers, who have left her while looking for some berries, and she wanders an unknown distance to the environs of Comus. Like the Attendant Spirit, and later, Eve, she was "all ear" and had been attracted by the sounds. The disguised Comus "reasons" with her, offers help, retreats with her to his castle, reveals himself as a dire magician, offers her a potion, threatens her to no avail, and is stopped in his hellish assault only as the brothers, with the Attendant Spirit and the magic herb Haemony, burst into the castle. Ultimately the Attendant Spirit and the brothers must call upon Sabrina, a water nymph who breaks the spell and cures all:

Shepherd 'tis my office best
To help ensnared chastity;
Brightest Lady look on me,
Thus I sprinkle on thy breast
Drops that from my fountain pure
I have kept of precious cure,
Thrice upon thy finger's tip,
Thrice upon thy rubied lip;
Next this marble venom'd seat
Smear'd with gums of glutinous heat
I touch with chaste palms moist and cold.
Now the spell hath lost his hold.   (908-919)

The Lady is then restored to her brothers and enters into the presence of her father, having been tried and proven in her virtue; and the celebration commences as the masque ends. Clearly the material reminds us of so many children's stories that it becomes almost archetypal. A look at even so late (1927) a concoction as Deane and Balderston's dramatization of Bram Stoker's Dracula will show that Milton's plot had a profound influence on later dramas exploring this kind of material.

Perhaps it is best to think of Comus as drawing on archetypes and becoming itself a model, if not type, which influenced literature for children in later ages. Surely, the master of so many genres in his own right: the sonnet, the pastoral elegy, the ode, the "twinned" poems, the Christian epic, the brief epic, the tragedy, could surprise no one by inventing a new genre for the circle of his own acquaintance: the children's romance. The circumstances surrounding the masque would warrant it, as would his interest in specific literary genres. For one who loved and respected children as much as Milton did (see Of Education), it is only fitting and reasonable that he should make such a contribution to their enjoyment.

THE HUMANIST TEACHES CHILDREN'S LITERATURE:
SOME CONSIDERATIONS *

Francis J. Molson

In 1969 the National Council of Teachers of English released the report of its
ad hoc committee on the teaching of children's literature in colleges and universities. [1] Observers who have suspected that the teaching of children's literature,
generally speaking, leaves much to be desired can find ample evidence in the report to confirm their suspicions. For instance, the report finds that about half
of those teachers of children's literature who responded to the committee's survey indicated that they had not taken any undergraduate work in children's literature. [2] Moreover, forty percent of the respondents had no graduate course
work in the subject. [3] Although the report does not state what percentage of those
without undergraduate preparation is also included among those with no graduate
preparation, still with the percentages in both categories so high, 50% and 40%
respectively, the chances are good that the number of those with no formal preparation at both levels is significantly and distressingly high. Another provocative finding is that seventy-five percent of the respondents either majored or
minored in English. [4] Unfortunately, the report provides no unambiguous data
that might indicate the number of English majors or minors included among those
having no undergraduate course in children's literature. Thus, while there is no
conclusive evidence that only English departments have ignored the importance
of children's literature, still English departments, willy-nilly, the largest "pro-
vider" of children's literature instructors, must take the chief blame for the in-
adequacies in the preparation of those who go on to teach children's literature in
colleges and universities.

The reasons for English departments' reluctance to take children's literature
seriously as a legitimate object of scholarship and criticism are not now my
prime concern. We all recognize that the reluctance has existed, and it has
been responsible, to a large extent, for the humanist's slow involvement in children's literature. This reluctance has also contributed to the confusion and conflict swirling about the definition of children's literature as an academic discipline, and the assignment of responsibility for the design and control of courses
in children's literature—in particular the introductory course—within the university. Even though John Rowe Townsend is speaking to the causes he finds
for the near-chaotic state of assessing juvenile books, his remarks also apply
to that confusion and conflict surrounding children's literature and its teaching:

----

* Given at the Modern Language Association Seminar on Children's Literature,
New York City, December 27, 1972.

The second cause of confusion is that children's literature is a
part of the field, or adjoins the field, of many different specialists;
yet it is the <u>major</u> concern of relatively few, and those not the
most highly placed in the professional or academic pecking-order.
Furthermore, the few to whom children's literature is central
cannot expect, within one working lifetime, to master sufficient
knowledge of the related fields to meet the experts on their own
ground and at their own level. And yet, while the children's literature person cannot operate at a professional level in all these
various fields, the people operating in the various fields can and
quite properly do take an interest in children's reading as it affects
their own specialities, and are able to quite frequently pronounce
upon it. But, understandably, such people are often unaware of or
have not thought deeply about the aspects of children's literature
that do not impinge upon their own field. The subject is one on
which people are notoriously willing to pronounce with great con-
fidence but rather little knowledge. Consequently, we have a flow
of apparently authoritative comment by people who are undoubtedly
experts but who are not actually experts on this. [5]

I submit that it will not lessen the confusion Townsend decries to have the humanist withdraw from or unduly compromise his stake in the teaching of children's
literature. On the contrary, what is needed is a clear statement of the legitimacy of the humanist's claim and an acceptance, especially by the humanist
himself, of the implications of that legitimacy. (In this paper the term humanist
describes any one trained in literature as humane study and committed to any
facet of literary studies.)

It is increasingly irritating for the humanist professionally involved in children's literature to insist on what should be, by now, evident. That is, the humanist can be legitimately interested in children's literature because all phases
of literary studies attract him, and children's books are frequently literature.
Moreover, the humanist is often vitally interested in children's literature because he cares about children and the books they read. Yet, perhaps because
some of us have come only recently to the humanistic study of children's literature, for the immediate future we should reconcile ourselves to the necessity of
spelling out our stake in children's literature. As Professor Butler stated, in
Volume One of <u>Children's Literature</u>, we must educate our colleagues in the humanities to perceive that simplicity is not superficiality and that verbal sophistication does exist on various levels. To our colleagues in elementary education,
library science, and child psychology we must reiterate that no one discipline has
a monopoly on caring about children. Further, I find it objectionable that in
some colleges the humanist is expected to demonstrate, so to speak, his care for
children by adopting in his own classes methods and media other disciplines have
devised to express their concern for children and their reading material. The
humanist should oppose attempts by other disciplines unilaterally to approve the
content or methods of his courses in children's literature or to pass on his cre-

dentials. [6] Humanists must insist on their own autonomy when passing on the professional competence of their colleagues in children's literature. This seminar and its journal point, I should think, to our eventual autonomy.

The humanist does have, then, a legitimate interest in children's literature, but so have other disciplines. The humanist must concede the legitimacy of these interests without carping or imputing inferiority to these disciplines. Personally, I might doubt the validity of bibliotherapy, but my objections must be put on a level comparable to that the bibliotherapist operates on. I cannot simply dismiss his claim because of my own professional bias. At the same time I would like to caution the bibliotherapist that using Charlotte's Web exclusively to allay a child's fear of death or grief at the death of a beloved pet neglects the book's stylistic merits and demeans an artifact to a mere tool.

A second point: wherever the humanist has responsibility for the introductory course in children's literature, he must not attempt to be all things to his students, regardless of the pressures put upon him. Rather, he should do that for which he is trained or wants to do: for instance, to discuss the relation between children's books and society's desire to control its children; or to discuss narrative strategies in Victorian children's books. Why must he be expected to provide units on the making of picture books, bibliotherapy, reading and interest levels, selecting materials for the library, or classroom methods of presenting children's books? Is it really feasible for most of us to acquire in one working lifetime the competence of the reading specialist, the school librarian, the child psychologist, the early childhood specialist, and the art and graphic expert? If we try, we present their speciality in our classes with a superficial acquaintance that barely distinguishes us from our students. Some of us are so busy being Jacks in everybody else's trade that we are unable to be the Master we are supposed to be in our own.

I submit, further, that within the introductory course the use of the typical anthology works against the students' acquiring an attitude towards books essential to a humanistic approach to children's literature. The one semester romp through disparate selections hardly provides an opportunity to gain respect for literary values, for question of meaning and artistry. It is important for the prospective elementary teacher to attain this respect for the books children read, for respecting children's books goes hand in hand with respecting children as persons: to patronize a child's book is to patronize the child. It is no argument in favor of the anthology to point out that it is used within the English major program. For in the latter the negative effects of the anthology, in particular, the extensive but superficial reading, are offset, at least theoretically, by the English major's later intensive work in period and genre courses. But in the case of the elementary education major who is most likely to enroll in the introductory course, what subsequent course or formal educational experience compensates for the customary shallowness of reading? What supplements the extensive reliance on the anthology compilers' and instructor's dicta about value and meaning? What subsequent course encourages respect for children's books as books and not mere instructional media? Whenever I am depressed over what apparently goes on in some children's literature courses I can't help suspecting that many college and university faculties, in spite of public utterances to the contrary, continue to look down upon elementary education majors and express their disdain by requiring them to enroll in courses where, in effect, they are denied opportunity to seek and attain mastery within any of the traditional arts or sciences.

Our options, I suggest, concerning the introductory children's literature course are limited. (1) We can teach the course as our humanist training and inclination direct and tell other interests to mind their own business. (2) We can voluntarily restrict our participation to a smaller segment of the course as presently constituted and ask other disciplines to help us teach the course. (3) Or, best yet, we can invite the other disciplines to join with us and demand fundamental changes in the introductory course. I suggest, for instance, a genuinely interdepartmental, two-semester course in which each discipline contributes its distinctive perspective without fear of offending anyone or encroaching on another's speciality. Such a course should not be controlled by one department, nor structured upon one approach, nor directed by one method.

Earlier I remarked on the autonomy humanists should have in assessing a colleague's competence in children's literature. To effect such autonomy and to staff adequately the introductory course, including innovative, interdisciplinary courses, requires professional training that reflects the rigor and openness of the best liberal arts graduate instruction. It is only to be realistic today to point out that there can be no irresponsible proliferation of graduate programs in the humanistic study of children's literature. Yet even though but few programs may be established, let us hope that their prime concern will be the preparation of teachers and scholars who will acknowledge that the phrase "children's literature" is made up of two terms, "children" and "literature."

NOTES

[1] Teaching Children's Literature in Colleges and Universities, ed. Elliott D. Landau (Champaign, 1968).

[2] Landau, Table 15, p. 14.

[3] Landau, Table 16, p. 15.

[4] Landau, Table 13, 1. 13.

[5] "Standards of Criticism For Children's Literature," Top of the News, 27:4 (June 1971), pp. 375-376.

FANTASY IN A MYTHLESS AGE

John S. Morris

According to the <u>Oxford English Dictionary</u>, two of the meanings of the root word from which the word "fantasy" is derived, i.e., φαντασία , are

   (1) appearance - often a spectral apparition, phantom; and

   (2) imagination.

The common present-day meaning of fantasy is "caprice, whim, fanciful invention." Both of the root meanings suggest that the word fantasy is used to represent a discontinuity with known reality:

   (a) Appearance. That which is given to us with a vision which is "unearthly"—the spectral apparition which cannot be tested by the senses, but is 'known' to be present as that which is "unreal"—the phantom is an unreal specter that nevertheless has real power over us in its presence.

   (b) Imagination as "the process of forming mental representations of things not present" thus also has the meaning of that which is somehow "unreal," unexpected, fanciful. It is also extravagant or visionary fancy.

The characteristic features of fantasy—invention, unreality, the unearthly, and the imaginative—show us that a distinction should be drawn between the literature of fantasy and fiction. Fiction, in its usual sense, carries with it the notion of imagination; but it is as an imaginative arrangement of that which is rooted in our everyday experience that fiction can be called imaginative. One definition of fiction is: "The action of 'feigning' or inventing imaginary incidents, existences, states of things whether for the purpose of deception or otherwise" (O. E. D.). Fiction simply suggests that it is a rearrangement of the <u>ordinary</u> rather than that it is the "extra-ordinary." It has about it a suggestion that it has the power to deceive us because what it deals with is so like our world. Fantasy, however, does not simply rearrange the ordinary, but presents us instead with the extraordinary. The "appearance" is an extraordinary appearance. A phantom, after all, is not simply something seen with the eyes, but is that which, by its inexplicable presence, throws us into a state of terror because it is not of this world.

A fundamental characteristic of the literature of fantasy, therefore is that it not only is imaginative but is in some way or other "not of this world." Science fiction can be classified as fantasy because much of its action takes place "outside of this world" in some other planet or galaxy. This extra-terrestial location is very significant. The science fiction stories of C. S. Lewis imagine a world, quite different from ours, which is peopled by beings quite distinguishable from humans. Tolkien's novels create an even more imaginary world with its own language system, its own logic, and its own system of rewards. It is a fantastic creation, not peopled by creatures which we would immediately be comfortable with should we meet on on the street.

Literature of the occult also can be considered as fantasy because it suggests this same "other-worldliness." In Charles Williams' novels events occur in this world, but this world is taken up into a world of supernatural phenomena: the dead still walk the streets, time scales merge with each other, unearthly powers converge upon objects, and so on. These worlds are all quite fantastic.

The "other worldly" character of fantasy calls myth to mind. Myth after all, appears to us to be fantasy. Whatever else they are, myths are fantastic stories. They are stories about the birth of the gods, the first impact of the gods in the world. We call any fictitious story that we know to be fraudulent a "myth." But a "myth," as distinguished from saga or legend, while in a sense fictitious, involves "supernatural passions, actions or events." But we should remember that the man who lived in the world for whom the myth was meaningful did not see the myth as a fantastic invention. It was for him the completely normal way of living in the world. The myth for him was the story which gave shape and form to his own perception of a unified world, and which played a part in his dealing with the very real problems of his existence in this world. It pictured a way of life which embraced the whole of his existence, and related that existence to the totality of all existence. His birth was related to the Beginnings, his death was related to the End of Days, his experience of the passing of time was placed in the perspective of the eternal motion of the Sun. Myth always pointed to that which is encompassed in a total value structure which put the elements of "the world" in their place within a sacred cosmos.

The imaginative grasp of experience that issues forth in myth is a grasp of an order of being where sacred power dwells, in which history, the time of our living, has boundaries that are set for us. From that order is felt to emanate the power of our individual lives. Eliade has said:

> The man of the archaic societies tends to live as much as possible in the sacred or in close proximity to consecrated objects. The tendency is perfectly understandable, because, for primitives as for the man of all pre-modern societies, the sacred is equivalent to a power, and in the last analysis to reality. The sacred is saturated with being. Sacred power means reality and at the same time enduringness and efficacity. [1]

Indeed, unreality for primitive man is the profane—that which is for us the real. This appears to us to be an inversion of our scheme of things, for what we call the real world is the world of chairs and tables and sticks and stones. Primitive man, on the other hand, saw power in the world because it was created by the gods. The gods showed themselves to men through cosmic life; this was the real. Human life was not individual, separated, and remote; men and women were not isolated fragmented dots in a world of isolated fragmented things, but were united with the cosmic power. "In living, religious man is never alone, part of the world lives in him,"[2] and it is in knowing his world that he knows himself. It is his very living in a world which has its values given, its structure determined, its reality guaranteed by something other than himself that makes it possible for this self-discovery to take place. To quote Eliade again:

> The sacred is pre-eminently the real, at once power, efficacity,
> the source of life and fecundity. Religious man's desire to live
> in the sacred is in fact equivalent to his desire to take up his abode
> in objective reality, not to let himself be paralyzed by the never
> ceasing relativity of purely subjective experiences, to live in a real
> and effective world, and not in an illusion. [3]

Note again how things have been turned on their head from our perspective. What is real for us lacks reality for archaic man. Its illusory quality arises precisely because the subjective world is fragmented and has no point of contact with the power of renewal which the cosmic world presents; the subjective world leaves man at the mercy of whim and leaves him without structure and order. The subjective world is a representation of chaos because it suggests the very lack of order which the power of the gods gives to existence.

Harvey Cox has argued that the path for the reception of science in our world was laid down by the way in which the Hebrew treated myth. [4] They took God out of the order of the world and made him the Creator of the world. No element of the world had any sacred power. Thus the world was de-sacralized. However, Cox's observation can be quite misleading, for the Hebrew did not suggest that the order of the world had any meaning apart from the Creator. The power of creation was made manifest in every created being. The order of the world is given and God-made: hence the value of the world. The world is good; life is not possible outside of this given order and has no value apart from it. The power of life is likewise found within the social order which is similarly brought into being, or created, by the divine act—the speaking of the divine word through Moses at Sinai. While in the Hebrew myth the world is de-sacralized in the sense that there is no element in the world that has divine power in itself, nothing in the world can have meaning, value or significance apart from its being a part of an order of existence which is given point and purpose by the acts of God.

What has happened in the modern rush to technocracy is that we have created a world in which particular ends control our approaches to existence, and knowledge becomes the ability to explain phenomena and to understand the explanations. Committed to such an approach to the world, our grasp of life is defined by desire and the satisfaction of wants; we enter what might be called a one-dimensional world. The real is the tangible, and the deepest satisfaction is the explanation that is sufficient unto our day: all else is fleeting experience and passing feeling which has no worth beyond its present happening. Anything out of this world is understood to be illusion and a grasping at straws. The imaginative is dismissed as fanciful. Religion itself is an illusion, which if it is useful might be given a place because it helps, or it is damned again as fanciful and imaginative and is only a help to the weak-kneed.

Myth, then—including Hebrew myth—performed some characteristic functions for archaic man:

> (1) Myth was the verbal declaration of the Act in which order is established over chaos.

> (2) Myth was the verbal declaration of the Act that sustains that order.

> (3) Participation in the declaration of the myth enabled the individual to participate in its creative and sustaining power as he lived his life as a journey towards the achievement of an end.

The literature of fantasy, inasmuch as it is "unearthly," "extra-ordinary," and "supernatural," is a creative attempt to re-experience the fundamental life-giving forces that myth provided for archaic man. It does so, often quite self-consciously, quite clearly in a meaningful way inasmuch as the literature of fantasy is not only written but quite obviously read a good deal.

Some theologians have told us that we live in a "secular age," the age when the Supernatural is no longer acceptable intellectual coinage, when the power of being is nothing more than an electrical discharge, an age in which something must be given an explanation, or explained in principle to be accepted as meaningful. Yet in an age when this is so, it is odd that literature of fantasy has caught on with such force and has such living power. Its symbols must still have power; that they must would suggest that the theologians of secularism have thrown away the baby with the bath water. Human life is not easily lived without the active powers of imagination which catch on to the symbols of the Absolute, which are presented in myth and fantasy.

I want now to show some of the ways in which the three characteristic features of myth just mentioned are worked out in some modern fantasies.

I. Myth as the declaration in word of the Act in which order is established over chaos.

J. R. R. Tolkien and Charles Williams return again and again to this theme of the power of creation and its manifestation in the life of each element of the cosmos. Tolkien has a small and touching description of Aragorn's discovery of a sapling at the time of his deepest despair. Bearing "one small cluster of flowers whose white petals shone like the sunlit snow," it was a "scion of the Eldest of Trees." Gandalf says of it: "though the fruit of the Tree comes seldom to ripeness, yet the life within may then lie sleeping through many long years, and none can foretell the time in which it will awake." [5] Within the context of Aragorn's despair and the imminent danger of defeat at the hands of the destructive forces of the world this was a sign that order would be maintained despite the possibilities of the return of chaos with barrenness and darkness. The whole setting of the Trilogy, The Lord of The Rings, suggests this same sense of order which has been established and is being maintained.

The secret of life lies in the necessity for the maintainance of order within a cosmos that could ever return to chaos. Charles Williams expresses this also in his War in Heaven in a scene in which the Archdeacon along with some of the central characters in the book celebrate the Holy Communion. As the Archdeacon leads the communicants in worship he comes to the reading of the Scriptures:

> And God said: "Let us make man, in our image, after our likeness . . . in the image of God created He him, male and female created He them" . . . And the Priest King's voice closed on the Gospel: "Behold, I make all things new."

> But the Archdeacon, hearing all these words, trembled a little as he knelt. The thoughts with which he approached the Mysteries faded; the Mysteries themselves faded. He distinguished no longer word from Act; he was in the presence, he was part of the Act which far away issued in those faint words, "Let us make Man"—Creation rose and flowed out and wheeled to its august return—"in our image, after our likeness"—the great pronouns were the sound of that return. [6]

Man discovers at the heart of the Universe, not an inert given—an empty time from X to X in which he has to live, but the power of a sustained order which he must accept as a part of himself if he is going to live. Time becomes important only insofar as the individual manifests in his journey through life the creative power that sustains the fundamental ordering of existence, which enables —not simply allows—man to be. It is only insofar as man enters into this fundamental unity with man who was and is created, and is thus obedient to that power which provides the ordering of Being, that man's life is itself ordered in the true sense. All other human life is disorder and chaos. I will touch on this point again later in the paper.

II. Myth is the declaration in word of the Act that sustains that order, for without that order there could only be chaos.

Fantasy has as a central theme some contest, some struggle which is of Cosmic importance. Chaos is always threatening—and without this sustaining power the struggle could end only in chaos. Further, this sustaining of order is due to an act of some sort, often an act of will, which briefly conquers and controls chaos. But chaos continues to threaten. The journey or quest undertaken always involves a moment which discovers the enormity of the struggle—one in which the travellers may participate, but in which they are deeply aware of the clash of forces which are completely beyond them. Let me give a biblical illustration of what I mean.

God's answer to Job's demand for justification is a question: "Can you draw out Leviathan with a fishhook, or press down his tongue with a cord? Can you put a rope in his nose, or pierce his jaw with a hook?" (Job 41:1-2). Leviathan—the Sea Monster—associated with primeval chaos, is controlled and ordered by God. Man lives in a world ordered by God and without the power that makes existence and order possible, life cannot be sustained. Man cannot and does not create the world in which he lives. Nor can he, the biblical story suggests, create the values of the world in which he lives without a disordering effect upon his existence.

Tolkien's The Lord of The Rings opens with Bilbo, the Hobbit, leaving home to go east. He leaves the ring, the magic ring he had found on his previous journey, along with his other possessions with his cousin Frodo Baggins. Years later Frodo learns the real significance of the ring. Far back in the Second Age the Elven-Smiths of Gregion, controlled by Sauron, had forged the Rings of Power; but Sauron lost the one ring which he had forged himself and into which he let a great part of his power pass. It was this ring that Bilbo found in Gollum's Cave in the Misty Mountains.

Sauron is again preparing for all-out war, but he lacks one thing—the Ring—that will give him strength and knowledge to cover the whole land in "a second darkness." He knows where the ring is. Thus in order to save the world from this dark chaos, Frodo must take the ring and put it forever beyond his grasp. This is to be Frodo's quest.

The power of Evil is not the power of a counter world, but the power of no-order in this world. Darkness, which makes it impossible for us to differentiate between things, is thus chaos or lack of order. Sauron symbolizes a parasitic power, it must feed upon light if it is to be powerful. In discussing Evil as it appears in the Trilogy, Gunnar Urang quotes Frodo's remark about the orcs: "The shadow that bred them can only mock, it cannot make: not real new things of its own. I don't think it gave life to the orcs, it only ruined them and twisted them; and if they are to live at all, they have to live like other living creatures." Urang comments on this passage:

> Evil represents a privation of being. It is always the Dark Shadow; its blackness is the privation of light, its shadowiness the privation of substance. Its most fearful emissaries are the winged Nazgul, wraiths whose black robes cover nothingness. [7]

But to say that Evil is a privation of being is not to say that it is nothing. Evil is a power because in negating being it implies the active rejection of the created order of things and therefore the rejection of the creative power of being. The victory of the powers of darkness represents a victory for chaos because it implies the loss of the order and structure of being.

Again, in Charles Williams' War in Heaven the Graal, which is the central symbol for the life-giving force of creation in the book, becomes the center of an attack by Manasseh who worships its opposite, the power of destruction. In one incident in the book this disintegrative power is directed towards the Graal. The

Archdeacon, and his friends Kenneth Mornington and the Duke of Ridings, who
have taken it upon themselves to protect the Graal from attack, find themselves
at the center of a "supernatural" attack upon the Graal. The Archdeacon commands them to pray.

> "Against what shall we pray?" the Duke cried.
> "Against nothing," the Archdeacon said. "Pray that he who made
> the universe may sustain the universe, that in all things there may
> be delight in the justice of His will." [8]

But it is characteristic of fantastic literature that the powers of creation always defeat the powers of Evil. The creative forces always are maintained despite weakness and rejection. This is not simply a case of the "good guys" always
winning, but as Urang has said of The Lord of The Rings:

> Considered allegorically (it) speaks not only of the nature of the
> struggle against evil, the inescapability of involvement, the fact of
> freedom, the qualities of heroism, and the possibility for real loss.
> It also declares the viability of hope. It has a "happy ending." Frodo
> and Sam, their Quest achieved, wake in the sweet air of Ithilien.
> They see Gandalf again, and their other friends. They hear themselves
> acclaimed: "Long live the Halflings! Praise them with great praise!"
> They are seated in exaltation upon the throne of Aragorn. A minstrel
> of Gondor begins to sing the lay of Frodo and the Nine Fingers and the
> Ring of Doom. And then Sam, we are told, "laughed aloud for sheer
> delight, and he stood up and cried: 'O great glory and splendor! And
> all my wishes have come true!' And then he wept."
>
> (p. 119)

Tolkien in an essay contributed to a book in honor of Charles Williams, talks of
the part that hope plays in fairy stories. The eucatastrophe, the sum of events
leading to the happy ending, is a necessary part of such stories, not because hope
is meant to hide from us the harsh realities of existence, but because existence
itself presupposes the "good news" of the sustaining power of order—which is,
finally, the power of good.

III. Participation in the declaration of the myth enables the individual to participate in the creative power that sustains life.

Fantasy, of course, is not just story, it is enchantment. Otherwise only
some external features would distinguish it from fiction, and it would have no
power over us. Enchantment is the state of being under the domination of an
extrinsic power—usually a power which does not have a natural explanation. One
of the reasons why Tolkien is popular and Charles Williams is not, it can be surmised, is that Tolkien locates his story in a mythic world which is entirely self-
contained. He brings us into the created fantastic world and slowly allows the
symbols of power to work within us. Charles Williams, on the other hand, im-
poses upon our natural order another order, the occult and the supernatural, and
merely shows us how enchantment works. Tolkien allows us to participate in the

strange world which then, with its deep and meaningful symbols, casts us under its spell.

For enchantment is not simply being engrossed in a story so that we enter its world for a short time; rather, it becomes our world: we are caught up in it so that our very being is changed, in the way that perceiving the most powerful symbols alters our being. We can resist this world by rejecting it, but we do that at our peril. Chaos lurks around the corner. When Frodo hears the history of the ring and the implications that history has for what he is, he has no choice but to go on the journey, even though, as he points out, it is a strange world—it is not to find a treasure, but to give away a treasure, to return the ring to its rightful place.

The enchantment of the story lies beyond itself, and it is in this ability of fantasy to enchant us that we find the source of its power. We can be enthralled by a tale, we can be fascinated, we can be absorbed, but enchantment takes us beyond the tale and beyond ourselves.

It is this "going beyond" that implies that fantasy does not simply give us self-awareness or insight into our lives. The best fantasy points further beyond itself. Ancient man understood that to participate in myth was to participate in creation and in creating. Fantasy suggests in an analogous way that human power is limited, that the transitoriness of life is not accidental but is a limitation fully grasped only in relation to the power of creation.

Fantasy cannot be accepted without openness to the possibility of enchantment. Without that it is simply non-sense. To enter into the fantastic world we must suspend our view of the ordinariness of the world and accept the fantastic without question as reality. We so often think of fantasy literature as appropriate for children precisely because they are able to suspend judgment about their everyday world quite easily. Tolkien remarks that a child does not ask whether someone in a fantastic story is real or whether he or she exists, but wants to know "Was he good?" or "Was he wicked?" [10] The child is interested in getting clear the right and the wrong side. The question about the reality of the story world is one of value, not of existence.

If we read the literature of fantasy, and if we accept its world through its enchantments, we are forced into adopting, even for a short while, a new standpoint for ourselves—a standpoint which may centrally embody a system of values quite different from our own everyday values.

We ordinarily accept only the values generated from our experience, and we ordinarily understand values in terms of our interests and desires or in the best interests of a group or society. We thus treat value judgments either as emotive (good as my desire) or as objectively ascertainable in terms of some clear conception of group interest. Fantasy takes these questions of value out of the spheres of emotion and interest completely. The prime achievement of fantasy is that it makes the value of any element within the "real" world depend upon its relation to a quite different order of being. Through fantasy we understand our world as limited by its relationship with a different order of being, and we perceive that an awareness of this limitation is fundamental to a proper understanding of our world. Fantasy, therefore, warns us of the danger of turning to some element within the natural order as that which can grant us the power of life, and suggests instead that we are able to live fully only when we accept a basic sense of dependence upon an order beyond ourselves. Fantasy demonstrates the contingency of one part of our ordinary world and thus suggests the contingency of all its parts and of the whole itself; fantasy thus makes us comprehend the need for a secure reality on which to found our being. Our humanity is symbolized by our power to say 'no' to ourselves, to forbid a desired action. Such an ability must come from beyond the flux of our desires and passions; a moral absolute of some sort is presupposed. [11] Such a moral demand comes from "outside" our world, from that which is "beyond" us.

In reaching out to the fantastic one reaches out quite consciously into another dimension of reality. In this "other" dimension one enters into a world which is conceived as a counterpoint to the world in which the normal life is lived. It is in this "otherness" of the fantastic world that its importance lies, for the "otherness" represents a dissociation from the ordinary world of our normal life which leads us to see clearly that there are other standpoints from which life can be viewed. This is not to say that archaic man, who lived by the structure of his myths, simply adopted a standpoint from which he could view life. To say this would be far too misleading, because for such a man the myth world was his world. But, nevertheless, in living in such a world the world of animal desire is over-ridden because life is measured by the sacred absolutes of the myth and not by the appetites. Fantasy cannot be myth, however much its structure is myth-like, because it cannot have the power to ensnare us so completely that it becomes our total reality. But its mythological structure involves us in a self-consistent world where a different reality affects us perceptibly. Fantasy can only give us a standpoint; though, since it wins us with its enchantments and its spells, this standpoint has a deep and vital significance. This sense of a "deeper" reality attracts us to fantasy and its enchantment haunts us thereafter.

Thus fantasy, when we accept its enticements and its enchantments, forces us to examine our fundamental assumptions about our life. Reality is not what we ordinarily make it; it is less easily assumable than we think. It is moreover the very cradle of our existence, the very sphere of our lives. Fantasy invites us to look again at that cradle, that upholding sphere of existence; We thus look at ourselves from a standpoint quite distinct from our usual egocentric stance, and we are perturbed. For fantasy demonstrates the contingency of what was felt to be a secure element of the reality within which we implicitly define ourselves. It thus strikes very close to home, challenging our definitions of ourselves in a most basic way.

A journey taken in the realm of fantasy is taken at one's peril. Along the way questions will be asked which have no easy answer. But to take that journey is

to rediscover the self related to the world in a deeply meaningful though somewhat discomforting way.

---

1 Mircea Eliade, The Sacred and The Profane: The Nature of Religion (New York: Harper, 1961), p. 12.

2 Eliade, p. 166.

3 Eliade, p. 28.

4 Harvey Cox, The Secular City (New York: Macmillan Co., 1965).

5 J. R. R. Tolkien, The Return of The King: Being the Third Part of The Lord of The Rings (New York: Ballantine Books, 1970), pp. 308-309.

6 Charles Williams, War in Heaven (London: Faber and Faber, 1962), pp. 253-254.

7 Gunnar Urang, Shadows of Heaven: Religion and Fantasy in the Writing of C. S. Lewis, Charles Williams and J. R. R. Tolkien (Philadelphia: Pilgrim Press, 1971), p. 109.

8 Williams, p. 140.

9 C. S. Lewis, ed., Essays Presented to Charles Williams (Grand Rapids, Michigan: Eerdmans, 1968).

10 Lewis, p. 61.

11 John Oman in his The Natural and The Supernatural (Cambridge, Cambridge University Press, 1931) makes this interesting observation: ". . . the re-cognition of anything as sacred, as of an absolute value above desire and even above life, was the well-spring of all endeavour after emancipation from a material world merely appealing to man's appetites, because this alone in his life was not measured by them. Even in its most material forms, therefore, he was finding a higher power which made this victory over the material world possible. . . . This valuation as sacred, therefore, we ought to esteem as the spring of all self-mastery and all mastery over the world, as the sublime attainment by which man became truly man" (p. 92).

SCIENCE FICTION AND THE ADOLESCENT

Thomas J. Roberts

> "It's a poor sort of memory that only works backwards."
> —Through the Looking Glass

"The phases of being a science-fiction reader can be traced and charted," says Donald A. Wollheim in The Universe Makers. "So many read it for one year, so many for two, so many for life. For instance, reading it exclusively can be as compulsive as a narcotic for a period of an intelligent teen-ager's life. The length of time as I see it—and I have seen and talked with and corresponded with hundreds and hundreds of such readers in my lifetime—is about four or five years of the most intense reading—usually exclusive, all other literature being shoved aside. After that a falling off, rather rapid (often due to college entry or military life or the hard stuff of getting a job for the first time). There is, I suspect, something like an 80 percent turnover in the mass of readers of science fiction every five years."

Science fiction has many shapes. It is a mode, not a genre, which is to say that its traditions and content vary with the media in which it appears. The science fiction television series (Star Trek) is governed by different conditions than the feature film (2001: A Space Odyssey). Just as science fiction radio (X-One) is beginning to fade from human memory, a new oral tradition is beginning to emerge on records with The Firesign Theatre's Don't Crush That Dwarf and I Think We're All Bozos on This Bus. Even the lowly comic strip (Alex Raymond's Flash Gordon) is actually rather different from both the old comic books and the new underground comics (Planet Stories; Fantagor). But it is science fiction prose—by far the most sophisticated and demanding of all these genres—that is capturing that adolescent reader. We seriously underestimate him if we suppose we understand science fiction prose merely because we have watched The Creature from the Black Lagoon and read Flash Gordon when we were younger. It would be like supposing we know Moby-Dick because we have seen John Huston's film. The science fiction film may be lovable but it is stupid. Science fiction prose is often clumsily written but it is intelligent.

It may surprise some nonreaders to learn that within science fiction prose itself there is a tangle of conflicting traditions. Samuel J. Lundwall, in his study, Science Fiction, identifies five strands: pure adventure (e.g., Edgar Rice Burroughs, The Moons of Mars); horror (the stories of H. P. Lovecraft); sword and sorcery (Tolkien, Lord of the Rings); social satire (Huxley's Brave New World; Pohl and Kornbluth's Gravy Planet); scientific speculation (Hal Clement's Mission of Gravity); and literary experiment (Harlan Ellison's anthology Dangerous Visions). One of the leading magazines makes this mixture of subgenres explicit;

it calls itself <u>The Magazine of Fantasy and Science Fiction</u>. The truth is that a large part of science fiction is not about science at all; it is about the supernatural. And much of the rest of it is either covertly or quite openly doubtful about scientific values: we all think of Ray Bradbury as a writer of science fiction but he knows very little about modern science and is blatantly antagonistic to it. The adolescent who likes Isaac Asimov's stories about robots (<u>Caves of Steel</u>; <u>I, Robot</u>) probably also likes Tolkien's <u>Lord of the Rings</u>. In some of the best stories, magic and science are deliberately intertwined. There is nothing quite like Jack Vance's <u>Dying Earth</u> and Roger Zelazny's <u>Jack of Shadows</u> in the motion picture, or in any of the classic literary genres. Science fiction stories are often simple, but the genre itself is not simple.

Finally, some science fiction is written for adults and some for adolescents. This is so well recognized by readers of the genre that <u>Luna Monthly</u>, which is devoted to news about science fiction, has a special section of reviews titled "Lilliputia." There are some good novels which only the exceptional adolescent will find absorbing: Stapledon's <u>Last and First Men</u> and <u>Star Maker</u>, and Frank Herbert's <u>Dune</u>, and John Brunner's <u>Stand on Zanzibar</u>, and the oeuvre of H. G. Wells (when read as anything more than gadget-stories). He feels more at ease with simpler books like Arthur C. Clarke's <u>Childhood's End</u> and E. E. Smith's <u>Gray Lensman</u> than with, say, Walter Miller's <u>Canticle for Leibowitz</u>. It is wrong—inaccurate to say the least—to defend adolescent interest in the genre by citing books that will sustain the serious attention of adults.

C. S. Lewis once observed that it is the mark of the serious reader that he returns to certain important books again and again; but I think this is not (or only rarely) true of the serious reader in adolescence. He reads voraciously, drunkenly. He does not return to a book he loved. As soon as he has finished one book he reaches hungrily for something new. In a sense, he is not reading the books, he is reading the genre itself. Only later, and only if he continues to read, will he develop a private canon of books that have earned his continuing attention. Reading by genre is a different style of reading. It has its own logic, its own rationale, its own satisfactions.

Adolescent science fiction is a fictional analogue of those Jacques Cousteau films I suppose everyone has seen. Cousteau is giving us an exotic world invaded by men equipped with exotic devices for survival. Make some of those strange creatures Cousteau finds under the sea intelligent and make that equipment even more exotic and we have the world of technological science fiction. Replace that equipment with strange (but carefully defined) mental powers or with ancient charms and spells and we have moved into the world of supernatural science fiction. In either event, the emphases will be on the alien creatures and on the equipment, not on the people who do the adventuring. (Adult science fiction manifests moral and philosophical and theological concerns and gives greater emphasis to the people in that strange new world, but it is the adolescent variety that interests us.)

What is it in this imagined reality that a certain kind of adolescent finds important? The answer cannot be given in two paragraphs, but a couple of its features are worth remarking. First, science fiction, like Cousteau, shows men working closely with machines. Serious writing (and of course much science fiction too) admits the existence of the machine but treats it as pure menace. There are some notable exceptions to this—Melville's love of the technical apparatus of whaling, Beckett's use of a tape-recorder as a character in <u>Krapp's Last Tape</u>—but the serious writer at his most characteristic moments is as bigoted about the technician and machinery as any aging racist could be about Blacks. A profound concern about technology is appropriate to our times, but it does seem odd that writers should be so unqualifiedly hostile when, in all probability, they can still remember with great affection the first bicycles they ever owned, when they take pride in their high fidelity sound equipment, when they reach their friends normally by telephone, and when—as they must recognize—they may be kept alive and productive later by heart-pacers. Ursula K. Le Guin spoke truly: "For modern man, nature is technological." The adolescent knows this without knowing that he knows it, and he finds the world in which he meets "slow glass" and "body shields" and "space skimmers" and "hyperdrives" as realistic in its own way as the worlds of Emile Zola and Frank Norris are in their ways. Science fiction understands the machine intuitively much better than contemporary serious writing does; it, too, often presents the machine as an alien which has invaded our world from within us; it, too, often presents it as irrelevant; but it also presents it as the tool and companion it has come to be. The adolescent is reading a literature which at this moment in our cultural history is unique in its imaginative exploration of man-machine relationships.

Then, there are also those exotic intelligences—not just the bug-eyed monsters of the motion picture and the old fashioned science fiction novel (Wyndham's <u>Day of the Triffids</u>) but the alien life-forms, alien intelligences, alien psychologies to which so much of the science fiction writer's imagination is devoted. Whether it be the sorcerer of Tolkien's stories, or a shape-shifting carnivore in Weinbaum's "Martian Odyssey," or the intelligent and benign virus in Clement's <u>Needle</u>, or the flame-throwing plants in Aldiss's <u>Long Afternoon of Earth</u>, or the bisexual humanoids in Le Guin's <u>Left Hand of Darkness</u>, it is the alien which captures most of the reader's attention. Just as <u>Gulliver's Travels</u> and the <u>Odyssey</u> and Mandeville's <u>Travels</u> did in their own day, these stories make manifest the unadmitted uneasiness we have about the obvious. Like us, the adolescent works with categories that usually serve well enough in his dealings with others. He thinks he knows what a high school English teacher is like, what congressmen are like, what career soldiers are like, what actors are like; but the individual teachers and congressmen and soldiers and athletes he actually gets to know have a perverse way of not quite fitting his pigeonholes. He thinks he knows what he himself is; but he finds himself being surprised now and then by something he has done unconsciously—an "accidental" remark that gives someone else pain, his inability to remember somebody's name when he has to introduce him, a sudden spurt of joy when something nice happens to someone he thinks he dislikes. For him (as for us) nothing quite fits that grid his culture and his experience and his reflection has constructed in his brain. In the science fiction aliens, his unadmitted sense of the mysteriousness of others is given the objective correlative, as Grierson and Eliot called it, for feelings that are always inside him. He is in the process of shifting from a world centered upon him to one in which he is just an individual in a crowd of people whose inbuilt purposes are taking them in other directions. He will come to accept this more easily, I suspect, when the otherness is given an unmistakably alien form; he will learn later—as King Lear did—that all the rest of us are aliens too.

Adolescent science fiction shares this interest in the machine and the alien with adult science fiction, but it has other features which repel experienced readers. For one thing, the stories are thickly smeared with sentimental lard. The work of Cordwainer Smith (e.g., "Scanners Live in Vain") offers a fictional universe so bizarre that it is outstanding even within the genre, but the price an adult must pay to share Smith's vision is very heavy: We must swallow a sentimentality of characterization and event that we find almost indigestible. But now we must ask ourselves two questions students of children's literature have no doubt raised many times before. Are we never to say that a book is excellent for adolescents unless it is also a good book for adults? Must we measure adolescent tastes only by their similarity to adult tastes? When I reflect on the long history of my own reading preferences I find that there was no slow evolution but rather a series of abrupt metamorphoses. Perhaps we are butterflies now, but once we were caterpillars and what satisfies us as butterflies was not what we needed then. I am not displeased, today, to recall that I preferred Robert Heinlein's stories to Scott's Ivanhoe—a book my own high school teachers forced upon me with only the best intentions.

Science fiction includes some of the many forms the ancient tradition of fantasy is taking today. I suppose no one who has ever looked into the genre has failed to notice this, and yet it does not seem to be generally appreciated. It is a simple fact that the adult reader of science fiction is also interested in Kafka's Metamorphoses and Jorge Luis Borges's Labyrinths and that the adolescent reads the stories of John Collier and Saki too. The Lord of the Rings, a fantasy, might easily be transformed from its subgenre to the other. Put the story into outer space and have the adventurers move from one planet to another. Make Gandolf a super scientist. Make the different peoples different species found on those different planets. (The thematic content would hardly be affected: no one thinks of Frank Herbert's Dune as fantasy per se and yet it presents a more complex fictional universe than Tolkien did, it deals with prescience and the prophet, and it raises ultimate humanistic questions—in, I feel, a more sophisticated and disturbing way.) How different, after all, is a wizard with a magic wand from a scientist with a microminiaturized matter-transformer? The reader does not understand how either gadget works. People who would like to believe for a while in magic will prefer the wizard. People who would like to believe in the unending progress of technology will prefer the scientist. It is a matter of one's willingness to suspend certain kinds of disbelief, and not others, when one chooses between them.

Most of science fiction purports to be about the future, and it is either openly fantastic or a translation of the fantastic into super science. It is, then, a projection into an imagined future of the concerns and wonders of the past, a presentation of that future in the language of the past. "It is a poor sort of memory that only works backwards." For the adolescent, "real" life does lie in the future; it will begin when he is released from school. He finds in even the most technological science fiction an impression of that life in which the ancient worries of man appear once again: love and hate, victory and defeat, honor and shame—and always difficulties, terrors, problems, crises in an unfamiliar world he did not make and will never fully understand. In short, what is implicit in Chaucer and Shakespeare and Austen and Dickens and Shaw and Faulkner is made so explicit in science fiction that even inexperienced readers cannot miss it.

True, most of these science fiction stories the adolescent devours are worth no more than one reading, but this does not argue that the genre itself is not worth his attention. The corpus of the genre—the total of all the stories it has generated—constitutes for him one immense collage; it is a loose-leaf book whose chapters are novels and whose subchapters are short stories, which he may enter at any point and explore in whatever sequence interest and chance should suggest. Science fiction is a subliterary genre—subliterary because so few, if any, of its stories will sustain the continued attention of thoughtful readers—which closely parallels the junk sculpture of our age. It is not a story-by-story but a story-with-story analysis that it requires. The first approach will prove that the whole is composed of junk parts but it will miss the interaction of those parts. It will not see that one flawed story may complement another flawed story and the whole become greater than the sum of its parts.

But one might reply, this argument makes it possible to defend any literary genre that has ever emerged and obliterates distinctions in value. Not so. Of adolescent and adult science fiction I think this is true, but not of most other genres. Spasmodic poetry and the western and the "academic" novel never achieved significance. I do not know enough about children's literary genres to identify the significant among them, but it seems to me that the only other subliterary adult genre for which the same claim can be made is the mystery novel—a web of such subgenres as the novel of detection (Agatha Christie's And Then There Were None), the thriller (Eric Ambler's Coffin for Dimitrios), police-procedure stories (William P. McGivern's novels), and especially the tradition which emerged from Black Mask magazine (Dashiell Hammett's Red Harvest). Some genres do not merit the attention of adults or adolescents.

To dismiss books written for children as unimportant because they do not interest adult minds and to dismiss—however regretfully—the children who do prefer them to adult books is, often, to do both an injustice. It fails to recognize that the adolescent mind has its own nonadult requirements and that some adolescent genres have an internal complexity and a pertinence that transcends the limitations of the stories that emerge from them. I think no better example of such an injustice can be found than in the contemporary dismissal of adolescent science fiction by thoughtful readers.

HOW IT DEVELOPED THAT BOTANY WAS THE SCIENCE THOUGHT MOST SUITABLE FOR VICTORIAN YOUNG LADIES

Emanuel D. Rudolph

During the second quarter of the nineteenth century in the United States the notion that botany was the science especially suited to women became prevalent. "Botany is peculiarly fitted for introduction into a girls' school," one essay concludes. "It is admirably adapted to the tastes, feelings, and capacities of females, as is demonstrated by the fact that the majority of our botanists are females. Boys are less easily interested in it; more apt to be careless and harsh in their treatment of specimens, and too much attached to rude and boisterous sports. Girls, on the contrary, are apt to take delight in examining the most minute peculiarities of flowers, in pressing and preserving specimens, and in delineating the most remarkable with the lead pencil, or in water colours. Their enthusiasm, therefore, will generally be easily awakened."[1] This notion is echoed by Almira Hart Lincoln Phelps, an important educator of the period, and a sister of Emma Willard, who was the founder of the first girls' school in the United States.[2] In her Familiar Lectures on Botany of 1829 she states her case for girls' botany. The statement appeared unchanged in all editions as late as 1860: "The study of Botany seems peculiarly adapted to females; the objects of its investigation are beautiful and delicate; its pursuit leading to exercise in the open air is conducive to health and cheerfulness. Botany is not a sedentary study which can be acquired in the library; but the objects of the science are scattered over the surface of the earth, along the banks of the winding brooks, or the borders of precipices, the sides of mountains, and the depths of the forest."[3]

To discover the origins of these quaint notions one must venture backward toward France and England in the third quarter of the eighteenth century. At least part of the credit for the idea that ladies should best be botanists must be given to the famous author and philosopher Jean Jacques Rousseau. His 1771 Essais élémentaires sur la botanique was Englished six years later under the fateful title, Elements of Botany Addressed to a Lady.[4] The English title is not altogether inappropriate, since Rousseau does address the volume to a lady who wishes her daughter to observe plants and determine their classification according to the then popular Linnaean system. He writes: "I think your idea of amusing the vivacity of your daughter a little, and exercising her attention upon such agreeable and varied objects as plants, is excellent: though I should not have ventured to play the pedant so far as to propose it of myself. Since however it comes from you, I approve it with my heart, and will even assist you in it; convinced that, at all times of life, the study of nature abates the taste for frivolous amusements, prevents the tumult of the passions, and provides the mind with a nourishment which is salutary, by filling it with an object most worthy of its contemplation."[5] And later: "Since you continue, dear cousin, to pursue, with your daughter, that peaceable and delightful study which fills up those voids in our time too often dedicated by others to idleness, or something worse, with interesting observations on nature; I will resume the interrupted thread of our vegetable tribes." [6]

Rousseau, however, would be surprised (not to say dismayed) to find laid to his charge the idea that lady scientists should be botanists, for neither in this work, nor in his educational philosophy in Emile, does he suggest that botany is the best or only science for girls. In fact, he says that exact science is not at all suitable for girls: "An inquiry into abstract and speculative truths, into the principles, and axioms of sciences and every thing that render our ideas more general, is not the province of women. Their studies ought to be all practical; it is their business to apply the principles discovered by man, and to make the observations by which our sex is induced to establish those principles. . . . With regard to works of genius, they surpass their comprehension, neither have they sufficient attention and precision to succeed in the mathematics; and as for natural philosophy, it belongs only to that sex which is most active, sees most objects, is possessed of most strength, and exercises 't the most, to judge of the relations of sensible beings, and of the laws of nature." [7] Still, I believe that Rousseau can be given indirect credit for the idea of botany as the girls' science because he influenced others, particularly female English writers, who popularized the elegance of botany as a science when the Linnaean system was used as an aid to learning about plants and how to classify them.

In England during the late eighteenth and early nineteenth centuries writers of children's books on botany were often women. One of them, Mrs. Maria Elizabeth Jackson, who wrote anonymously, was much influenced by Rousseau in her botanical works. [8] Her Sketches of the Physiology of Vegetable Life states: "The taste for botany which has of late years so generally prevailed amongst all ranks and ages of society, and more peculiarly manifested itself in the younger part of the female sex, has long rendered me desirous to attempt to lead the more inquiring minds of those engaged in this interesting and rational pursuit, to a deeper investigation of the habits and properties of that division of organized nature denominated the vegetable kingdom, than is usually entered into by students of the technical part of the science." [9] Priscilla Wakefield, prolific writer of children's natural history works, [10] offered botany to the young reader with the advice that, "Botany is a branch of Natural History that possesses many advantages; it contributes to health of body and cheerfulness of disposition, by presenting an inducement to take air and exercise; it is adapted to the simplest capacity, and the objects of its investigations offer themselves without expense or difficulty, which renders them attainable to every rank in life; but with all these allurements, till of late years, it has been confined to the circle of the learned, which may be attributed to those books that treated of it, being principally written in Latin; a difficulty that deterred many, particularly the female sex, from attempting to obtain the knowledge of a science, thus defended, as it were, from their approach." [11] And yet other female writers of the period, Elizabeth and Sarah Fitton, [12] recommend botany as a study because, "What Miss Edgeworth

93

has said of Chemistry (in Letters for Literary Ladies) may with equal truth be applied to Botany, and may serve to recommend the study of it, as a branch of general education: 'It is not a science of parade, it affords occupation and infinite variety, it demands no bodily strength, it can be pursued in retirement; there is no danger of its inflaming the imagination, because the mind is intent upon realities. The knowledge that is acquired is exact; and the pleasure of the pursuit is a sufficient reward for the long labour.' " In the work mentioned, Miss Edgeworth also notes: "Botany has become fashionable; in time it may become useful, if it be not so already . . . Chemistry will follow botany; chemistry is a science particularly suited to women, suited to their talents and to their situation." [13] In reading the works of these women it is apparent that they have not selected botany over other sciences, such as chemistry, zoology or astronomy as being more suitable for girls. Though she wrote a botanical work, Conversations on Vegetable Physiology, the most famous female writer of scientific books for the young of this period, Mrs. Jane Marcet, best known for her Conversations on Chemistry, believed that any science was suitable for girls to learn provided it was presented simply. [14] Thus, the British writers of children's botanical works of the late eighteenth and early nineteenth centuries do not make a special point of botany as the science for young girls even though they wrote works for the young. In practice, as Archer says about British schools of the late nineteenth century, "Botany, always popular in girl's schools, began to be taught so as to produce scientific habits of the mind." [15]

How, then, can we account for the popular association of ladies and botany in the United States, which the quotations at the beginning of this essay attest? The key is perhaps in the attitudes of Almira Hart Lincoln Phelps, the prominent educator quoted at the outset of this piece, and in the influence of Amos Eaton, an energetic teacher of botany and other subjects, upon her and countless other students. [16] Amos Eaton did not write a textbook of botany, but rather a manual for the identification of plants according to the Linnaean system. In the introduction to his 3rd edition of 1822, he says: "The recommendation of the study of botany to the attention of ladies, subscribed by the late governor Strong of Massachusetts, and others, which was published in the second edition, is unnecessary at this day; for I believe more than half the botanists of New England and New York are ladies." [17] And it is apparent that by his welcoming women into his classes not only in botany, but in mineralogy and geology, he converted many, including Mrs. Phelps, to botany. In a letter to John Torrey, an eminent botanist of the time, Eaton writes: "It is among the hobbies of Troy folks (and I ride it the hardest) to make botany a part of the common school learning in the summer season. We intend to have our Yankee girls teach it." [18] Eaton's lessons were learned well by Mrs. Phelps, whose books became widely used in schools and home. She confided to William Darlington, a Pennsylvanis botanist, in 1857: "It is certain that about one hundred and fifty thousand of my Botany have been sold; if the work has been so simple as to be popular, it has certainly done something towards diffusing a taste for the science where otherwise its first principles might never have been known." [19]

Americans of the mid-nineteenth century, with the sudden extension of formal education to women, seemed to embrace, in many quarters, Mrs. Phelps' idea that botany was the science most suitable for girls. Others, including Emma Willard, did not believe that any science should be omitted from the training of girls. "Natural philosophy has not often been taught to our sex. Yet why should we be kept in ignorance of the great machinery of nature, and left to the vulgar notion, that nothing is curious but what deviates from her common course? If mothers were acquainted with this science, they would communicate very many of its principles to their children in early youth. From the bursting of an egg buried in the fire, I have heard an intelligent mother, lead her prattling inquirer, to understand the cause of the earthquake. . . . A knowledge of natural philosophy is calculated to heighten the moral taste, by bringing to view the majesty and beauty of order and design; and to enliven piety, by enabling the mind more clearly to perceive, throughout the manifold works of God, that wisdom, in which he hath made them all."[20] By the last quarter of the century, the teaching of many sciences to girls won the day in the United States. It was only in the popular mind that the notion of botany as a "girls' science" persisted. Vigorous spokesmen for scientific botany using the natural rather than the Linnaean system, such as Asa Gray in the United States, wrote the new texts and some of the children's books about botany, and it was they who set the new tone.

Linnaeus put all plants into a system that was understandable, making it possible to classify them by counting the sexual organs in their flowers. Rousseau by writing his Letters on the Elements of Botany Addressed to a Lady helped to make botany a "fashionable" pursuit for women and a science worthy of being taught to their daughters. British female writers of the late eighteenth and early nineteenth centuries wrote many botanical works for children; while they did think it eminently suitable for ladies, they did not claim it as the science most suitable for them. Apparently this claim was made by some American writers, but most particularly by Almira Hart Lincoln Phelps. Thus, in the United States, between 1826 and 1846, botany acquired the reputation of being a girls' science and that association persisted much longer in the popular mind.

---

[1] "Botany for Schools," American Jour. of Education, 4 (1829), 168-175. The piece was probably written by William Russell, who edited the journal from 1826-1829. He later established a school for girls in connection with Germantown Academy in Philadelphia.

[2] See E. L. Bolzau, Almira Hart Lincoln Phelps: Her Life and Work, Philadelphia, 1936. Her Familiar Lectures on Botany. Including practical and elementary botany, with generic and specific descriptions of the most common native and foreign plants and a vocabulary of botanical terms. For the use of higher schools and academies, went through many editions and reprintings between 1829 and 1868. Her other more simplified work is: Botany for Beginners: an introduction to Mrs. Lincoln's lectures on botany. For the use of common schools and the younger pupils of higher schools and academies (Hartford, 1831); it had a number of editions between 1831 and 1867.

3 Familiar Lectures on Botany (Hartford: H. and F. J. Huntington, 1829), p. 12.

4 The first English edition of the Essais élémentaires was translated by Thomas Martyn (London: White and Son, 1775)

5 From the seventh English edition, Letters on the Elements of Botany, addressed to a lady, by the celebrated J. J. Rousseau. Translated into English, with notes, and twenty-four additional letters, fully explaining the system of Linnaeus, by Thomas Martyn, B. D. F. R. & L. S. S. Regius Professor of Botany in the University of Cambridge. (London: John White, 1807), p. 19.

6 Elements of Botany, p. 33.

7 Emilius; or, an essay on education, translated from the French by Mr. Nugent. 2 vols. (London: J. Nourse and P. Vaillant, 1763), p. 229.

8 Her strictly botanical works: Botanical dialogues, between Hortensia and her four children, Charles, Harriet, Juliette and Henry. Designed for the use of schools. By a lady. (London: J. Johnson, 1797). Botanical lectures. By a lady. Altered from "Botanical dialogues for the use of schools," and adapted to the use of persons of all ages, by the same author. (London: J. Johnson, 1804). Sketches of the physiology of vegetable life. By the authoress of "Botanical dialogues." (London: John Hatchard, 1811). She is not treated in the Dictionary of National Biography. G. E. Fussell, "Some lady botanists of the nineteenth century. III. Mrs. Maria Elizabeth Jackson," The Gardeners' Chronicle, 130 (1951), pp. 63-64.

9 Vegetable Life, p. 1.

10 Priscilla Wakefield née Bell, (1751-1832). See Dictionary of National Biography, and G. E. Fussell, "Some Lady Botanists of the Nineteenth Century. I. Priscilla Wakefield," The Gardeners' Chronicle, 128 (1950), pp. 130-131. In addition to her An Introduction to Botany in a series of familiar letters (of which there were at least 11 British editions, 1796-1841, 2 French editions, 1801-1802, and 3 American editions, 1811-1818), she published numerous works for children, among which are the following, dealing with natural history: Domestic Recreation: or dialogues illustrative of natural and scientific subjects, London, 1805; An Introduction to the Natural History and Classification of Insects, in a series of letters, London, 1816: Instinct Displayed, or facts exemplifying the sagacity of various species of animals, London, 1811; A Catechism of Botany, London, 1817 [?].

11 Priscilla Wakefield, An Introduction to Botany, in a series of letters, with illustrative engravings, 2nd edition (London: E. Newbery, 1798), p. 11.

12 On the sisters Fitton see G. E. Fussell, "Some lady botanists of the nineteenth century. IV. Elizabeth and Sarah Mary Fitton," The Gardeners' Chronicle, 130 (1951), pp. 179-180. Their anonymous Conversations on Botany (London, 1817), went through at least 9 editions between 1817 and 1840. The quotation here is from the 1820 edition.

13 Maria Edgeworth was a popular writer in her day. See I. C. Clarke, _Maria Edgeworth, her family and friends_ (London: Hutchinson, 1950); P. H. Newby, Maria Edgeworth (London: Barker, 1950); and S. W. Patterson, _Rousseau's Emile and Early Children's Literature_ (Metuchen, N.J.: The Scarecrow Press, 1971). The quotation here is from Miss Edgeworth's _Letters for Literary Ladies, to which is added an essay on the science of self-justification_ (George Town: Joseph Milligan, 1810), pp. 39–40.

14 Jane Marcet (1769-1858) was an important and popular interpreter of science. See _Dictionary of National Biography_; E. V. Armstrong, "Jane Marcet and her Conversations on chemistry," _Jour. Chemical Education,_ 15 (1938), pp. 53-57; J. Read, _Humour and Humanism in Chemistry_ (London: 1947), pp. 176-191; and G. E. Fussell, "Some lady botanists of the nineteenth century. V. Jane Marcet," _The Gardeners' Chronicle,_ 130 (1951), p. 238.

15 R. L. Archer, _Secondary education in the nineteenth century_ (Cambridge: Cambridge University Press, 1928), p. 144.

16 See E. M. McAllister, _Amos Eaton, Scientist and Educator,_ 1776-1842 (Philadelphia: University of Pennsylvania Press).

17 _Manual of Botany, for the northern and middle states of America_ (Albany: Websters and Skinners, 1822). p. 11.

18 Letter to John Torrey, Feb. 4, 1824, as quoted in McAllister, _Amos Eaton,_ p. 220.

19 Letter to William Darlington, Dec. 9, 1857, in the William Darlington papers at The New York Historical Society.

20 Emma Willard, _A plan for improving female education_ (Middlebury, Vermont: Middlebury College, 1819), p. 19.

FIVE WAYS AND ONE OF LOOKING AT MOTHER GOOSE

Wilson Currin Snipes

In the following remarks I propose to discuss briefly five ways of approaching the literary work of a single author. Each approach, to simplify the difference among the approaches, is governed by a central question:

(1) The Biographical Approach: what kind of person was or is the artist?
(2) The Socio-cultural Approach: what are the characteristics of the age?
(3) The Humanistic Approach: what are the ethical qualities of the literary work?
(4) The Formalist Approach: what is the character of the work of art itself?
(5) The Psychological-Psychoanalytic Approach: what is the psychic life of the artist?

Obviously these questions are oversimplifications of the critical views represented, but they are indicative of the critical approaches of many contemporary, practicing critics. They are stances people adopt when they read literature seriously as literature. Now let's take a look at the five in theory and in application to Mother Goose.

I. The Biographical Approach

Many of us studied literature through what is commonly described as the biographical approach. E. M. W. Tillyard in "The Personal Heresy" states this position: "I believe we read Keats in some measure because his poetry gives a version of a remarkable personality of which another version is his life." I recall seeing a biography of Picasso that illustrates Tillyard's remarks: on the top of each page one could see the art work Picasso produced at a particular time; on the bottom of each page in prose was a description of what Picasso was doing in his daily life besides painting: his friends, mistresses, social and political life. The primary characteristic of this approach is that we study the work of art in the context of the artist's development. Hence, we study Emerson's "Compensation" essay in terms of Emerson's development. We are interested in the man Emerson in relation to the art of a man named Emerson.

The biographical critic would ask: What kind of person was Mrs. Goose, the author of the "Mother Goose Rhymes"? Of course we should be better able to answer this question had Mrs. Goose left an autobiography, a diary, a few letters, or had her friends left Memoirs of Mother Goose, or Mother Goose's Trip to Banbury Cross, but even without these the biographical critic reads Mrs.

Goose's poems biographically. Thus the biographical critic can say that Mrs. Goose was a village busy-body, one who knew many intimate details of the life of her community (based on Mrs. Goose's detailed knowledge of Jack Horner, Mrs. McShuttle, Doctor Foster, Jack and Mrs. Sprat, Old Mother Hubbard, and Simple Simon). She liked children: witness her acquaintance with Lucy Lockett, Kitty Fisher, Miss Muffett, Georgie Porgie, Mary, Bo-Peep, Little Boy Blue, and others. She had a special interest in animals—kittens, mice, donkeys, rats, sheep, black hens, dogs, robin redbreasts. She followed some questionable eating habits "pease porridge nine days old"; she had a strong aversion to stealing—remember the Knave of Hearts who "after being beaten full sore, vowed he'd steal no more." Some biographical critics argue she had strong moral qualities. She would not lend Dapple-Gray again to a woman who whipped him, slashed him, and rode him through the mire. She objected to those who washed clothes on Saturday—"Oh, they are sluts indeed." In "Hush-A-Bye" Mrs. Goose said, "Hush-a-bye, baby, daddy is near; mamma is a lady, and that's very clear." Other critics have argued that Mrs. Goose was highly immoral. Remember "There was an old woman who lived in a shoe, she had so many children she didn't know what to do." Certainly Mrs. Goose loved the seasons of the year. In "The Year" she speaks of April as a time that "brings the primrose sweet, scatters daisies at our feet." Or "Fresh October brings the pheasant, then to gather nuts is pleasant." Or, to show Mrs. Goose's lightness, she described the seasons as follows:

> Spring is showery, flowery, bowery;
> Summer: hoppy, croppy, poppy;
> Autumn: wheezy, sneezy, freezy;
> Winter: slippy, drippy, nippy.

Mrs. Goose emphasized the importance of motherhood through such poems as "Rock-A-Bye, Baby"; "Sleep, Baby, Sleep"; "Diddle, Diddle, Dumpling"; "Dance, Little Baby"; "Clap Handies"; and "Pat-A-Cake! Pat-A-Cake!"

Based on such deductions from the corpus of Mrs. Goose's works the biographical critics would probably divide into three groups in their evaluations and interpretations of Mrs. Goose's character: in the first group a C. Frederick Postlethwaite said, "Mrs. Goose had an imagination that belongs to all ages." A rural physician, a kindly one, who lived between Claypool Hill and Taswell, Virginia, said, "Anyone who sees a cow jumping over a moon or a dish running away with a spoon is in immediate need of psychiatric help." A third group of critics, represented by a well known member of Alcoholics Anonymous, said, "A member of our organization would have talked with Mrs. Goose at any time she wished." Hence the biographical critics may have concluded that Mrs. Goose was highly-imaginative, mentally ill, or a confirmed alcoholic.

II. The Socio-cultural Approach

David Daiches in "Fiction and Civilization" represents those who insist on approaching the work of art through its socio-cultural milieu; Daiches states,

"We affirm dogmatically that that critical approach is more useful which involves relating the art of fiction at any given time to the civilization of which it is a part, and endeavoring to see all other questions of form, technique, style, subject matter against the background of this relationship." To illustrate, Shakespeare's Hamlet must be considered as work of art against a late sixteenth and early seventeenth century background. Fundamental to the socio-cultural approach is this question: what is the character of the civilization of which Mrs. Goose is a part?

The socio-cultural critic of Mother Goose would be particularly interested in the background of Mrs. Goose's rhymes. What are some of the specific characteristics of Mrs. Goose's civilization? In "Old Mother Hubbard" we learn that there were bakers to bake bread, joiners to build coffins, fishmongers to catch fish, fruiterers to sell fruit, tailors to make clothes, barbers to make wigs, taverners to sell white and red wine, cobblers to mend shoes. These descriptions would suggest that Mrs. Goose lived in a world of guilds; her friends and acquaintances were craftsmen. Next, notice the richness of rural imagery in Mrs. Goose's poems. Think only of "Little Boy Blue"—poems filled with sheep, cows, corn, haycocks, mowing, candlesticks, farmers, ravens, mares, rams, market days, and such. A third characteristic of Mrs. Goose's world involves a monarch: "Old King Cole"; "a princess who has lost her shoe"; "a little girl who has been gathering roses to give to the queen"; "an old woman who fell asleep on the king's highway"; "a pussycat who has been to London to look at the queen"; a past that involves the "Good King Arthur" and "Hector Protector being sent to the queen."

Mrs. Goose lived in a religious age: "Little Fred always said his prayers when he went to bed." In "Matthew, Mark, Luke and John" we hear Mrs. Goose saying "Bless the bed that I lie on! Four corners to my bed, Four angels overhead." In "Christmas" the wish that "God bless you"; in "A Week of Birthdays" the conclusion "But the child that's born on the Sabbath day is blithe and bonny, and good and gay." Perhaps the best overview of the religious customs of Mrs. Goose's time is provided by "The Death and Burial of Poor Cock Robin." You will recall that the fish, birds, animals and insects participated in this death and burial. Remember "Who killed Cock Robin?" "I," said the sparrow, "With my bow and arrow, I killed Cock Robin." A sequence followed involving the murder, a witness the fly, a fish who caught the blood, a beetle who made his shroud, a lark who served as the clerk, an owl who would dig his grave, a rook who would be the parson, a thrush who would sing a psalm, a dove who would be the chief mourner, a bull who would toll the bell.

Many other comments may be made about the civilization to which Mrs. Goose belonged: Her people were seafaring people ("Dance to your Daddie," "I Saw a Ship," "Bobby Shaftoe"); folklore of her day included "Robin Hood," "Pancake Day," and "when good King Arthur lived"; her world included superstitions involving sneezing, three straws, "A Sunshiny Shower," "Pins," "Dreams"— remember in "Jack and Jill" after Jack fell down and broke his crown, he went to bed and plastered his head with "vinegar and brown paper." And then there is:

The fair maid who, the first of May,
Goes to the fields at break of day,
And washes in dew from the hawthorn tree,
Will ever after handsome be.

Mrs. Goose's world involved thieves, huntsmen who hunted both with bows and arrows and with guns and bullets (obviously a transitional period), and a domestic life that centered around the fireplace, drinking, porridge, broth, curds and whey, the dairy, hoeing and mowing, reeling and spinning and singing.

It should be clear that the socio-cultural critic would pursue these many suggestions found in Mrs. Goose's poems—or rural imagery, monarchy, dress, foodstuffs, romantic notions, superstitions. And based on his examinations of these in Mother Goose's world he would see the poems in the socio-cultural context.

III. The Humanist Approach

The humanist critic asks: what are the ethical qualities to be found in Mrs. Goose's work? Douglas Bush describes his personal faith in an essay entitled "The Humanist Critic": "I believe (1) that criticism should use all helpful means and methods for the study of literature; (2) that historical knowledge and aesthetic analysis need to work together, and preferably in the same mind, not in different minds; (3) that . . . the scholar or critic cannot be content with the elucidation of works of art, central as that function is; (4) that he has the further and traditional function of actively conserving the ethical and cultural inheritance that we are in danger of losing altogether; (5) and that he has a social or . . . a missionary obligation to labor to convert the heathen.   (6) If my position is naive, reactionary, and unrealistic, I can only say that I would rather go to hell with a Christian Platonist than to heaven with a naturalistic positivist."

Mrs. Goose made clear the importance of moral responsibilities: Little Boy should be tending his sheep; Tom the Piper's Son was beaten for stealing a pig; Taffy who stole a piece of beef was beaten on the head; and, Little Johnny Green who put pussy in the well was considered a naughty boy (Little Johnny Stout who got pussy out of the well should have been given a good licking for going into the well). In "The Clock" Mrs. Goose summarizes her concept of moral responsibility:

There's a neat little clock—
In the schoolroom it stands—
And it points to the time
With its two little hands.

And may we, like the clock,
Keep a face clean and bright,
With hands ever ready
To do what is right.

Mrs. Goose was a philosophical woman. Remember her "Birds of a Feather flock together," or her "Little girl with a curl right in the middle of her forehead," who was either good or horrid.

Typically Mrs. Goose believed strongly in the importance of marriage. According to Mrs. Goose the progress of true love is as follows:

> One, he loves; two, he loves;
> Three, he loves, they say;
> Four, he loves with all his heart;
> Five, he casts away.
> Six, he loves; seven, she loves;
> Eight, they both love.
> Nine, he comes; ten, he tarries;
> Eleven, he courts; twelve, he marries.

There are no alternatives.

Mrs. Goose had the realistic streak of a charter member of the American Chamber of Commerce. Remember in "Simple Simon":

> Simple Simon met a pieman going to the fair,
> Says Simple Simon to the pieman, "Let me taste your ware."
>
> Says the pieman to Simple Simon, "Show me first your penny."
> Says Simple Simon to the pieman, "Indeed, I have not any."

Would someone care to guess whether or not Simple Simon was given a taste of pie?

Mrs. Goose believed in a fair day's work for a fair day's pay. Remember "Seesaw, Margery Daw": "Jackey shall have but a penny a day because he can't work any faster." Remember Mrs. Goose's famous axiom: "For early to bed and early to rise is a way to be healthy, wealthy and wise."

The humanistic critic would say that Mrs. Goose was a common sense philosopher, one who emphasized moral responsibility, one who recognized the social and ethical significance of man, one who held a realistic view toward the problems of daily life.

IV. The Formalist Approach

The new critic asks: what is the character of the work of art itself? This position was stated by Cleanth Brooks in "The Formalist Critic." He affirms (1) that literary criticism is a description and an evaluation of its object; (2) that the primary concern of criticism is with the problem of unity—the kind of whole which the literary work forms or fails to form, and the relation of the various parts to each other in building up this whole; (3) that the formal relations in a work of literature may include, but certainly exceed, those of logic; (4) that in a successful work, form and content cannot be separated; (5) that form is meaning; (6) that literature is ultimately metaphorical and symbolic; (7) that the general and the universal are not seized upon by abstraction, but got at through the concrete and the particular; (8) that literature is not a surrogate for religion; (9) that, as Allen Tate says, ' specific moral problems ' are the subject matter of literature, but that the purpose of literature is not to point a moral; (10) that the principles of criticism define the area relevant to literary criticism; they do not constitute a method for carrying out the criticism. What would the new critic say of Mrs. Goose's works?

Among other things he would say her works are playful ("Dance, Thumbkin, Dance"), musical ("The Cat and the Fiddle"), imaginative ("I Had a Little Nut Tree"), humorous ("Where Are You Going, My Pretty Maid?"), imagistic ("Pease Porridge hot"), symbolic ("I had a little husband"), paradoxical ("Henry was a worthy king"). Perhaps the best way to show the new critic's position is to suggest some of these characteristics in Humpty Dumpty:

> Humpty Dumpty sat on a wall,
> Humpty Dumpty had a great fall;
> All the King's horses and all the King's men
> Cannot put Humpty Dumpty together again.

To begin with, what is a Humpty Dumpty? A swift glance at the Oxford English Dictionary will reveal that "humpty-dumpty" has a number of lexical meanings.

(1) Around 1698 "humpty-dumpty" referred to a kind of liquor. That doesn't fit the rhyme.
(2) Around 1700 "humpty-dumpty" meant "a drink made with ale boiled with brandy." Although the idea of the drink sitting on the wall is far removed, the idea of the drink as a symbol of the drinker is not too wild.
(3) A "humpty-dumpty" may refer to a "short, dumpy, hump-shouldered person," or "a short, clumsy sort of person." This is possible.
(4) Or a game called "humpty-dumpty."
(5) Or someone who is "short and fat."
(6) Or it may be "applied to a mechanical rhythm."
(7) Or Lewis Carroll's conception in Through the Looking Glass: "It's very provoking—to be called an egg, very!"

Traditionally, Humpty Dumpty is associated with an egg. As a playful piece, eggs don't sit on walls. As an imaginative thing, eggs can sit on walls, but eggs that do, fall off walls. Hence, practically, eggs should not sit on walls. Secondly, an egg is what a goose lays. Could it be that Humpty Dumpty belonged to Mrs. Goose? Hence, this poem is autobiographical. Or eggs are symbols of fertility and life. Remember "Humpty had a great fall"; so too did Adam. Is this poem a study of original sin? Finally, Humpty Dumpty may refer to the fact of being born. Each of these views the new critic would carefully examine, not reglecting to point out that the spondee at the end of line two emphasizes the abrupt end of the fall.

V. The Psychological and Psychoanalytical Approach

The psychological-psychoanalytic critic often begins with his theory and applies it to a given work of art, a character in a work, a phrase; then, if he is ambitious, he goes behind the work of art and comments on the psychic life of the artist. Herbert Read in "Psychoanalysis and Criticism" explains the position of this group of critics: "Psychoanalysis finds in art," he writes, "a system of symbols, representing a hidden reality, and by analysis it can testify to the purposive genuineness of the symbols; it can also testify to the faithfulness, the richness, and the range of the mind behind the symbol."

Such an analysis as we have begun of Humpty Dumpty may be applied to Mother Goose's works in order that we may discover the hidden life behind the art, behind the symbols of her poems.

One of the most interesting poems suited to the psychoanalytic critic's approach is the familiar "One, two, buckle my shoe. . . . " In this poem we see the values parents teach girls as they grow. Remember, "Three, four, shut the door; / Five, six, pick up sticks. . . . / Thirteen, fourteen, maids a-courting; / Fifteen, sixteen, maids a-kissing; / Seventeen, eighteen, maids a-waiting"; / And "Nineteen, twenty" gives the editors of the nursery rhymes problems in the text I have used; the line reads "Nineteen, twenty, my stomach's empty." In context, in the series involving courting-kissing-waiting, obviously this last line does not refer to the stomach being empty. In The Tall Book of Mother Goose the sequence doesn't make sense: 13, 14, maids are courting; 15, 16, maids in the kitchen; 17, 18, maids are waiting; and 19, 20, my platter's empty. I am prone to think the editor has taken privileges with Mrs. Goose's verses. It may be that the House Un-American Activities Committee will investigate both sides of the matter; or the Illinois American Legion will attack Mrs. Goose for indecency; or the American Civil Liberties Union will defend Mrs. Goose against the American Legion attack.

What might the Freudian critic do with the "Humpty-Dumpty" poem? What kind of "hidden reality" in Mrs. Goose's life do we find waiting for us in the poem? Can we invoke such a logic as the following: geese lay eggs; a goose will lay a goose egg; Mother Goose lays goose eggs; Humpty-Dumpty is a goose egg, one of Mother Goose's goose eggs, in fact, one of her goslings. Now the question occurs, why would Mrs. Goose want "All the King's horses and all the King's men" to put Humpty back "together again"? Could it be that Mrs. Goose did not want to have Humpty? An indiscretion, perhaps? The fund of possibilities to the psychological-psycholanalytic critic are limitless.

Remember, too, that our consideration of Mrs. Goose has been somewhat limited, for we have not at all considered Mr. Gander:

> Old Mother Goose, when
> She wanted to wander,
> Would ride through the air
> On a very fine gander.

PRICKLES UNDER THE FROCK

Seth Sicroff

Beatrix Potter's prose style bears a resemblance to Mrs. Tiggywinkle's plain print frock; underneath the deceptively simple dress there are prickles. The apparently simple, guileless point of view of the narrator is betrayed by an understated humor which depends on the complications of word games and the interplay between details of text and illustration. The premise of anthropomorphism is not accepted and ignored, but continually recalled to mind by sly references and incongruities. To see the importance of the deliberately bland and aphoristic sentence structure, one need only compare the taut understatement of Potter's "your Father had an accident there; he was put in a pie by Mrs. McGregor" with the wordy French translation: "Un accident affreux arriva a votre pauvre père dans ce maudit jardin. Il fut attrapé et mis en pâté par Madame McGregor." In this case, less _is_ more.

Beatrix Potter has a feel for unusual words, which glow "with a hard and gem-like flame" against the backdrop of deliberate simplicity. In most of the books, there are one or two of these elegant words: Tommy Brock snored "apoplectically" in The Tale of Mr. Tod, and in The Tale of the Flopsy Bunnies, the effect of the lettuce is very "soporific."[1] In these passages, the word draws attention to an important idea. The soporific effect of eating lettuce is responsible for the rabbits' capture; Tommy Brock's deceptively apoplectic appearance encouraged Mr. Tod to risk setting the booby trap. In most cases, these incongruously elegant words are used in such a way as to emphasize the incongruity of the characterization. Jemima's high aspirations move her to complain of the "superfluous hen." The technical language in Ginger and Pickles suggests the awesome complexity of the problems besetting the dog and the cat: "Send in all the bills again to everybody, 'with compts', replied Ginger."

Potter indulges in a number of little games which remind the reader of the ambiguous position of her inventions, between man and beast. An important trick is juxtaposition, as in Mr. Tod:

> Mr. Tod was coming up Bull Banks, and he was in the very worst of tempers. First he had been upset by breaking the plate. It was his own fault; but it was a china plate, the last of the dinner service that had belonged to his grandmother, old Vixen Tod. Then the midges had been very bad. And he had failed to catch a hen pheasant on her nest.

Sentimental human regrets are set cheek by jowl with the practical concerns of a wild predator.

The juxtaposition is of a more complicated sort when mother pigs give advice.

In <u>The Tale of Pigling Bland</u>, Aunt Pettitoes gave these instructions to her children, before they set off to market:

> "Now Pigling Bland; son Pigling Bland, you must go to market.
> Take your brother Alexander by the hand. Mind your Sunday clothes,
> and remember to blow your nose"—(Aunt Pettitoes passed round the
> handkerchief again)—"beware of traps, hen roosts, bacon and eggs;
> always walk upon your hind legs."

Aunt Dorcas gave similarly garbled instructions to Robinson:

> "Now take care of yourself in Stymouth, Nephew Robinson. Beware
> of gunpowder, and ships' cooks, and pantechnicons, and sausages,
> and shoes, and ships, and sealing-wax."

The reminders on manners and the errands might have been addressed to a human child. "Bacon and eggs," "shoes," "sausages," and "sealing-wax" are objects which represent death to pigs. Some of the advice means nothing, except in retrospect, later on. "Hen roosts" prove a dangerous locale to Pigling Bland—though how Aunt Pettitoes could have foreseen this is beyond explanation. The reason for avoiding ships' cooks is clarified when one kidnaps Robinson, and the need for prudence with respect to sausages and wax is also elaborated later on in <u>Little Pig Robinson</u>:

> Old Mr. Mumby was a deaf old man in spectacles, who kept a general store. He sold almost anything you can imagine, except ham—
> a circumstance much approved by Aunt Dorcas. It was the only general
> store in Stymouth where you could not find displayed upon the counter
> a large dish, containing strings of thin, pale-coloured, repulsively un-
> cooked sausages, and rolled bacon hanging from the ceiling.
> "What pleasure," said Aunt Dorcas feelingly—"What possible plea-
> sure can there be in entering a shop where you knock against a ham?
> A ham that may have belonged to a dear second cousin?"
>
> . . . Finally (the man) begged to have the honour of showing him
> over a ship engaged in the ginger trade, commanded by Captain Barna-
> bas Butcher, named the "Pound of Candles."
> Robinson did not very much like the name. It reminded him of tallow,
> of lard, of crackle and trimmings of bacon.

(One wonders at the menace posed by "pantechnicons"—moving vans; was it simply that the noise of passing carts prevented Robinson from hearing old Mr. Mumby's anxious warning?)

The little reminders about the double nature of the characters do not emerge inevitably from the dialogue and the action. Potter's complicity is apparent not only in the improbability of some of the things said by characters, but also in the peculiar vocabulary of the narrator. When she tells us that "Timmy Willie had been reared on roots and salad" (<u>Johnny Town-mouse</u>), she is slyly mixing mouse and human realities. Mr. Brown, in <u>Squirrel Nutkin</u>, is clearly not

dressed in human clothing, but Potter tells us that he puts the unfortunate squir-
rel in his waistcoat pocket. Again, some of the animals do live in houses, but
others live in less human abodes. The mice who wink at Peter in the garden, we
are told, are "sitting on their doorsteps," although the picture shows them sitting in an ordinary niche. Certain loaded phrases acquire a generalized meaning. Mrs. McGregor's example of making rabbit pie is followed, improbably
enough, by Mr. Brock ("Tommy Brock did occasionally eat rabbit-pie . . . "
Mr. Tod). The phrase, which makes some sense in the domestic context of Mrs.
McGregor's home, has been exported to the woodlands. The reverse occurs with
the phrase "rabbit tobacco." This makes some sense as an item in Old Mrs.
Rabbit's shop: "she also sold herbs, and rosemary tea, and rabbit-tobacco
(which is what we call lavender)." But when Mr. and Mrs. McGregor start talking about buying rabbit tobacco (Flopsy Bunnies), it is Potter who is winking at
us.

The above examples are relatively logical, compared with some of the other
tricks by which Potter recalls the basic absurdity of the stories. When Pigling
Bland approaches Piperson's farm, the hens try to warn him away, in very peculiar language:

> "Bacon and eggs, bacon and eggs!" clucked a hen on a perch.
> "Trap, trap, trap! cackle, cackle, cackle!" scolded the disturbed
> cockerel. "To market, to market! jiggetty jig!" clucked a broody
> white hen roosting next to him.

There is no intrinsic logic in what the hens say; rather, their words, like the
Pie's "gammon and spinach," are logically non-sensical, like real-life chicken
garble. Again, like the Pie's "gammon and spinach," which are foods and therefore somehow relevant to Duchess's strangulation, the words are sensible to the
other party (and to the reader). "Bacon and eggs," "henhouse," and "trap"
have come to mean the equivalent of "danger." "To market, to market! jiggetty
jig" is a line from a nursery rhyme, which we may understand as either a reminder to Bland of his destination, or a prediction of Piperson's intention "to
catch six fowls to take to market in the morning."

Potter's nonsense is often of the sort that draws attention to her art rather
than to her "subject." The fact that Aunt Pettitoes gives her instructions in
rhymed verse, and that Aunt Dorcas gives hers in alliterative doggerel, does not
tell anything particular about the pigs. Instead, Potter develops a personal way
of looking at things in terms of nursery rhymes, incongruities, and puns.

The puns are often of a peculiar sort: although many are spoken between
characters, the joke is usually between author and reader. Ribby seems to be as
little responsible for the humor of her puns as for the humor of cats' wearing
clothes: "He's a bad kitten, Cousin Tabitha; he made a cat's cradle of my best
bonnet last time I came to tea. Where have you looked for him?" (The Roly-poly
Pudding). The same is true of Duchess's pun in The Pie and the Patty Pan:
"Shall I run for the doctor? I will just look up the spoons!" "Oh, yes, yes! fetch
Dr. Maggotty, my dear Ribby: he is a Pie himself, he will certainly understand."

The pictures play an indispensable role as a complement to the text. It is important to be able to see Peter Rabbit's world—the scenery, the little houses, and especially the dressed-up animals. But the illustrations do not simply show what is going on in the text.

Chronologically, the pictures are not limited to the scene described in the text. In Johnny Town-mouse, when the country mouse is explaining his tastes to the town mice, there is a flashback illustration of the way life used to be, when he was in the country. In Two Bad Mice, there are pictures drawn, as it were, in the conditional tense. "The little girl that the doll's house belonged to said, 'I will get a doll dressed like a policeman!'" The accompanying picture shows how the mice would react to this: Hunca-Munca is holding up her baby to meet the policeman, while two other mice crawl in at the window. On the next page, the nurse says she will set a trap; the picture shows how Hunca-Munca and Tom Thumb would teach their little children to deal with a mouse-trap.

In many cases, details are introduced in the pictures before they are mentioned in the text. In The Tailor of Gloucester, the text makes no mention of the mice until the bottom of page fourteen except "accidentally," when the tailor refers to the scraps as "tippets for mice and ribbons for mobs" (p. 13). Yet in the first illustration of the book, there are three mice inconspicuously stealing scraps of cloth behind the tailor's back, and in the next illustrations we are given pictorial evidence of the mice's craftsmanship, thirty pages before we are told as much in the text. In Jemima Puddle-duck the same thing happens. In the illustration of Jemima addressing the other animals in the barn, there is an egg hidden under the trough; later, we are told that although Jemima hid her eggs, they were always found and removed. The facing picture shows this happening, but there is also another egg under the rhubarb leaf which the boy does not seem to have noticed.

Often the pictures are necessary to explain the text. For example, when Potter tells us, in Benjamin Bunny, that "Peter let the pocket-handkerchief go again," we would be unsure of the significance of that remark, without the picture. Peter's clumsiness is due to apprehension: hand touching his chin, he is listening for sounds of the approach of Mr. McGregor. Sometimes the pictures tell the story more precisely than the text. The "pocket-handkerchief" worn by Peter is not rabbit-size, but man-sized; the discrepancies with regard to the mice's doorstep and Old Mr. Brown's waistcoat are similar.

In many instances, the illustrations allow the reader a more accurate perception of what is going on than that of a relatively naive narrator. For example, the narrator of Jemima Puddle-duck seems to share the duck's simple point of view. Nowhere in the text is the "sandy whiskered gentleman" explicitly identified as a fox. Where the text tells us simply that "the gentleman opened the door and showed Jemima in . . . " and that "she was rather surprised to find such a vast quantity of feathers. But it was very comfortable; and she made a nest without any trouble at all," the pictures show the fox snickering behind her back, and a barrel-full of chicken parts in the corner. In another tale, when Ginger and Pickles are forced to close up shop, the narrator tells us that "Ginger is living in the warren, I do not know what occupation he pursues; he looks stout and comfortable. Pickles is at present a gameskeeper." The pictures make it clear that both have turned to poaching.

The fact that one can read the books over and over, forwards and even backwards, and still discover, at each reading, new and amusing details, is an important factor in the popularity of Beatrix Potter's stories. Potter's art is not polemic, elegiac, or philosophical, but it is amusing and intelligent. She does not take sides, or choose between animals and humans, or reality and fantasy. The distinctive quality of her work is a function of her ability to maintain a consistent literary world which exists between reality and fantasy, denying neither.

The various Tales are published by Frederick Warne & Co. Ltd., London and New York.

Beatrix Potter
Frontispiece to "Tailor of Gloucester."
Courtesy, The Tate Gallery, London.

JOHN DOUGH AND THE CHERUB *

Martin Gardner

After Lyman Frank Baum's fantastic success in 1900 with The Wonderful
Wizard of Oz, and his equally astonishing success two years later with the stage
musical based on the book, Baum was at the height of his fame and creative
energy. His second Oz book, The Marvelous Land of Oz, in many ways even
better than its predecessor, was published in 1904 by Reilly and Britton, a small
Chicago house that would publish all of Baum's Oz books and almost all of his
juveniles not about Oz. Queen Zixi of Ix, which some critics consider the best of
non-Oz fantasies, was serialized in St. Nicholas and published as a book in 1905.

Edward William Bok (later famous for his autobiography, The Americaniza-
tion of Edward Bok) was then editor-in-chief of The Ladies' Home Journal. We
know from a 1912 letter of Baum to his publisher, Frank Reilly, that sometime
before 1906 Bok met with Baum and offered him $2,500 for serial rights to a
new fantasy. [1] Baum responded with an early draft of John Dough in which Chick
the Cherub did not appear. Bok returned the manuscript, asking Baum to add a
human child to the tale.

"I had either a grouch or the big-head," Baum said in his letter to Reilly,
"and refused to alter the text." But after some second thoughts he decided that
Bok was right. He rewrote the story, introducing a child with whom young readers could identify, and gave the manuscript to Reilly. The book's working title
was John Dough, the Baker's Man. John Rea Neill, who had illustrated the second Oz book (and would illustrate all subsequent Oz books by Baum and his successor, Ruth Plumly Thompson, as well as three Oz books of his own), did the
pictures for John Dough.

In a copy of the first edition of John Dough and the Cherub, published by Reilly
and Britton in 1906, [2] Baum wrote the following inscription to his son, Robert:
"Too bad this wasn't an Oz book, but I like the story just as well. This was the
first creation of a gingerbread man and John Dough was original with this story."

Why did Baum underline "first creation" ? Dick Martin, in his article cited
in the footnote, gives the reason. The words imply that he invented John Dough
before the production in New York in 1906, the very year Baum's book was published, of a musical comedy called The Gingerbread Man. The play and lyrics
were by Frederick Ranken, the music by A. Baldwin Sloane. "It, too," writes
Martin, "involved a gingerbread man magically brought to life, and (to twist the

* This paper will be the introduction to a facsimile of the first edition of John
Dough and the Cherub to be published by Dover Publications, Inc., New York.

arm of coincidence a little further) he was also named John Dough. Here the parallel ends—the plot and characters of the Ranken-Sloane musical are quite different from those of Baum's book. On the other hand, the 1902 musical comedy of The Wizard of Oz bore little resemblence to Baum's original book—so perhaps there is a connection—and a mystery yet to be solved."

John Dough and the Cherub is not, in my opinion, among Baum's best fantasies, but that doesn't mean it is not worth reading. It is typical Baum, funny and exciting, packed with Ozzy characters and episodes, and with outrageous surprises on almost every page. The book has its spots of humdrum writing, and some of its ideas are hackneyed, but it is hard to imagine a young reader, even today, who would be bored by the tale.

For readers unfamiliar with John Dough, a capsule summary of the plot may be helpful. A baker, making a large gingerbread man to celebrate the Fourth of July, accidentally mixes an Arabian Elixir of Life into the dough. John Dough comes alive, walks out of the bakery, and is carried by a skyrocket to the Isle of Phreex. Chick the Cherub, one of the island's "freaks," helps him escape (from a pursuing Arab who wants to eat him to acquire the elixir's power) in an airship with flapping wings.

After some adventures in the Palace of Romance (where Chick, like Scheherazade, forestalls their execution by telling an endless tale), they arrive on an island inhabited by the evil Mifkets. Para Bruin, a rubber bear, joins them. They are rescued from the Mifkets by the King of the Beavers. After a brief stop on Pirate Island, they come to the twin countries of Hiland and Loland where John Dough fulfills an old prophecy about the coming of a ruler who is not flesh and blood. John is crowned King Dough the First, the bear becomes a sort of court jester, and Chick "rules the ruler" as Head Booleywag.

There are many reasons for supposing that Baum hoped to make a musical out of the story. He had tried without success to put his second Oz book on the stage (as The Woggle-Bug, which had a short woggle in 1905) and in 1913 he would try again with the musical, The Tik-Tok Man of Oz. Michael Hearn, author of The Annotated Wizard of Oz, believes that many of John Dough's defects can be attributed to Baum's intent to dramatize it. The episode on Pirate Island, for instance, does nothing for the plot, but pirates had been a big success in Maud Adams' Peter Pan and would have added considerable color to a stage version. Of course any hope for dramatizing John Dough was dashed by the Ranken-Sloane production.

Ironically, it is Chick, added to the story as an afterthought, who dominates the narrative. Is Chick a boy or a girl? Baum does not tell us. All masculine and feminine pronouns are avoided (often awkwardly, as when Chick is referred to as "it"), and at the book's close, when Chick grows up as the Head Booleywag (Prime Minister) of Hiland and Loland, we still do not know if the Booleywag is a man or woman.

Baum and his publisher exploited the mystery for all the publicity they could get. A mustard-colored contest blank, tipped in the book's early printings, offered cash prizes for the best statement of why readers thought Chick a boy or a girl. It is amusing to learn that the contest left the question unresolved. Although no documentation has yet been found, Baum's son, Frank, who collaborated with Russell P. MacFall on a biography of his father (To Please a Child), told MacFall that the first prize of $100 was divided between two contestants. One asserted that Chick was a boy, the other that Chick was a girl. [3]

Several press clippings about the contest are preserved in Baum's scrapbooks. One newspaper story (see The Baum Bugle, Spring, 1967) compares the mystery to Frank Stockton's famous "Lady or the Tiger?" story, then continues with what surely is a fabricated conversation. Asked by his publisher if Chick is a boy or girl, Baum reacts with amazement. "Doesn't it tell in the story?" Informed that it does not, Baum replies: "I cannot remember that Chick the Cherub impressed me as other than a joyous, sweet, venturesome and loveable child. Who cares whether it is a boy or a girl?"

Unsatisfied, the publisher questions his office staff only to get contradictory opinions. A second appeal is made to Baum. All he will say is, "Leave it to the children."

Another clipping, reproduced in the same issue of The Baum Bugle, shows three pictures of Chick, drawn by Neill to promote the story's serialization in 1906 newspapers. In the center picture, Chick wears the sexless pajamas and sandles that Chick wears in the book. On one side we see how the child would look if dressed like a boy, on the other, if dressed like a girl.

Chick the Cherub
Boy or Girl? Baum never said.
Illustration by John Rea Neill.
From John Dough and the Cherub
(1906)
Courtesy, Martin Gardner

John Dough provides little information about Chick's background aside from the fact that Chick is the world's first incubator baby. This explains Chick's residence on the Isle of Phreex (Freaks) and probably why Baum chooses the name "Chick." (As Baum well knew—his first book was on chicken rearing—incubators were used for hatching chicken eggs long before they were used for prematurely born human babies.) Like most of Baum's child protagonists, nothing is said about Chick's father or mother. Indeed, the implication is that the Cherub has no parents. We do know that Chick is at least eight, blonde, blue-eyed, and curly-headed. The child is always happy, always frank, clever, "wise for one so young," creative, brave, unprejudiced, and friendly. Chick likes to use the latest slang. Anyone the child particularly admires is "all right." One of the Cherub's talents is producing an ear-splitting whistle.

Above all, Chick is an adventurer of the open road. The child doesn't care where it is (page 286). Chick is equally unconcerned with what happens: "I'm not afraid. Anything suits me" (page 275). "What's the use of staying outside, when the door's open?" (page 298). "It doesn't matter where we go, so long as we keep going" (page 273). Compare that last remark with this dialogue from Jack Kerouac's On The Road: "Where we going, man?" "I don't know but we gotta go."

In sum, Chick is a sandle-footed highway freak—a flower child of the counter-culture, self-sufficient, androgynous, parentless, and happily "into" oatmeal and cream instead of drugs.

Chick's companion, John Dough (an obvious pun on John Doe), is the book's principal "non-meat" personage. He is a life-size gingerbread French gentleman, with top hat and candy cane, made by Jules Grogrande (gros and grande?), a Parisian baker who has settled in an unidentified American city. The powerful Arabian elixir which brings John to life makes him wise and strong, and capable of speaking all languages, modern and classic. (Since John Doe is everyman, Hearn has observed, it is natural that he speak all languages.) He suffers occasionally from soggy feet, chipping, and loose glass eyes. Like the Scarecrow and Tin Woodman, he neither eats nor sleeps, though he is capable of drinking. He is deemed "all right" by Chick because, in spite of his dread of being eaten, he restores Princess Jacquelin to health by allowing her to nibble the stump of his left hand. (Note how cleverly Neill conceals John's mutilated hand in most of the pictures, after John's fingers have been eaten by Ooboo, and before the hand is finally restored.)

Para Bruin, the third member of the book's unlikely trio of adventurers, is one of Baum's most lovable creations. He is made of indestructible para rubber, hollow like a rubber ball, kind and harmless (how could his rubber teeth harm anyone?), and a ham vaudevillian who loves to roll up like a ball and bounce from high places to amuse the crowd. It is to his credit that he doesn't love everybody. I can still remember the satisfaction I felt as a child when Para Bruin bounced down from the sky to demolish Sport, surely one of the most unpleasant characters in all of Baum's fantasies.

Para Bruin attacks some Mifkets
Illustration by John Rea Neill
From John Dough and the Cherub
(1906)
Courtesy, Martin Gardner

Chick, John Dough, and Para Bruin attend Ozma's birthday party at the close of The Road to Oz. His "Gracious and Most Edible Majesty" brings Ozma a gingerbread crown as a gift. When Dorothy asks Button-Bright if Chick is a boy or girl, Button-Bright responds with his usual, "Don't Know." Para Bruin is amazed by all the strange people he sees in Oz. Button-Bright asks if John Dough is good to eat. "Too good to eat," says Chick, and the Scarecrow assures John that visitors to Oz are never eaten. Chick informs Billina, a yellow hen, that it (Chick) never had any parents.

> "My chicks have a parent," the hen replies, "and I'm it."
> "I'm glad of that," says Chick, "because they'll have more fun worrying you than if they were brought up by an incubator. The incubator never worries, you know."

There are scores of lesser characters in John Dough, both meat and meatless. Duo, the two-headed dog, anticipates the Pushmi-Pullyu of Hugh Lofting's Dr. Doolittle books. [4] Sir Austin Alfred is a spoonerism on Sir Alfred Austin, poet laureate of England in 1906. Tietjamus Toips, whose symphony is harder to understand than one by Vogner (Wagner), plays on the name of Paul Tietjans, a friend of Baum who composed the music for The Wizard of Oz musical. The name is also a pun on "pajama tops." Is Sir Pryse Bocks, inventor of the rain-repelling tube, a spoonerism on "Bok's price"—Bok's demand that Baum add a child to the tale? More likely (as David Greene called to my attention) the name refers to the popular prize contest which The Ladies' Home Journal sponsored every month. Suggestions were mailed to "Mr. Bok's personal box," and (Greene adds), with "Sir" before the name it becomes "surprise box." Maria Simpson, the name of the Lady Executioner, is so artificially presented that Greene thinks it must refer either to someone readers of 1906 would recognize or to one of Baum's personal friends.

On page 233 John Dough, angry at the macaw who is laughing at him, calls the bird a "rampsy." What is a rampsy? The answer lies in an obscure spot: a short story called "Nelebel's Fairyland" which Baum wrote exclusively for The Russ (June, 1905), a college paper published in San Diego. The story (reprinted in The Baum Bugle, Christmas, 1962) gives added facts about the immortals who live in the Forest of Burzee, south of Oz, and who figure prominently in Baum's two earlier fantasies, The Life and Adventures of Santa Claus and Queen Zixi of Ix. It seems that Queen Lulea, "annoyed at the awkwardness of the huge gigans, transformed them into rampsies—the smallest of all immortals." So far as I know, it is the only other reference to rampsies in all of Baum's writings.

There are four fat ladies in John Dough: Madame Tina, the baker's wife; Bebe Celeste, one of the freaks of Phreex; the mother of the Princess; and the Lolander who bakes a new hand for John Dough the First. Baum is no doubt reminding his readers about the hazards of eating too much French pastry.

Taking cues from some references to Hiland and Loland in The Magic of Oz, James E. Haff, cartographer of the official map of Oz (available from the International Wizard of Oz Club, which publishes The Baum Bugle, 220 North 11th Street, Escanaba, Michigan, 49829) places the island in the Nonestic Ocean, due east of Oz. The four smaller islands of the story form a chain extending to the northeast. The Isle of Phreex is mentioned on page 20 of Rinkitink in Oz, and the same book, page 294, also refers to the Mifkets, whose island is the second to be visited by John Dough. The Mifkets should not be confused with the Mifkits, in John R. Neill's Scalawagons of Oz. Mifkits can remove their heads and hurl them at enemies. They are probably identical with Baum's Scoodlers, in The Road to Oz. The King of the Beavers and his subjects, who live under the waterfall on Mifket Island, reappear in Jack Snow's The Shaggy Man of Oz.

The ersatz General of Phreex, whose entire body has been replaced by artificial parts, raises the same perplexing metaphysical questions about personal identity as does the Tin Woodman. Ali Dubh's Elixir of Life is similar to the Powder of Life that vivifies Jack Pumpkinhead and the Sawhorse in The Marvelous Land of Oz. The Beaver king's Magic Box anticipates Ozma's Magic Picture, which in turn foreshadows the television screen. The electrically operated ornithopter—it works so well that its inventor, Imar, is in disgrace among his fellow cranks—recalls the flying Gump of the second Oz book. As MacFall points out in his biography of Baum, the Wright brother's flight had taken place in 1903, only a year before the second Oz book, and Baum had been quick to introduce flying ships into his stories. Two of Baum's pseudonymous books for teen-age girls, The Flying Girl and The Flying Girl and Her Chum, were about a girl aviator.

(above)
Dust jacket (not cover) of first state
of John Dough and the Cherub
Courtesy, The Baum Bugle

(right)
Front cover of the first edition of
John Dough and the Cherub
Courtesy, The Baum Bugle

The humor in John Dough ranges from low-level word play ("I'm sure I couldn't agree with anyone who ate me," John declares; I counted more than fifteen puns on words relating to food alone) to occasional remarks of existential import. John cannot recall when he was not alive. He informs a lady who thinks he ought not to be alive that he cannot help it. And on another occasion he observes that "it is better to be wrong than to be nothing." (Remember "Better Red than dead"?)

In 1910 the Selig Polyscope Company, Chicago, released a one-reel film of John Dough, starring Joseph Schrode as the gingerbread man and a girl named Grace Elder as Chick. The Selig studios had made most of the film a few years earlier for Baum's ill-fated series of "radio plays." These plays, each based on one of Baum's fantasies, had nothing to do with "radio" as the term is understood today. They were a curious mix of live actors, silent film clips (made by Selig and hand-tinted in France), colored stereoptican slides, live orchestral music, and commentary by Baum himself. Baum stood on the side of the screen with a pointer, and at times moved into the film by walking off the stage and onto the screen. In 1908 Baum and one of his sons, who served as projectionist, toured fourteen cities with this remarkable show, starting in Grand Rapids and ending in New York.

The project was a financial bust. Selig obtained rights to the films, and by patching them together and adding more footage, they produced four one-reelers, one of which was John Dough. The film seems not to have survived. In its radio play form it followed the book closely (omitting the eating of part of John by the Princess, and the visit to Pirate Island), but the movie version had a much different ending. According to Richard A. Mills (see his article on the radio plays, The Baum Bugle, Christmas, 1970), Chick somehow manages to meet with Ozma who prophecies:

> The throne of Lo-Hi shall vacant be
> Until the coming by air or sea
> Of an overbaked man and Cherub wee.

John Dough then arrives in Oz to fulfil the prophecy and be crowned king of Lo-Hi. [5] One of the highlights of the original film (presumably also of the 1910 version) was the Fourth of July fireworks scene in which John is carried into the clouds by a giant skyrocket. In an article on the radio plays which Baum wrote for the New York Herald (September 26, 1909), he explains how stop-action photography was used to substitute a dummy for the live actor, just before take-off, and to replace the dummy with the actor after the dummy falls to the ground.

It seems to me that John Dough, even today, could be the basis for a delightful stage or motion picture musical. Little is dated about its characters, plot or humor. Is that smiling, long-haired Cherub, on the side of the highway with upraised thumb, a boy or a girl? Think of the fun that public relations men could have with a new, unknown child star whose sexual identity is not known to the public! And what could be more appropriate now than John Dough's final moral?

Hiland and Loland, where Chick, John and the rubber bear settle at last, are two rival cultures, flourishing side by side, each firmly convinced of its own superiority, each regarding its neighbors as uncouth barbarians. The wall that separates the tall, thin Highlanders from the short, fat Lolanders is no higher than the old Great Wall of China or the new Berlin Wall, or a hundred other "walls" that these material structures symbolize. Baum's vigorous plea for tolerance and understanding of alien ways is one that he would stress again in Sky Island, where he describes the equally irrational rivalry between the Pinks and the Blues. Need anyone be reminded that it is a moral on which the world's fate may depend?

(I wish to thank David Greene, James Haff, Michael Hearn, Dick Martin, Fred Meyer and Justin Schiller for their help in writing this article.)

---

1 Baum's letter is quoted by David Greene in The Baum Bugle, 1971, pg. 15.

2 There were four issues of the first edition. The first has the misprint "cage" (for "cave") on page 275, line 10. The second state corrects the error. The third (and all later printings) has no back cover picture, and "Co." is omitted after the publisher's imprint on the spine. This imprint is reset in capitals on the spine of the fourth issue.

The second edition, published about 1920 by Reilly and Lee, eliminated color from the head pieces and most of the full-page illustrations, retaining color on twelve full-page plates. The same company's next and last edition, circa 1930, drops all color plates except the frontispiece. A paperback edition, newly illustrated by a young Chinese artist, Lau Shiu Fan, was published in English in Hong Kong, by Opium Books, in 1966. For additional bibliographic details see Dick Martin's report on John Dough in The Baum Bugle, Spring, 1969.

A small book called The Gingerbread Man was published by Reilly and Britton in 1917 as one of Baum's six "Snuggle Tales" books. It reprints the first four chapters of John Dough, and adds a new chapter, "Safe at Last," that tells of John's arrival on the Isle of Phreex.

3 Perhaps a reader in Chicago can run down the contest results. According to the contest blank, the judges were Baum, the Chicago author Henry M. Hyde, and Wilbur D. Nesbit of the Chicago Evening Post. Was the book serialized in the Post? If so, the Post probably announced the outcome of the contest. The contest blank gave December 31, 1906, as the closing date, and said that prize-winners would be announced about January 15, 1907.

4 Michael Hearn has noticed that John Dolittle, M.D., is John Do with "little" tacked on, and that both Dr. Dolittle and John Dough were capable of speaking all bird and animal languages.

5 The only known source for the film's plot is a garbled synopsis that appeared in Moving Picture World sometime in December, 1910.

THE WIZARDESS OF OZ *

Russel B. Nye

It would have been difficult to think of anyone better fitted to take over the mantle of L. Frank Baum than Ruth Plumly Thompson, whose nineteen chronicles of Ozland and dozens of additions to its population have become as famous in their own right as Baum's originals. Growing up as she did in a family environment of security, closeness, love, and activity, she came to the task of continuing the Oz series with the keen sense of participation in the life of the young and the respect for its attitudes and goals that Baum's successor had to have to be successful. John R. Neill, who illustrated all of the Oz books done under her name, recognized this at once. He wrote Reilly and Lee, after he had finished reading the manuscript of Kabumpo in Oz, that "the whimsical, the humor, the interest, and the zip of the book" marked her as eminently qualified to carry on. Certainly Neill's judgment has been validated by time and a million readers.

Yet Miss Thompson, in continuing the series, did much more than merely follow out the patterns established by Baum. The briskness of pace of the books that followed Kabumpo was hers, the characters she introduced attracted loyal followers in their own right, and the concepts that underlay her Land of Oz developed it into a country not quite the same as that one Dorothy was blown into so many books before. She brought to her task a briskness of mood and a freshness of imagination, an enthusiasm and gusto, that were her own and which consistently marked her books throughout. As one young reader told her, she had "a more exciting way of writing"—a way of making the reader, another said, "feel more at home inside your books." There is, as one surveys the range of Miss Thompson's Oz, a good deal of truth in these observations. Her books were pervaded, in a way that Baum's were not, with a sense of sheer light-heartedness, of fun and good nature, that is peculiarly her own. As she once said, writing the Oz books "is either easy or impossible, and if they are not fun for you to write, they will not be fun to read." Somewhat dismayed at the gravity with which some Oz Club members have approached her books, she remarked recently: "They take it seriously. I just have fun with it."

This, I think, may well be the key to Ruth Plumly Thompson's Oz—that is, the different quality of imagination, as distinct from Baum's, that is operative in her books. Baum, especially in his later books, seems to have considered Oz with a somewhat detached calculation, fitting together his plots and characterizations with rather careful intent. His interest in dramatic writing, in adult fic-

* Reprinted from The Baum Bugle, Autumn, 1965, by permission of The International Wizard of Oz Club.

tion, and in designing an American fairy-tale genre predisposed him to his own particular kind of creative approach. There is, as I have pointed out elsewhere, a strain of moralism in Baum's work, a strain of satire—gentle, implicit, but persistently there—and a strain of thoughtful humor that lends his narratives of Oz a third dimension unusual in American juvenile literature.

Ruth Plumly Thompson's Oz, it seems to me, is a truer world of fun and fantasy, and a less complex one. I have not been able to feel in her books the same depth of characterization that the earlier Baum books display, nor the sense of geographic volume present in Dorothy's Oz. Miss Thompson's is a different, individualized inventiveness, no less valid in its final effect, but operating horizontally on a different plane. There is, in the final analysis, a flavor of playfulness in her books, the impression that a quite unserious diversion is being played out between writer and reader in which both win. Her writing, she has explained, is the result of a kind of free-association reverie in which writer and reader are swept away into an inward, non-logical world where anything good and funlike can happen. There is a capricious quality in the Thompson Oz books that gives them a timbre of fantasy unlike Baum's; this is, I think, their most distinctive characteristic.

Miss Thompson's remarks on how this comes about provide an insight into the highly personalized creative process that produced the people and places and things in her vision of Oz. "Just close your eyes," she writes, "or gaze up at the sky, or off over the tree-tops, and presto! the magic door will open and you're off and away . . . What happens afterwards surprises me as utterly as it does the children." Where you land, then, in Ruth Plumly Thompson's books, is two steps further away from reality, and a step closer to pure fantasy, than Baum's Oz.

The Thompson Oz adventures were set against widely differing backdrops, displaying great diversity of scenery and equally great versatility of description. The familiar landscape of Oz was always there, but Miss Thompson's explorations of it opened up a great deal of new territory. The Orientalism of Silver Island was an aspect of Oz never before examined; the medievalism of the story of the Yellow Knight gave a kind of historicity to Oz it had not before possessed, linking it both with the Arthurian tradition and the faery-land of Scott. The sea-background of the Nonestic, and the Blue Forest of the bandits, described with brief authenticity, put Oz closer to the pirate-world of Stevenson and the ancient forests of Robin Hood. Miss Thompson's virtuosity in background description was a contribution of real importance to the Oz series; for sheer delicacy and perceptiveness in description probably nothing in Baum's series, nor in her own later books, exceeds the passages which deal with the Sapphire City of Oz. Umbrella Island, on the other hand, is perhaps the most inventive of all her backgrounds, conceived with unusual thoroughness and detail and integrated most carefully into the plot which uses the umbrella theme as an effective agent in influencing the action.

The basic plot pattern of Miss Thompson's books was the quest, the oldest of all mythic plots and the traditional sequential pattern of the classic folk and fairy tale. There were nineteen quests—with <u>Speedy in Oz</u> providing a possible exception in that here it is less clearly defined than in the others—each in search of something different, valuable, and attainable. Pompadore, Randy, the Yellow Knight, or Notta Bit More, searched and found; it is the success of the quest, as well as its value, which made the books particularly satisfying to the young reader. The quests might vary—from Mombi's attempt to control the King of Oz to invisible Ruggedo's endeavor to conquer Oz—but the essential element of search and discovery is always present.

But it is in characterization, probably, that Miss Thompson's stories of Oz found their primary excellence. Her creations, like Baum's, were likely to be unforgettable, sometimes less solidly fleshed out but each possessed of a quirk or trait that individualized it and fixed it in the galaxy of Oz. Her human characters—Sir Hokus of Pokes, Grampa, Captain Salt, Realbad, Speedy, to name a few—have a gentle appeal that reminds one very much of Baum's similar skill with rounded types. The fairy-tale people, one stage removed from humanity, are marked with that satisfactory unreality such characters should have—the Silver Princess, the Lost King, the Gnome King, the Purple Prince. One of the best creations of all in this genre (and incidentally Miss Thompson's favorite) is Jinnicky, the Red Jinn of Ev—rascal, ruler, and wizard, who ranks with the Tin Woodman and Jack Pumpkinhead themselves as someone to remember. Miss Thompson also developed in her stories a variety of trick characters which Baum had introduced but which she extended into a consistent type, such as Kuma Party who actually comes apart, the elastic Reachard who could reach anything, Handy Mandy of the seven arms, and Herby the Medicine Man who had a real medicine chest in his chest.

It is the animals, however, who really make Ruth Plumly Thompson's Oz what it is. Five of them appear in title roles with books of their own—Cowardly Lion, the Hungry Tiger, Kabumpo the Elephant, the Giant Horse, and the Wishing Horse. She also populated Ozland with a whole zoo of minor beasts—Pigasus the poetical pig, Roger the Read Bird, the Bananny Goat (Miss Thompson had a penchant for puns), Terrybubble the bony dinosaur who discovered Umbrella Island—and others who exemplify the amazing fertility of her invention. The Thompson books taken as a whole display a distinctively close relationship between the child's world and the animal world, establishing a connection among writer, reader, and specially-created animal that carries with it something of the rapport that marked the medieval bestiary. Whether she did it consciously or not, Miss Thompson caught superbly in her stories the intimate anthropomorphism of the traditional folktale; rarely has it been conceived with greater sensitivity and/or handled with more understanding than in her version of Oz. The elegant elephant, Kabumpo, with his pompous pride and his kind and loyal heart, is a major creation, equal to Baum's best, and one of the most memorable additions to the wonderful richness of Oz.

For nineteen Christmases beginning in 1921, boys and girls could expect to find another Oz book under the tree, or on birthdays discover still another hither-to unexplored corner of Oz, people with new and familiar characters. With no intent to diminish the great honor due L. Frank Baum, the Master of Oz, it is reasonable to say that Ruth Plumly Thompson in her way made Oz her own, and fully deserved the right of Royal Succession that Reilly and Lee gave her over that fabled, familiar land. Because of her, the Yellow Brick Road not only re-mained open to beckon generations of young people toward its goals, but stretched on beyond the horizons of the land Baum first found long ago. For this we grate-fully concede our debt.

Ruth Plumly Thompson lives in Malvern, Pennsylvania and the Oz Club has just published her twentieth Oz novel, Yankee in Oz. [1] (In 1918, The Perhappsy Chaps, her first book, was published.) She was born in Philadelphia and lived most of her life there; she edited the children's page in the Ledger, wrote ad-vertising booklets of fairy tales for Colgate, Royal Baking Powder, and other firms; wrote stories for King Comics, Ace Comics and Magic Comics; served as advisory editor for David McKay Company; wrote for numerous children's magazines; and did radio and television plays for children. She produced nine-teen Oz books published by Reilly and Lee, her last appearing in 1939. In the twenties she also did a musical stage version of The Wizard. "Exploring the Land of Oz," she said in 1965, "has been an enchanting and wonderful exper-ience, and the children and I have had tremendous fun together."

---

[1] A complete bibliography of her work appears in The Baum Bugle, Magazine of the International Wizard of Oz Club, Escanaba, Michigan, (Autumn, 1965) and an addendum in the issue of Autumn, 1970.

LEO LIONNI, ARTIST AND PHILOSOPHER *

Annabelle Simon Cahn

Leo Lionni has had a long, varied, and influential career in the visual arts as a painter, graphic designer, writer, and teacher, but his distinctive production has gained its widest audience as a result of the children's books he has written and illustrated. Conceived at the rate of one each year for the past twelve years, these stories are didactic both in word and image, and the cumulative corpus makes a significant statement about Lionni's thought.

His work retains some of the characteristic visual qualities of the 1950's, a design image he influenced and fostered. He continues to have his texts set in Century, a turn-of-the-century font which he revived. His illustrations tend toward flat, poster-like layouts affected by Klee, Matisse, Miro, and Jean Arp. Snippits of printed paper incorporated into complex collages are the artistic mainstay of his books (Fig. 1). Many papers are monoprints of his own fabrication. All share a visual uniformity of repeated surface decoration. Wrapping papers, wall papers, printed Japanese paper (sometimes ornamenting imported goods), marble papers (better known on bookbindings), William Morris designs, doilied, stenciled, potato-printed, flour-pasted, crayoned, watercolored, pastelled, inked, roughly torn or just left alone, they are combined in a rich admixture of flat, simple, chunky forms laid down as a series of interrelated patterned surfaces to achieve a limited, lateral, diorama-like sense of space. Contrasting artistic techniques and mixed media are frequently used in conjunction with these small-patterned papers to lend emphasis to contrasting ideas or states of mind. There is a recurring interplay between opaque and transparent effects, marrying crayon or mat tempera paint with transparent inks, or pen and ink with opulent papers.

Lionni's interest in Surrealism influenced his books. On My Beach There Are Many Pebbles (1961) is devoted to the zoomorphic and anthropomorphic possibilities of striations and faults in pebbles worn by the sea. The Biggest House (1968), concerning the foolish aspirations and ultimate demise of a snail, exploits inconsistencies of scale to distort the natural optical relationship of reader to object. His involvement with the principles of Surrealism in also evident in the recent paintings of "moon-flowers" (metallic plants with amorphous, sometimes flat backgrounds), sculptural collages of branches cast in a Lionni-devised variant of the lost-wax process (using the casting metal to burn out and replace the wooden

* I wish to thank Leo Lionni for the rewarding time spent with him in Porcignano and acknowledge his stimulating essay, "My Books for Children," Wilson Library Bulletin, 39 (1964), 142-145.

limbs), and elegant drawings and lithographs of imaginative and imaginary plants (resembling vegetation in its diseased or deformed state in the lineage of seventeenth and eighteenth century botanical drawings).

Examples of all of these are visible in his studio today. They are a logical and understandable outgrowth of the artistic and philosophical thinking of his student days when Surrealism was most influential. But this is only one aspect of the history of imagery which has captured his fancy. Early printed books and popular wood cuts have been particularly appealing to him. As co-editor of Print magazine, a trade journal for the advertising and printing industries, he devoted his column, "The Lion's Tail," principally to aspects of the history of the graphic arts. His interest in surface decoration and patterned surfaces has, over the years, led him to an appreciation of many ornamental arts, with preference given to Persian and Turkish tile-work, Mughal Indian miniatures and Early Christian mosaics. Visual references to the decorative arts have frequently been incorporated into his designs, especially during his tenure as art director of Fortune magazine.

Not only are Lionni's books visually stimulating, but the texts are thoughtful and philosophical: the succinct prose is colorful, sometimes whimsical, sometimes poetic, and always didactic. The stories are essentially contemporary parables. In the best fabulist tradition, most of Lionni's tales center around animal heroes—an age-old device used to make the critical message or moral more palatable to a potentially resistent readership. Fables have long enjoyed favor among illustrators and producers of books, and a number of artists and graphic designers attracted to early printed books have made editions of Aesop: Alexander Calder (New York, 1931) and Antonio Frasconi (Museum of Modern Art, 1954), to note but two. Lionni himself used these editions in his column in the 1956 issue of Print magazine.

When Lionni came to produce his own fables, he strove for the same readership as the ancient writers of parables, who were not solely concerned with a juvenile audience. Indeed, according to Lionni, his books are concerned largely with adult problems. Nonetheless, because of the format of the books and our recent tendency to relegate illustrated books to the realm of juvenalia, children have become, unintentionally, his direct audience.

By electing the vehicle of illustrated stories, Lionni, perhaps unconsciously, takes advantage of notions concerning the function of children's books prevalent in late nineteenth-century England. A number of writers and artists of the Arts and Crafts movement voiced the belief that the most expedient way to influence or reform the direction of society was to present one's ideas to children, thought to be inherently brighter, more creative and open than their parents, and as yet unblemished or repressed by education. This appeal to youth, as much a sentimental hearkening after responses of simplicity and fresh wonderment as a desire to institute change, was thought to be most effective if the impact was through the presentation of well-designed topical books at an early age. No one understood this better than the illustrator Walter Crane, who not only included a rhyme concerning the relationship of the arts and politics in his own moralized fables, Baby's Own Aesop, but had also written,

> The ineffacable quality of these early pictorial and literary impressions affords the strongest plea for good art in the nursery and the schoolroom. Every child, one might say every human being, takes in more through the eyes than the ears, and I think much more advantage might be taken of this fact.

Lionni understood this well, being part of a generation of graphic designers who found justification for his profession in the larger scheme of aesthetic reform. The ideological sentiments of this generation of commercial designers used modern art as a political point of view; many were motivated by a sense that good design could stimulate social change. Lionni himself, speaking at the International Design Conference at Aspen, Colorado in 1958, said that the designer

> is expected primarily to incorporate the values received and return them in symbolic form. He is expected to arrange the discs in conformity with his society's scale of values, not with his own . . . If he believes in his power to alter society's scale of values, he must question whether there is a basic scale of values at all . . . His dilemma, while peculiar to his propagandistic functions, is in a sense symbolic of the fundamental dilemma of all designers . . . In the honest attempt to find answers, we may expect to recognize more clearly our functions, our potentials, our responsibilities. This clarification, in turn, should affect tangibly the things we make— and, perhaps, the world in which we live.

Keeping this in mind, we must now turn to the nature of his production.

His first book, little yellow, little blue (1959), is now a well-established classic. In the torn-paper collages of the illustrations, Lionni applied bold torn color forms (not unlike the 1940's collages of Jean Arp) to a story reminiscent of El Lissitzsky's Two Squares, but centered in two shapes, yellow and blue (Fig. 2). They are shown as dear friends playing together, and their love for one another leads them to melt together into green. The story reads not only as a very simple lesson in color theory—what happens when blue and yellow mix— but also as a parable concerning integration, identity, and social acceptance. Now, green, the result of the fused shapes, each original color loses its own properties and characteristics, and neither blue or yellow is recognized nor wanted by his family. In keeping with the cultural optimism of the early 1960's, the work was initially viewed as a strong plea for integration; but the perspective of years makes this less clear, for the story also pleads for the retention of individual differences.

As in most fables, Lionni's heroes are found in situations of distress, but they are not outwitted by their adversaries and resolve their difficulties in a multitude of ways. For example, a resourceful inchworm, working as a useful member of society to advance practical knowledge by measuring the length of

One day, when there was no one in the house, Alexander heard a squeak in Annie's room. He sneaked in and what did he see? Another mouse. But not an ordinary mouse like himself. Instead of legs it had two little wheels, and on its back there was a key.

"Who are you?" asked Alexander.

How they love to play at *Hide-and-Seek*

(above)
Alexander and the
wind-up mouse
Leo Lionni, 1969
(Cahn photo)

(left)
little blue, little yellow
Leo Lionni, 1959
(Cahn photo)

126

various birds (Inch by Inch, 1960) is called upon to measure the song of a night-ingale or be eaten for breakfast, and "inches out of sight." Swimmy (1963), a stereotype of the hero distinguished by his deeds as well as his physique, is a small black fish whose leadership and intelligence lead him to organize a school which teaches red fish to compensate for their small size by swimming together in formation to imitate the shape of the larger fish who harass them.

In this latter book, Lionni touches on several issues to which he has returned periodically—individual and group relations, the singularity of each individual and the place of each individual in society. In the book which followed Swimmy, a little bird born without wings is granted his wish for golden feathers, but loses his friends with this bequest only to regain them again when the last of his golden treasure is replaced by a real feather. Now he can no longer be outwardly dif-ferentiated from the others, and is left only with his memories (Tico and the Golden Feathers, 1964).

More recently, Lionni has turned to the old Platonic dilemma concerning the essential nature of things. A tadpole and a minnow, inseparable friends in in-fancy, come to argue as the tadpole begins to take on his adult characteristics (Fish is Fish, 1970). When, upon maturity, the frog quits the pond and does not return for many weeks and then only to tell his old friend of the wonders of the world, the fish completely misinterprets the significance of the frog's adven-tures. As in Medieval Bestiaries where creatures frequently take on vain pur-suits and come to be castigated for ill-conceived plans, the fish tries to quit his home, and only after an almost fatal mishap does he realize his own essential properties and limitations as well as the beauty of his own aquatic world. Vis-ually, there is a brilliant contrast between the pen-and-ink renderings of the fish's imagination and the softer-edged crayoning of his actual surroundings.

In the past few years, Lionni has begun to use the mouse as his hero or anti-hero, as the case would be, and with each new fable the swift-footed rodent has become the personification of certain ideas.

For instance, Lionni has conjured up a poetic mouse (Frederick, 1967), who, unlike the unfortunate cicada who sang all summer in LaFontaine's fable, does not suffer the consequences of a summer think-and-song fest. While he does not materially contribute to the family efforts to store goods for the winter, he is ul-timately recognized as a stimulating member of this small community. Freder-ick, basically a flower child—a sleepy-eyed mouse holding what looks surpris-inly like a poppy—is a fine example of the contemplative and creative Melan-cholia, one of the Four Humours. Frederick's poetry, iconoclastically animis-tic, depends on an ordered, almost encyclopedic, universe. Standing high above his brothers (who are huddled close together to keep warm in the rocks away from the snow), he tells them of the beauty of various colors and finally recites this poem—

> Who scatters snowflakes? Who melts the ice?
> Who spoils the weather? Who makes it nice?

Who grows the four-leaf clover in June?
Who dims the daylight? Who lights the moon?

Four little field mice who live in the sky.
Four little field mice . . . like you and I.

One is the Springmouse who turns on the showers.
Then comes the Summer who paints the flowers.
The Fallmouse is next with walnuts and wheat.
And Winter is last . . . with little cold feet.

Aren't we lucky the seasons are four?
Think of a year with one less . . . or one more!

In contrast to the poetic Frederick, Lionni then turned to a country mouse-city mouse parable. Alexander, a real mouse, is jealous of the fleeting comfort of a mechanical mouse, Willy, who, though unable to move freely, is content with his lot because "everyone loves him" (Alexander and the Wind-Up Mouse, 1969). In his desire to become transformed into a mechanical mouse, Alexander undertakes a grail-like quest for a purple pebble which will realize this wish. Alexander recognizes his folly when he discovers his wind-up friend in a box of discarded toys. In this tale, Lionni contrasted the constraints and impermanent satisfactions of the life of the gray-flannel mouse, Willy, a mechanical plaything of society—wound and enjoyed while working and productive, and then discarded when no longer useful—to the life of greater frustration, but larger possibilities, personified by Alexander.

His most recent book (Theodore and the Talking Mushroom, 1971) is concerned with false messiahs and the giving of religious power. Without the expanded prose of Jonathan Swift's Tale of a Tub or Anatole France's Penguin Island, Lionni has encapsulated the pseudo-religious experience. Theodore (the name itself conjures up Byzantium) is an undistinguished mouse who lives in an old tree stump together with a lizard, a frog and a turtle, each of whom boasts of exceptional talents. Chancing upon a mushroom that makes a noise not unlike the "bloop" of the soul reaching nirvana, the mouse convinces his friends that it is an oracular message from the toadstool which places the mouse above all other animals.

In their blind acceptance of this statement, they concoct an eclectic and pantheistic movement. In Buddha-like fashion along with tribute bearers and triumphant processions the mouse rides on a garland of flowers placed on the back of the turtle (long a mythological symbol of the curvature of the earth). These pseudo-religious trappings are sold to the "pagans," though the fragile position of the false messiah is revealed, the fraud is uncovered, and the mouse discredited. The whole story reads like refracted Near Eastern or Indian myth. Earth-toned papers are used for the bulk of the collages and stand in stark contrast to the acid blue mushroom head, the crisp outlines of the garlands of flowers, and the pen-and-inked undeserved crown.

Born of Judeo-Christian parents in Amsterdam in 1910, Lionni's cultural and religious heritage was rich. His mother was a singer; his father a diamond cutter, a confirmed Socialist and a lover of Oriental rugs, fine furniture and other objects of fine craftsmanship and beauty. Already sensitized to political ideas and artistic values, he grew up in the decade after the First World War and was exposed to the iconoclasm of the most productive twentieth-century movements. Surrealism was at its most influential moment. Bound by heritage and influenced by heresy, Lionni found the admixture stimulating. The germinal ideas for the Alphabet Tree (1968), which shows individual letters learning to join together to make words and sentences owes something to Judeo-Christian myth and medieval legends about naming letters and animals. Medieval geneological tables like the Tree of Jesse, or alphabet charts, such as Abecedaria, used well into the nineteenth century, lent some visual inspiration to the pictorial format. The world of medieval literature provided Lionni with other inspiration: bestiaries and Gothic encyclopedias are reflected in such parables in Fish is Fish and The Biggest House.

Lionni's artistic life has been varied. He is listed in Who's Who in American Art as a painter, designer, educator, and critic. He came to America in 1939, and after that time was, among other things, art director of Fortune magazine (1949 to 1960), making it one of the artistically most influential periodicals: head of the graphic department of the Parson's School of Design; designer for Olivetti when large corporations were just beginning to see the merits of contemporary design; and co-editor of Print magazine.

Lionni explores the full range of artistic alternatives in any given phase of his work. When he works on his books, the idea and the text are first polished, which is surprising for a man of such visual orientation. Noting the prominence he gives to puns and word-play, however, the textual priority seems inevitable. His texts seem to reflect the verbal clarity and succinctness which comes from the practiced used of English as a second language and, perhaps, from the conciseness inherent in advertising. Once the text has been refined, the illustrations are considered and quickly follow, bringing the work into focus.

Lionni has returned to Italy, where he spent his university days as a student of economics (he holds a doctorate in the subject). He divides his time between a house of his own design overlooking the Bay of Genoa and a farmhouse in the Chianti hills which contains carefully collected, jewel-like mementi of numerous travels. Embroidered cloths and hammered brass trunks from his days as crafts advisor to India, Indonesian wayang puppets, and African sculpture are carefully though casually arranged against the white walls.

The house inspires reflection upon the recommendation in The Biggest House (1968) to keep one's possessions light enough to be free at all times to go out into the world. For as one looks at Lionni's physical surroundings, the artistic souvenirs of a life which has been filled with interesting alternatives, one recognizes the value of the messages built into Lionni's texts—well-considered and lived truisms useful to us all.

CHILDREN'S BOOKS BY FAMOUS WRITERS FOR ADULTS *

Marilyn Apseloff

It is unfortunate that Children's Literature is not sufficiently understood or appreciated by scholars. Perhaps one way to illuminate their darkness is to point out that many of the famous figures that scholars discuss in their teaching and writing have found stimulation and satisfaction in the challenge of writing for children as well as adults. This essay deals principally with the children's books of five celebrated twentieth-century writers: Aldous Huxley, James Joyce, Arthur Miller, William Faulkner, and E. E. Cummings.

Some of these authors, it is true, wrote only one book and that for a particular child, as Aldous Huxley did with The Crows of Pearblossom, written in 1944 as a gift for his niece. Some books in this category were obviously not intended for publication, but were published posthumously: thus we have E. E. Cummings' Fairy Tales "written for Cummings' daughter, Nancy, when she was a very little girl";[1] The Cat and the Devil by James Joyce, a picture book made from a letter Joyce wrote to his grandson, Stevie, from Villers-sur-mer in Calvados in August, 1936;[2] and The Wishing Tree by William Faulkner, February, 1927, made available by Victoria Fielden, to whom that particular version was given.[3] Playwright Arthur Miller has also tried his hand at writing a children's book: the result was Jane's Blanket, recently reissued by Viking.

C. S. Lewis has created the fantasy land of Narnia in the seven books that make up that series, the last one winning for him the Carnegie Medal for the best-written children's book of 1957. About children's books he said:

> No book is really worth reading at the age of ten which is not equally (and often far more) worth reading at the age of fifty . . . the only imaginative works we ought to grow out of are those which it would have been better not to have read at all. [4]

He further states that "a children's story which is enjoyed only by children is a bad children's story. The good ones last."[5]

Robert Graves has produced both poetry and prose for children, among them The Big Green Book, perhaps his most amusing contribution, delightfully illustrated by Maurice Sendak. Novelist Graham Greene wrote four adventure stories for children;[6] it was his belief that:

> Perhaps it is only in childhood that books have any deep influence on our lives. . . . in childhood all books are books of divination, tell-

* Given at the Seminar on Children's Literature, Modern Language Association, New York City, December 27, 1972.

ing us about the future. . . . What do we ever get nowadays from reading to equal the excitement and revelation in those first fourteen years? [7]

John Masefield, a Poet Laureate of England, wrote several books of fantasy and adventure. "He has that final gift of a good story-teller," his biographer, Margery Fisher, remarks: "he makes each of his readers feel that a story is being read to him, and to him alone, at the moment of reading. Timing, the choice of incident, the peculiar, special Masefield dialogue, the immediacy of the scene— all these things help to make his novels compelling." What the reader should keep in mind with all well-written children's books is what she has said about Masefield's fantasies The Midnight Folk and The Box of Delights:

> These fantasies are not to be reserved for children. . . . Written
> with the full strength of Masefield's imagination and artistry, they
> are stories that summon up the child and the poet in everyone. [8]

The list of prominent literary figures who have written for children is impressive and long—from the Russian writers (Tolstoy, Pushkin, Chekhov), to the French (Colette, Eugene Ionesco, Marcel Aymé), to contemporary Americans (John Ciardi, Randall Jarrell, Gwendolyn Brooks). Herein is a look at what five of them have accomplished. The books selected for this study are occasional ones; that is, they were written for a particular child rather than for a larger audience. However, that should not mean that they are then automatically of inferior literary merit because they were not originally intended for publication: the quality of Alice's Adventures Underground should dispel that theory. Most of Emily Dickinson's poetry was not written for publication either.

The Crows of Pearblossom by Aldous Huxley is a case in point. Written during the Christmas holiday of 1944 while he and his wife were staying with his niece, [9] the story contains specific references to places and people instantly recognizable to her; yet the fact that another child would not be familiar with such references would not destroy his pleasure in the book. Abraham and Amelia Crow, ourselves in feathers (Abraham "worked as Assistant Manager in the drugstore"), [10] have a problem: a Rattlesnake has been coming up out of his hole every morning and eating Amelia's newly laid egg while she is out shopping. Abraham goes to his friend Old Man Owl, "who worked on a night shift and slept all day" (p. 14)—an original way of explaining his nocturnal habits. He comes up with a solution to the problem. He makes two clay eggs for Amelia's nest, much to the glee of the Rattlesnake, who swallows both of them. He soon regrets his action, for a severe stomachache causes him to twist and turn himself into knots around two branches of the tree, until he is tied up for good. And what child (or adult, for that matter) would not feel abundant satisfaction upon reading the last two lines?

> Since that time, Mrs. Crow has successfully hatched out four families
> of seventeen children each. And she uses the snake as a clothesline
> on which to hang the little crows' diapers.
>
> (p. 32)

Could justice have been better or more originally served?

Throughout the story humor prevails, despite the seriousness of the situation for the crows. For example, when Amelia has told Abraham what has happened, she suggests "'Why don't you go down into the snake's hole and kill him?'" (p. 13). The ridiculousness of such an approach is apparent to all. Later, when Abraham and Old Man Owl land in the alfalfa patch and Abraham complains of the mud, Owl's response is "'Abraham, you talk too much. . . . Keep your beak shut and do exactly what I do'" (p. 16). Both that sentence and Amelia's words are repeated when the two join her with their finished product, and the repetition adds to the humor. And after the snake discovers the two eggs we have some amusing moralizing: "And he smacked his lips, for his mother had neglected his education and he had very bad manners" (p. 20); and again, when Amelia returns finding him safely tied up, "she felt very brave and proceeded to give the snake a very long lecture on the wickedness of eating other people's eggs" (p. 30). There are other examples of humor that both adults and children can appreciate, for they are witty without being erudite, understandable without being condescending. A word must be said about the illustrations, too, for they capture the humor and mood of the story, as well as its plot, to perfection.

The Cat and the Devil also reflects the tongue-in-cheek humor of its author, as James Joyce tells his grandson how the bridge across the Loire River at Beaugency was created in one night. Before that, the people had to cross it in a boat, an inconvenience that they wished to correct. And the humor begins: "The Devil, who is always reading the newspapers, heard about this sad state of theirs."[11] He goes to call on the Lord Mayor who "always had a great golden chain round his neck even when he was fast asleep in bed with his knees in his mouth" (pp. 8-9). The Devil will make the bridge in exchange for the first person who shall cross it, and the Mayor agrees. When the townspeople awake and see it they exclaim, "O Loire, what a fine bridge!" (p. 12). The people flock to the bridge but stop short when they see the Devil on the other side; nobody dares to cross. The Mayor arrives with a cat in one arm and a bucket of water.

> All the people whispered to one another and the cat looked up at the
> Lord Mayor because in the town of Beaugency it was allowed that a
> cat should look at a lord mayor. . . . When the lord mayor came
> to the head of the bridge every man held his breath and every woman
> held her tongue.
>
> (pp. 25-26)

The Mayor puts the cat down and throws water at it, causing it to run into the arms of the Devil: "The devil was as angry as the devil himself" (p. 30). But, after launching a French tirade against the people of Beaugency, he retires with the cat, leaving them with their bridge. There is a postscript that again reflects the Joycean wit:

> P.S. The devil mostly speaks a language of his own called Bellsy-
> babble which he makes up as he goes along but when he is very

angry he can speak quite bad French very well though some who
have heard him say that he has a strong Dublin accent.
(p. 42)

Unless a child (or an unknowing adult, for that matter) is told at the beginning
that Joyce was from Dublin, most of the humor there is lost, although the sense
of it may not be. Here again we have a freshness, an originality of expression
flavored with Irish humor that results in an imaginative story that any child can
delight in.

A different kind of a story is Arthur Miller's Jane's Blanket. [12] It deals with
the problem exploited by Charles Schultz in his Peanuts cartoon—in this case a
little girl's love for and dependence upon a baby blanket in spite of attempts to get
her to part with it. The attachment begins in infancy and continues through the
toddler and pre-school years until Jane is going to school and is able to read and
do some of the shopping. One night Jane remembers her pink blanket and discovers that it isn't on her bed. Her mother gets it for her, and since it has ra-
velled and shrunk over the years to the size of a washcloth, Jane puts it on her
window sill until morning. When she awakens she discovers that a bird is pulling
threads out of it, and she is quite upset until her father explains that the bird is
using the threads to line her nest.

"Because it needs soft things to make a nest. It is taking the
threads to the nest and laying them inside, and when its baby
birds are born they will have a warm, soft place to live."
(p. 45)

He further explains to her that, although she cannot get it back from the nest
when the birds are through with it, " 'It will always be yours. . . . All you
have to do is remember it. Whenever you think of it, it's yours again' " (p. 45).
When the last thread has disappeared from the window sill Jane has her regrets,

But she was glad too. Because the birds were happy to be so nice
and warm at night, and she had helped to cover them so they could
sleep. She was glad that she was so big she didn't need her blanket
anymore.
(p. 47)

Here we have what appears to be a realistic anecdote, told in very simple
descriptive prose. In its style and language it would be best suited for a young
child, yet because of its length (forty-two pages of text and illustrations) the
young child might lose interest. And even a small child can sense when he is being preached to: a parent buying this book as a persuader for his own tot to give
up a favorite attachment should not be surprised to find that it has not worked.
Despite Arthur Miller's deserved reputation as a fine playwright, there is nothing
remarkably good about his children's book. Perhaps that is why he wrote no
others; writing good books for children is not an easy task.

The last two writers in this study both worked with fantasy, but the results
were quite different. E. E. Cummings' book, Fairy Tales, a collection of four
stories, was published after his death, as was William Faulkner's The Wishing

<u>Tree</u>. Faulkner uses the device of the dream for his fantasy, and the marvelous events that occur are explained to Dulcie by Maurice. He tells her that on the night before her birthday, "If you get into bed left foot first and turn the pillow over before you go to sleep, anything might happen" (p. 9). That refrain, that anything might happen, is echoed by Maurice as the search for the Wishing Tree unfolds in a mixture of southern setting and characters with the mysterious. It is a long story (seventy-eight pages of text and just a few illustrations) and an involved one that might be appreciated more by adults familiar with Faulkner's novels than by children, unless the children were southern, too, and would not be bothered by the dialect and the way some of the characters talk to each other:

> "I says, we don't want no old trash like him with us. I bet he's a tramp. I bet your mommer wouldn't like it if she knowed." (p. 20)

That's Alice's opinion of the old man, whose wife appears at the door and proceeds to throw things at him crying:

> "You lazy old scoundrel! . . . Sitting out here and gassing with strangers, and not a stick of wood to cook dinner with in the house!"
>
> (p. 21)

No wonder he sneaks off and joins the group in their search!

When a wonderful tree is finally discovered, the old man insists that it isn't the Wishing Tree but a mellomax tree, even though wishes start coming true for the travelers who have each picked a leaf. As they travel further in their search they come upon some soldiers: "'A soldier's life is awful hard,' Alice said."[13] There follows a section on a discussion of war, and Alice's husband comments:

> "I never seed a soldier yet that ever won anything in a war. But then, whitefolks' wars is always run funny. Next time the white-folks has a war, I think I ain't goin'. I think I'll jes' stay in the army instead."
>
> (p. 48)

How much understanding children would get out of this section is debatable, both because of the ideas and their presentation through conversations that are heavily dialectical. Later Dulcie gets separated from the others and comes upon the old man who remembers nothing about traveling with them and doesn't recognize Dulcie; this also could be bewildering to a child. Still later, reunited, the group comes upon Saint Francis, who tells them that the mellomax tree was the Wishing Tree, but who also explains that to make a wish from the tree would be selfish since all of the leaves would be gone in no time. They give him the leaves and he gives them each a bird in a cage in return, except for Alice's husband, who will help her take care of hers, and George, who ill-used his wishes (pp. 77-78). When Dulcie wakes up out of her dream her mother hands her a bird in a cage for her gift, the same as in the fantasy. The story ends with her moralizing on what Saint Francis said, and thinking about remembering to get into bed the right way again next year (p. 82).

Here, then, is a book with a limited appeal. Even though one might argue that the story is a fantasy and therefore a child doesn't have to understand all of it, even fantasy must operate logically and within the frame of reference of children. Imagination and wonder can take over if the writer gives children the basic realm or situations from which such a reaction can spring. In The Wishing Tree we have no readily identified fantasy land and no easily understood, familiar characters except for Dulcie, Dicky, and perhaps Maurice who works most of the magic. Setting the fantasy within a dream isn't enough; there must be more logic and coherence involved for the child reader in general to appreciate the tale. Obviously, Faulkner's intended audience, the little girl Victoria, knew the setting well and, I assume, was also familiar with the types of characters involved, if not with the characters themselves. But for an audience at large, the book would be confusing and therefore not effective.

E. E. Cummings' Fairy Tales was also written for a little girl, but he has avoided particularizing his stories. The result is that they can be read and enjoyed by everyone. There are four tales in all: "The Old Man Who Said 'Why'"; "The Elephant and the Butterfly"; "The House that Ate Mosquito Pie"; and "The Little Girl Named I." All are highly imaginative. Two are about love between highly disparate partners: an elephant and a butterfly in the second story, and a bird and a house in the third. The first story probably grew out of his daughter's insatiable question "Why?", one common to all young children at the pre-school level. A faerie agreed to go and stop the man on the moon from saying "why, " and when he got to the moon

> he saw a high rock, right on the very edge of the moon, and on the
> top of this rock there was a tall church, and on top of this church
> there was a slender steeple, and away up—right at the very top of
> this steeple—there was sitting a very very very very very very very
> old man with little green eyes and a big white beard and delicate
> hands like a doll's hands.
> (p. 12)

The faerie attempts to carry on a conversation with him, but to no avail, for he is constantly interrupted by "Why?". Finally, in exasperation the faerie warns him that if he says that again he will "fall from the moon all the way to the earth" (p. 14). And that is what happens, except that in the process he grows younger and younger until when he does finally reach the earth "he was about to be born" (p. 14). There the tale ends, with the implication that this explains why little children ask "Why?"

The two love tales are full of gentleness and delicacy and should be richly satisfying to children. For example, in "The Elephant and the Butterfly" is the following:

> So they came out together and the elephant's arm was very gently
> around the butterfly. Then the littlest tree said to his six friends:
> "I believe the butterfly loves the elephant as much as the elephant

loves the butterfly, and that makes me very happy, for they'll love each other always."

(p. 21)

In the next tale there is this description of the house before the bird comes:

> This house was tall and empty and had a great many windows. No-
> body lived in him because he stood on top of a high hill, away off
> from anywhere, with no one except the morning to play with and no
> one except the sunset to talk with and no one except the twilight to
> confide in. There was the afternoon, of course; but the afternoon
> rarely came near the house because the afternoon was too busy putting
> the moon to bed. And there was the night, too; but the night was
> fondest of wandering among all the bright and gentle kinds of flowers
> which you and I call "stars" because we don't know what they really
> may be.
>
> (p. 24)

Then the little bird arrives and the house asks her to live in him always:

> Then the bird thanked him and promised; and the house made all
> his rooms beautiful just by feeling happy. . . . When the bird
> woke up next morning, she found the house all filled with sunlight,
> and knew that she was happier than she had ever been before. So
> she sang to the house; and as for the house, he loved her so much
> he washed all his windows and wound up all his clocks and swept all
> his stairs and finally painted himself all over with fresh bright new
> paint.
>
> (pp. 27-28)

The final story is most representative of Cummings' style. It is presented in conversational form, the storyteller constantly stopping to ask his listener questions such as "And who do you suppose she meets?" and "What do you suppose this horse said?" (p. 32). After the little girl named I has met and invited several animals to come and have tea with her, which they weren't able to do for a variety of amusing reasons, she meets another little girl just like her and finds out that she is You:

> "You. That's who I am" she said "And You is my name because
> I'm You." . . . Then I said to You "Would you like to have some
> tea?" I said. And You said "Yes. I would" You said. So then
> You and I, we went to my house together to have some tea and then
> we had some fine hot tea I suppose and some delicious bread and
> butter too, with lots and lots and lots of jam.
>   And that's the end of this story.
>
> (p. 39)

Anyone who has read Cummings' poetry cannot fail to see its reflection in the style of his prose writing as well.

Thus, five writers, prominent for their adult works, made an attempt at writing for children; these efforts were highly personal in origin. Perhaps they felt as Graham Greene did—"Only in childhood do books make any deep impression on the human personality" [14]—and they wanted to contribute something to the special children for whom they wrote. Some were obviously more successful than others in reaching a larger audience as well. Of course the children themselves are unaware of the prominence of the authors. As Paul Hazard observes,

> The world of children is tolerant. It does not know about the pre-
> judices that sometimes can postpone the fame of great books indefi-
> nitely. It does not know about wars, how they destroy at a stroke
> values which once seemed established. It is more loyal than the
> world of adults which will not hesitate to scorn tomorrow the authors
> that it praises today, will even pretend to have forgotten their names.
> Its perception is more alert and sensitive, since it proceeds not
> by criticism but by instinct. [15]

[1] E. E. Cummings, Fairy Tales, illus. John Eaton (New York: Harcourt, Brace, & World, 1950), Dedication page.

[2] Richard Ellman, James Joyce, (New York: Oxford University Press, 1965), p. 703. The letter itself is printed in its entirety in a footnote, pp. 703-705.

[3] William Faulkner, The Wishing Tree (New York: Random House, 1964), a Dedication page and the Publisher's Note. Apparently Faulkner had made several copies of this particular story: "To Mrs. Brown's [the widow of one of Faulkner's former professors at the University of Mississippi] daughter, Margaret, Faulkner presented at about this time (1926), or a little later, the unpublished story, The Wishing Tree." See Michael Millgate, The Achievement of William Faulkner (London: Constable, 1965): there is "a much later typescript of the story which Faulkner inscribed for Phil Stone's son, his own godson, at Christmas, 1948" (pp. 10-11, 298).

[4] C. S. Lewis, "On Stories," Essays Presented to Charles Williams (London: Oxford, 1947), p. 100.

[5] C. S. Lewis, "On Three Ways of Writing for Children," Only Connect: Readings on Children's Literature, ed. Sheila Egoff, G. T. Stubbs, and L. F. Ashley (New York: Oxford, 1969), p. 210.

[6] The Little Train; The Little Fire-Engine; The Little Horse-Bus; and The Little Steam-Roller. All illustrated by Dorothy Craigie as mentioned in Bettina Hürlemann, Three Centuries of Children's Books in Europe, trans. Brian W. Alderson (London: Oxford, 1967), p. 262.

[7] Graham Greene, The Lost Childhood and Other Essays (London: Eyre and Spottiswoode, 1951), p. 13.

[8] Margery Fisher, John Masefield (New York: Walck, 1963), pp. 50, 53.

[9] Aldous Huxley, <u>The Crows of Pearblossom</u>, illus. Barbara Cooney (New York: Random House, 1967), Editor's Postscript.

[10] Ibid, p. 10. Since the pages in the book are not numbered, I have adopted the first page of text as page 3 and continued the numbering from there.

[11] James Joyce, <u>The Cat and the Devil</u>, illus. Richard Erdoes (New York: Dodd, Meade, 1964), p. 6. Since the pages in the book are not numbered, I have adopted the first page of text as page 3 and continued numbering from there.

[12] Arthur Miller, <u>Jane's Blanket</u>, illus. Emily A. McCully (New York: Viking, 1972).

[13] P. 42. A. A. Milne's poem "Buckingham Palace," from <u>When We Were Very Young</u> (New York: Dutton, 1924), contains the line:

"A soldier's life is terrible hard,"
Says Alice.

Since the book was an immediate success, it is possible that Faulkner had seen it and had remembered one of the most popular poems in the collection, or knew that it was a favorite of Victoria's.

[14] Graham Greene, "The Acceptance of the Regina Medal for Bertha Mahony Miller by Ruth Hill Viguers," <u>Horn Book</u>, 45 (October, 1969), p. 517.

[15] Paul Hazard, <u>Books, Children, and Men</u> (Boston: Horn Book, 1960), p. 147.

THE DEVIL HAS A DUBLIN ACCENT*

Alison White

Nursery rhymes and tales, and the books read in childhood have fired the imaginations of the world's great writers. This is of special interest in the case of James Joyce because his mind, supremely sophisticated though it was, renewed itself ceaselessly in the popular culture: folklore, puns, jokes, cartoons, politics, music-hall, street cries, games, or theater, Punch and Judy, books for children. Joyce's Dubliners, written early in this century, is a book of stories mainly about people as obscure and as odd as the characters of Edward Lear's cartoons, and as prone to folly. Joyce wrote Dubliners in his early twenties while his childhood memories were sharp, as indeed they remained to the end. Perhaps the young author recalled books of fairy tales which came on the market in the 1890's. His family was well-off then, and its many children were well-supplied with toys, books, and free time to browse in the book shops. Joseph Jacobs' English Fairy Tales, 1892, may have drawn his ten-year-old eye. Its tales had long been current orally, as they still are, and some of them had long been in print. Jacobs' first tale, "Teeny-Tiny," was copied word for word out of Halliwell's Nursery Rhymes and Tales, published in 1848. There Halliwell had explained "Teeny-Tiny" as a cante-fable, rhymes surviving in prose. Joyce may easily have heard or read the story. I've never yet met anyone who doesn't know about the teeny tiny woman who leaves her teeny tiny house to go to the teeny tiny graveyard. There she finds a teeny tiny bone for her teeny tiny soup. Later, from her teeny tiny bed she hears a great voice call, "GIVE ME MY BONE!"

In Joyce's Dubliners there is a story "Clay," first entitled "Hallow Eve." In it a tiny old maid, Maria, a laundry worker, spends Hallowe'en with a family. There, children blindfold Maria and guide her in a divination game: to choose a ring, for marriage; a prayer book, if she is to enter a convent; water, for crossing the sea. But, Maria touches a dish of clay, the symbol of death. Later, she pathetically sings "I Dreamt I Dwelt in Marble Halls" from Balfe's Bohemian Girl. . . . A sad tale's best for Hallowe'en. I never read this story without feeling that the leprechaun at Joyce's elbow led him to recall "Teeny-Tiny" and other nursery tales and rhymes as well. For he wrote that Maria "put her tiny dress-boots beside the foot of the bed." She had a "tiny, quavering voice," she "bent her tiny head"; laughing, "her minute body nearly shook itself asunder." The graveyard motif, the dish of clay, further recalls the teeny-tiny woman's ghoulish selection of a soupbone from the churchyard. And another

---

* Given at the Modern Language Association Seminar on Children's Literature, Chicago, Illinois, December 27, 1971.

child's tale of Joyce's youth comes to mind. Maria is like a household brownie.
"How can you expect Maria to crack nuts without a nutcracker?" asks her host.
Aside from being an indelicate allusion to Maria's profile, where "the tip of her
nose nearly touched the tip of her chin," this hints at her elfin faculties. In
1874, eight years before Joyce's birth, there was published Dinah Maria Mulock
Craik's Adventures of a Brownie. Brownie had "a very little mind like his little
body; but he did the best he could with it." The style is that of Joyce's story,
kept ever inside Maria's limited little mind. Maria sat "on the little stool . . .
with her toes barely touching the floor." Miss Mulock's Brownie "placed himself
on the milking stool, which was so high that his little legs were dangling halfway
down." Brownie turns a stone into a cake. It disappears. Maria buys a cake.
It disappears. Like Brownie, Maria does domestic magicking. At the laundry
she cut the barnbracks so well that you could not see where the knife had been.
(Last January in Dublin I cut a barnbrack and, in that sticky mess, no mere
mortal could have avoided leaving clumsy marks.) To this day in Ireland, a
barnbrack is served at Hallowe'en. It is a yeasty bread, heavy with fruit, into
which have been put a ring for a wedding, a rag for an old maid, a pea for poverty, a button for clothes, sixpence for riches, and a stick to beat your old man
with.

If I see Joyce's Maria as Teeny-Tiny and Brownie, I am in the company of
critics who have seen in her a Hallowe'en witch, the Irish Washerwoman, a wife
and mother manqué, Ireland, a saint, the Virgin Mary, and Mr. Punch—the last
because of her profile and her singing Punch's song from Balfe's opera. I feel
on surer ground, though, in tracking Maria to a limerick in The History of Sixteen Wonderful Old Women. This, the first book of limericks ever, came out in
1820. Edward Lear imitated it and so, I think, did Joyce, who was not the man
to pass up a limerick and who lived in Limerick's own country. In this 1820 book
the first rhyme, ironic and sour, is: "There liv'd an old Woman at Lynn
[Dublin?] / Whose nose very near touch'd her chin. / You may easy suppose /
She had plenty of beaux, / This charming old Woman of Lynn." Of Maria, Joyce
intones again and again that "the tip of her nose nearly touched the tip of her
chin." And, as for beaux, it is central to the story that Maria's "eyes shone
with disappointed shyness" at any mention of them. And this draws one to spec-
ulate that Joyce may have in some recess recalled that great figure in children's
literature, a countrywoman of his in Ireland, called by Byron "Maria the Great."
She was the eighteenth-century novelist and writer for children, Maria Edgeworth:
and her biography tells us that she never married "because she was dwarfish
and plain."

Often Joyce seems to survey his drab little Dubliners through the large end of
the opera glasses. In "A Little Cloud," (Notice little) the human "cloud" is a
glooming, sometimes glowing, visionary, shifting little office-worker called
"Little Chandler." T. Malone Chandler, "Tommy", he is called by a loud-
mouthed city slicker from London when the two engage in a Town Mouse and
Country Mouse exchange. And, indeed, Little Tommy Chandler is more of a
mouse than a man. "His hands were white and small, his frame was fragile . . .

He took the greatest care of his fair silken hair and moustache, and when he smiled you caught a glimpse of a row of childish white teeth." To his eyes there appeared a world of mice. "A horde of grimy children . . . squatted like mice . . . all that minute vermin-like life." Tommy Chandler lives in a prim, pretty prison of a house, with a mean-eyed wife. One remembers Mother Goose: "Little Tommy Tittlemouse / Lived in a little house." In the main, Dubliners presents small, dim people, poor and seedy, scuttling in the futile circles that define brown Dublin's spiritual sterility. They are the tarnished, faded images of Mother Goose's "Littles": Little Tommy Tittlemouse, Tiny Maria, the Pariah, grown to dusty adulthood and disenchantment.

But last, I wish to offer a brighter vision, though a diabolical one. This is of Joyce's only book for children. It is a good little book, akin to the comic fantasies of Ruskin, Thackeray, Dickens, and Thurber: Joyce's The Cat and the Devil, published in 1964 by Dodd Mead. Joyce wrote it in 1936, five years before his death, as a letter to his five-year-old grandson, Stephen James Joyce. Both were living in Paris. In this letter Joyce retold a folk tale of how the devil approached the lord mayor of Beaugency who "always had a great golden chain round his neck even when he was fast asleep in bed with his knees in his mouth." The devil bargained to throw an instant bridge across the Loire if he were given the first to cross it. The lord mayor set a cat down on the bridge and threw a bucket of water on it. "The cat who was now between the devil and the bucket of water" ran across and into the devil's arms. "The devil was as angry as the devil himself," but he accepted the cat, saying they would go "to warm themselves." P.S. by Joyce: "The Devil mostly speaks a language of his own called Bellsybabble which he makes up himself as he goes along, but when he is very angry he can speak quite bad French very well though some who have heard him say that he has a strong Dublin accent."

"SHOES OF SONG AND WINGS OF RHYME"
VACHEL LINDSAY'S POETRY FOR CHILDREN *

Blair Whitney

Vachel Lindsay committed suicide by drinking a bottle of Lysol. At the end he was completely broken, virtually bankrupt, no longer popular, desperately trying to regain the vigor and energy which characterized his best poetry and which sent him across the country in a furious, but ultimately futile attempt to convert America to his Gospel of Beauty. Like other Romantic poets, he worshipped the visionary gleam, and like them he admired the innocence of childhood, which he tried to retain throughout his life. His almost deliberate avoidance of family and financial responsibilities, his insistence that the Philistines were out to destroy him, and his refusal to recognize that his best work was done made him seem a kind of child himself. On the evening of his suicide, one biographer reveals, Lindsay railed at his wife for three hours.

Yet the very things which made Lindsay a failure as a responsible adult helped make him one of the best children's poets of this century. Critics of Lindsay may legitimately accuse him of lacking the coherent philosophy which enables a lyric poet to work beyond his youth, and they may term him a mere "music-maker," but these deficiencies make his poetry even more appealing to children. Although only a few of his poems are specifically for children, almost all his work may be read, recited, chanted, and sung by them. Always a superb entertainer whose reading audiences may have numbered in the millions, Lindsay was a master of the music of poetry, from the "Willy willy willy wah Hoo!" of "The Kallyope Yell" to the whispered close of "The Flower-Fed Buffaloes," and from the joyous hymn tune of "General Booth" to the jazzy "boomlay-boom" of "The Congo." Although he professed to hate jazz (Lindsay was for Temperance; jazz meant speak-easies), and although he was almost tone deaf, Lindsay was always a singer of words to improvised and borrowed tunes. He was exactly the right kind of poet for the new Jazz Age, though like a pop idol, he lacked the staying power to become a literary great in the usual sense. Scholars have him pigeon-holed as a good minor poet, worthy of a few pages in the anthologies, but children know otherwise.

Of all Lindsay's work, only a few poems are too advanced or too much of their own time ("Why I Voted the Socialist Ticket," for example) for younger readers. The others can be divided into three groups: poems about historical or legendary figures; moon-and-fairy poems; and poems about animals. The first group con-

---

* Given at the Modern Language Association Seminar on Children's Literature, New York City, December 27, 1972.

tains most of his best work. A celebrator of American heroes, Lindsay tried to create a sort of pantheon of demi-gods for Americans to draw inspiration from. These heroes, he believed, were men and women who understood the genius of America, and if Americans would but study these lives, they might be persuaded to overturn the capitalists in power and restore America's lost beauty. Brother of a missionary in China, Lindsay hoped in these poems to convert America to his own gospel, and he preached in rhymes which are full of music, full of vigor, full of life—and which catch children's fancy.

The first of these heroes and the subject of Lindsay's first successful poem is General William Booth of the Salvation Army. Lindsay's marginal notes call for this poem to be sung to the tune of "The Blood of the Lamb," accompanied by the bass drum, banjo, flute, and tambourine, but even without these instruments, it makes a joyful noise with its grand rhythm.

> Booth led boldly with his big bass drum—
> (Are you washed in the blood of the Lamb?)
> The Saints smiled gravely and they said: "He's come."
> (Are you washed in the blood of the Lamb?) [1]

Another religious hero is Daniel, cast into a den of ferocious, but delightfully growly lions.

> We want Daniel, Daniel, Daniel,
> We want Daniel, Daniel, Daniel.

"How Samson Bore Away the Gates of Gaza" is a similar piece with plenty of action and the striking refrain,

> Let Samson
> Be Coming
> Into Your Mind.

Like these poems of religious heroism, the poems about secular historical figures give life to abstractions in a way that few biographies can improve upon. They are certainly not expressions of impartial historical truth, but instead are celebrations of what Lindsay believed was best about this country. He makes his politicians into folk heroes of mythic proportions. William Jennings Bryan, whom Lindsay heard in 1896, becomes for him,

> The bard and the prophet of them all.
> Prairie avenger, mountain lion,
> Bryan, Bryan, Bryan, Bryan . . .

This hero is defeated by villains of monstrous proportions:

> Election night at midnight at midnight:
> Boy Bryan's defeat.
> Defeat of western silver.
> Defeat of the wheat.
> Victory of letterfiles

> And plutocrats in miles
> With dollar signs upon their coats,
> Diamond watchchains on their vests
> And spats on their feet.

Lindsay's Teddy Roosevelt is compared to Saul, and John Peter Altgeld, the great liberal governor of Illinois, is an eagle, forgotten but still living in the heart of mankind.

But above all these is Abraham Lincoln. The Lindsay home in Springfield, Illinois is only a few blocks from the only house Lincoln ever owned, and Vachel grew up with the Lincoln legend. In one of his most famous poems, "Abraham Lincoln Walks at Midnight," Lincoln returns to walk the streets of his home town.

> A bronzed, lank man! His suit of ancient black,
> A famous high top-hat and plain worn shawl
> Make him the quaint great figure that men love,
> The prairie lawyer, master of us all.

Lindsay invokes this ghost as a way of expressing his hope for an end to World War I.

> It breaks his heart that kings must murder still,
> That all his hours of travail here for men
> Seem yet in vain. And who will bring white peace
> That he may sleep upon his hill again?

Lindsay finds other images of the nation's strength in John L. Sullivan and in the Clark Mills statue of Andrew Jackson.

> Andrew Jackson was a Democrat,
> Defying kings in his old cocked hat.
> His vast steed rocked like a hobby-horse.
> But he sat straight up. He held his course.

This celebration of national heroes was not just simple patriotism. In the day of Babbitt and the Lost Generation, we had somehow forgotten our national destiny. Perhaps these poems might serve as a reminder.

The three poems on Johnny Appleseed are a good illustration of poems written with this motive. Lindsay finds John Chapman a kindred spirit, one who walked the nation dropping seeds as Lindsay dropped poems. These poems express the real meaning of Appleseed's life.

> Then
> The sun was their turned-up broken barrel,
> Out of which their juicy apples rolled,
> Down the repeated terraces,
> Thumping across the gold,
> An angel in each apple that touched the forest mold,
> A ballot-box in each apple,

A state capital in each apple,
Great high schools, great colleges,
All America in each apple,
Each red, rich, round, and bouncing moon
That touched the forest mold.
Like scrolls and rolled-up flags of silk,
He saw the fruits unfold,
And all out expectations in one wild-flower written dream.

Lindsay did not neglect the history of Afro-Americans in his heroic pantheon. Everyone knows "The Congo," but his trilogy in honor of Booker T. Washington, a Black sermon into which he weaves Simon Legree, John Brown, and Solomon and Sheba, is also notable. Lindsay did not understand Africa, and his poems may seem patronizing today, but they were certainly not intended in that spirit. It was he who gave the first public reading of Langston Hughes's poetry. Like his Blacks, Lindsay's Indians are usually noble savages. Pocahontas becomes the mother of us all, the spirit of America personified.

We here renounce our Teuton pride:
Our Norse and Slavic boasts have died:
Italian dreams are swept away,
And Celtic feuds are lost today . . .
She sings of lilacs, maples, wheat,
Her own soil sings beneath her feet,
Of springtime
And Virginia,
Our Mother, Pocahontas.

The second group of Lindsay's poems consists of the moon-and-fairy poems, the best known of which is probably "The Moon's the North Wind's Cooky." These poems are both more delicate and less successful than the rest of Lindsay's work. They sometimes resemble the poetry of Eugene Field. When they fail, it is usually because they are made too much of gossamer, without the sturdy homespun of Lindsay's best work. Yet a few are successful, especially "The Scissors-Grinder," which Lindsay subtitled "An Unconscious Prophecy Written in 1913," and in which an old man sees what is about to come.

The moon is but an emery-wheel
To whet the sword of God,
. . .
I see that sword each century, friend,
It means the world-war comes
With all its bloody, wicked chiefs
And hate-inflaming drums.

"The Lame Boy and the Fairy" is a pleasant fantasy which, though overly sentimental in lines like "Sleepy young fairy flowers," is still fairly fresh and vigorous. In the poem a lame boy meets a fairy who brings him gifts and calls him into an eternal heaven of childhood imagination.

145

A hundred years
And
A day,
There we will fly
And play
I-spy and cross-tag
And meet on the highway,
And call to the game
Little Red Riding Hood
Goldilocks, Santa Claus,
Every beloved
And heart-shaking name.

Like almost every other good children's author, Vachel Lindsay wrote about animals. Besides the Daniel lions, there are many more creatures in the Lindsay bestiary. His simplest poem was written for his three-year-old niece and is familiar to countless pre-schoolers.

There was a little turtle.
He lived in a box.
He swam in a puddle.
He climbed on the rocks.

He snapped at a mosquito.
He snapped at a flea.
He snapped at a minnow.
And he snapped at me.

He caught the mosquito.
He caught the flea.
He caught the minnow.
But he didn't catch me.

"The Flower-Fed Buffaloes" remind us of a lost America.

With the Blackfeet, lying low,
With the Pawnees, lying low,
Lying low.

But some buffaloes are not content to lie low. Instead, in "The Ghost of the Buffaloes," they come charging into our dreams, accompanied by their Indian hunters.

Buffaloes, buffaloes, thousands abreast,
A scourge and amazement, they swept to the west.
With black bobbing noses, with red rolling tongues,
Coughing forth steam from their leather-wrapped lungs . . .

Some of these animal poems are just for fun, but others have serious morals. "The Broncho that would not be Broken," written from one of Lindsay's actual experiences on his travels, is a good example. The colt in the poem is a grace-ful, noble, free creature who must be broken to the farm. They hitch him to a reaper, but he will not give in to his driver. The effort to fight free kills him, but his death is like that of a tragic hero.

> In that last afternoon your boyish heart broke.
> The hot wind came down like a sledge-hammer stroke.
> The blood-sucking flies to a rare feast awoke.
> And they searched out your wounds, your death-warrant tracing.
> And the merciful men, their religion enhancing,
> Stopped the red reaper, to give you a chance.
> Then you died on the prairie, and scorned all disgraces,,
> O broncho that would not be broken of dancing.

In all of Lindsay's best poetry is a sense of vitality and of strength, expressed in bold and musical rhythms. He saw himself as a bringer of gifts, the same gifts brought to the lame boy by the fairy, "shoes of song and wings of rhyme." If his readers and listeners enjoyed his poetry, they might then be converted into a nation appreciative of both the beauty of art and the beauty of action.

---

[1] Vachel Lindsay, Collected Poems (New York, 1930), p. 123. All other cita-tions are from this edition except "The Flower-Fed Buffaloes" from Selected Poems of Vachel Lindsay, ed. Hazelton Spencer (New York, 1931), p. 15.

"THE TONGUE OF GODS AND CHILDREN":
BLAKEAN INNOCENCE IN RANDALL JARRELL'S POETRY *

Bernard Horn

> To prefer the nest in the linden
> By Apartment Eleven, the Shoreham
> Arms, to Apartment Eleven
> Would be childish. But we are children.
>
> "Hope" (p. 305)[1]

For Randall Jarrell, while we are all, like children, powerless victims of a
destructive time, we are also unlike children because our imaginations have been
victimized. Consequently, the freshness of perception, the naive hope, and the
poignancy of childhood and childish things pervade his poetry. Only in William
Blake's Songs of Innocence do we find so rich an exploration of these matters, but
before I explore this quality of "innocence" more fully, I shall first make distinctions among the various ways childhood creeps into Jarrell's poems. First,
there are "The Owl's Bedtime Story" and the Bat-Poet's poems: lyrics, narratives, and descriptive poems primarily directed at an audience of children. Next,
there are poems like "The Marchen," "The Sleeping Beauty: Variation of the
Prince," and "Cinderella," that contain subject matter from "children's literature" but are directed at an adult audience. Finally, there is the largest group
of poems—some directed at adults, some at children, many at both—poems
either about childhood or narrated by children.

> (1) When the swans turned my sister into a swan
>   I would go to the lake, at night, from milking.
>
> "The Black Swan" (p. 54)

> (2) Never again will Orion
>   Fall on my speller through the star
>   Taped on the broken window by my cot.
>   My knee is ridged like corn
>   And the scab peels off it.
>
>   We are going to live in a new pumpkin
>   Under a gold star.
>
> "Moving" (p. 94)

---

* Given at the Modern Language Association Seminar on Children's Literature,
Chicago, Illinois, December 27, 1971.

(3) At home, in my flannel gown, like a bear to its floe,
    I clambered to bed; up the globe's impossible sides
    I sailed all night—till at last, with my black beard,
    My furs and my dogs, I stood at the northern pole.

                                    "90 North" (p. 113)

(4) Sometimes as I drive by the factory
    That manufactures, after so long, Vicks
    VapoRub Ointment, there rises over me
    A eucalyptus tree.

                                    "The Lost World" (p. 289)

(5) All night in the womb I heard the stories.
    My brother was a fish, began, "O fish!"
    And I listened till my gills began to fall.

                                    "A Little Poem" (p. 362)

            Piping down the valleys wild,
                Piping songs of pleasant glee,
            On a cloud I saw a child
                And he laughing said to me:

The last quotation, of course, is from Blake's "Introduction" to Songs of Innocence. Juxtaposing Blake's stanza with the fragments from Jarrell demonstrates
the kinship between the two poets. No poet since Blake has brought off so well
that quality of "innocence," that matter-of-fact acceptance of the supernatural,
of magic and mystery, that we call "childlike." Children's tales, Jarrell writes,

                    are full of sorcerers and ogres
            Because their lives are: the capricious infinite
            That, like parents, no one has yet escaped
            Except by luck or magic.

        "Children Selecting Books in a Library" (p. 106)

Magic. No roll of a snare drum. No blare of rhetorical trumpets. But simply,
"On a cloud I saw a child," or "When the swans turned my sister into a swan."

    Of course Jarrell is no mere Blake imitator, though that in itself would have
been quite an accomplishment; he is rather a modern partly disillusioned counterpart. Even in "The Black Swan," the poem closest to Blake, a quite un-
Blakean literal dream intrudes before the swan's song restores the magical world
of the child's imagination. In "Moving," my second example, Jarrell locates
the girl's monologue within a third person narrative. In "90 North," the Blake-
like opening turns out to be the stimulus for a bitter meditation in which an adult
speaker rejects the richly meaningful "Cloud-Cuckoo-Land" of childhood in the
face of existential woe "at the actual pole of my existence, / Where all that I have
done is meaningless." Similarly, "A Little Poem" ends:

                            149

I said, "O speak!" My brother smiled,
And I saw Nothing beckon from his lids,
The heart in his oiled breast was dumb as Time,
And his skill crackled with its empty blood.

In "The Lost World" and in "Thinking of the Lost World," poems explicitly
about his own childhood, childlike perception or sensation stimulates a Proustian
collapsing of time. Finally, the matter-of-fact childlike mind can perceive the
monstrous as well as the beautiful: in "A Nursery Rhyme," suddenly, with almost no preparation,

The orphan laterals the warden's head
To a manic who gains eleven yards,
Runs to the stands and assaults a nurse,
Is beaten to shreds by the fretting guards.

(p. 429)

Kafka, like Proust, lived between Blake and Jarrell.

In Jarrell, as in Blake, this innocence of perception is accompanied by naive
faith and matter-of-fact acceptance of the natural as well as the supernatural.
Innocence involves belief as well as perception. Both poets locate innocence
within the minds of their speakers, not within the world, and both achieve some
of their most poignant and powerful effects because of the discrepancy between a
speaker's naiveté in both belief and desire and the state of the world—compare
"The Chimney Sweep" and "The Little Black Boy" of Blake to "The State," "The
Truth," and "Protocols" by Jarrell. The "Lament of the Children of Israel in
Rome" has some of the power of "Holy Thursday":

Then we chorus, with the tongues
Of our fathers, to the harps,
In harmonies our sorrow sharpens,
David's Psalms, still unforgotten:
Till the tears begin to flow—
And once more, from our hearts,
The pain of a thousand years
Melts into hope for the Messiah.

(p. 451)

Jarrell also employs a matter-of-factness of tone, particularly with respect to
death, to intensify pathos in such well-known adult poems as "The Death of the
Ball Turret Gunner," "When I Was Home Last Christmas . . . ," and several
poems with a woman narrator, like "The Lost Children" and "The Player Piano."

Jarrell understands, perhaps too well, that because of our powerlessness and
vulnerability, tragic feelings have given way to pathos as the emotion of our
time—our ogres, if we can even locate them, seem omnipotent. It is not surprising then, that in two poems about patients—that is, vulnerable adults—Jar-

rell reveals why he is so preoccupied with childish and childlike subjects. Writing about the faith of patients in doctors, Jarrell writes,

> And their childishness is natural; here is this office
> The natural perplexities of their existence,
> The demands they can neither satisfy nor understand,
> Are reduced to the child's, "I hurt," the bare
> Intention of any beast to go on being.
>
> "A Utopian Journey" (p. 110)

All the patients in "The X-Ray Waiting Room in the Hospital"

> miss our underwear
> And the old days. These new, plain, mean
> Days of pain and care, this routine
> Misery has made us into cases, the one case
> The one doctor cures forever . . .
>
> (p. 297)

It is in the context of days like these that Jarrell evokes in his poems a world in which it is possible, through luck or magic, to defeat or escape from "that sick dream the waking call a world" (p. 357).

---

1 This and subsequent page numbers refer to Randall Jarrell, The Complete Poems (New York, 1969).

I would like to thank Professor Jack Davis for making this paper possible.

THE PROPER BRINGING UP OF YOUNG PIP *

Muriel Whitaker

Charles Dickens' description of how Mrs. Joe brought up young Pip "by hand" is usually regarded as an example of the author's penchant for grotesque exaggeration; yet an examination of English children's literature from the seventeenth century to the 1830's suggests that the view of the child held by Pip's sister conforms rather closely to that promulgated by many adult authors. The Puritans regarded the child as stained with sin, a "brand of hell"—"naterally wicious," as Mr. Hubble tersely puts it. In one of the earliest Puritan books for children, James Janeway's A Token for Children: being an Exact Account of the Conversion, Holy and Exemplary Lives, and Joyful Deaths of several young Children, [1] the author reminds parents that no child is too little to go to Hell. Even the gentle cleric, Isaac Watts, whose Divine Songs attempted in easy Language for the use of Children (London: M. Lawrence, 1715) was a best seller for two hundred years, [2] devotes many lines to describing the dreadful Hell, the everlasting Pains, the Darkness, Fire, and Chains that await the youthful sinner. That this view of the child's corruptness still prevailed in the nineteenth century is illustrated by the introductory chapter of The Boy's Week-day Book (London: Religious Tract Society, ca. 1850).

> How hard it is to imagine, when we look on a helpless infant smiling
> in the arms of its mother, or sleeping in its crib or cradle, that its
> little heart will soon burn with anger, its dimpled cheeks redden with
> rage, and its mild blue eyes sparkle with evil passions! . . . And
> yet, if we look around us, we must be convinced that, at a very early
> age the bad passions of the heart begin to show themselves, and re-
> quire every care to subdue them. Well may parents watch and pray
> over their tender offspring, that they may not be led into temptation,
> but be delivered from evil, and guided in their pilgrimage from earth
> to heaven. [3]

Parents, clerics, educators, even philosophers agreed that the child's viciousness could be curbed only by fear. "Correction, in itself, is not cruel," proclaimed Dr. Johnson. "Children, being not reasonable, can be governed only by fear. To impress this fear is therefore one of the first duties of those who have the care of children." [4]

Mrs. Joe was not remiss is carrying out this aspect of parental duty. Tickler, "worn smooth by collision with my tickled frame," was always ready to

---

* Given at the Modern Language Association Seminar on Children's Literature, December 27, 1972.

hand, supplemented by the thimble, the bottle of tar-water, and the strong right arm. She would have approved of the analogy frequently drawn between children and tops—"the faster they scourge them, the better they go." The child, for his part, was expected to be grateful for such marks of affection from parental figures who were regarded as God's viceroys on earth.

In addition to punishments of a physical nature, horrendous examples were employed to warn the child of the dangers inherent in almost every juvenile diversion. Between 1780 and 1850 a plethora of hortatory books appeared, including those with such delightful titles as The Daisy; or Cautionary Stories in Verse Adapted to the Ideas of Children from Four to Eight Years Old (London: John Harris, ca. 1840), Early Seeds to Produce Spring Flowers (London: William Darton, 1824), and Memoirs of The Little Man and the Little Maid (London: B. Tabart, 1807). [5] The scope and intention of these works is indicated by the full title of one of them, The Affectionate Parent's Gift, and the good child's reward; consisting of a series of poems and essays, on natural, moral and religious subjects, calculated to lead the tender minds of youth in the early practice of virtue and piety, and eternal happiness. To which is prefixed, an affectionate address on the duties and obligations they owe to God and their parents (London: T. Kelly, 1828).

The heroes and heroines—or perhaps one should say, the victims—in these tales and verses are bitten by dogs, kicked by horses, burnt by pokers, poisoned by fruit or liquor, run over by goats, tossed by bulls, crushed by stones, pierced by penknives, scalded by tea-kettles, and attacked by sharks while swimming in African waters. Miss Julia Sandford persists in swallowing thread which, tying together her bowels, produces fatal results. Harry, who enjoys catching fish with a hook, is himself impaled on a meat hook. A boy who has pulled out a goldfinch's feathers is punished when his father pulls out the child's hair and then dismisses him with the words, "Go from my presence, you cruel wicked boy, and never let me see your face till you are sensible of your monstrous crime." Poised before the bottle marked "Drink me," Lewis Carroll's Alice recalls "several nice little stories about children who had got burnt, and eaten up by wild beasts, and other unpleasant things, all because they would not remember the simple rules their friends had taught them."

Inevitably, the fate which befalls these accident-prone children results from disobedience, adults having provided ample warning which the young have disregarded. Hence, Mrs. Joe's comment, "If you bring the boy back with his head blown to bits by a musket, don't look to me to put it together again" is a characteristic adult reaction of the "Don't say I didn't warn you" type common in hortatory literature for children.

With the horrendous example so firmly established as a means of instruction, it is not surprising that the Gargerys' Christmas dinner should provide an occasion for touching up Pip with "moral goads." Mr. Wopsle points out that the festal pig is a text from which many a moral for the young may be deduced. In fact, it enables the guests to condemn simultaneously three of the most flagrant juvenile sins—gluttony, idleness, and ingratitude. In writing this passage, Dickens may have had in mind "The Pig," a selection in <u>Nursery Morals, chiefly in Monosyllables</u> (London: John J. Harris, 1818). After describing in vivid detail the dirtiness and gluttony of the animal, the anonymous author goes on to point out the resemblances between children and swine.

> Have you seen children devour sweets and delicates
> without end?
> Tarts, and cakes, and fruits?
> Then with greasy face and dirty hands
> fall asleep on the ground.
> Their clothes all spoiled.
> Their limbs all twisted.
> Well, are not such children as bad as pigs?
> Aye, and worse, much worse,
> For they know better.
> They have the choice to be clean if they please.

Pip, "enjoying himself with his elders and betters, and improving himself with their conversation, and rolling in the lap of luxury," is well aware that he is an arrant knave. Not only is he guilty of ingratitude to her who brought him up by hand but he is guilty of theft, a crime frequently condemned in children's literature of the period. Significantly, in the moral tales it is often coupled with ingratitude. The child thief begins by stealing from his parents, progressing from the theft of a pin or a piece of food to more valuable booty. A poem in <u>The Affectionate Parent's Gift</u> describes how a father takes his sons on an instructive tour of Newgate where they see "confin'd within a grated cell" a little boy who has robbed his parents. In the same work, the affectionate parent also arranges family outings to asylums for the blind and insane.

In view of the barbarous punishments meted out to child thieves in the tales, it is little wonder that Pip should be overwhelmed by terror and consciousness of sin. The stair boards cry out, "Stop thief!"; the gates and dykes exclaim, "A boy with somebody-else's pork pie!", the cattle salute him with, "Halloa, young thief!" Only the greater terrors of dismemberment, mutilation, and the eternal damnation of the forsworn compel him to carry out his attack on private property. All the same, he is convinced that like the child thief of <u>Tales from the Mountains</u> he is destined for the gibbet.

Telling lies is another crime frequently condemned in moral tales. Pip's admission that he has lied in describing his visit to Miss Havisham so horrifies Joe that for the only time he assumes the role of hortatory parent.

> " . . . lies is lies. Howsoever they come, they didn't ought to
> come, and they come from the father of lies, and work round to
> the same . . . If you can't get to be uncommon through going
> straight, you'll never get to do it through going crooked. So don't
> tell no more on 'em, Pip, and live well and die happy."

Joe's treatment of Pip is infinitely compassionate compared with that depicted in Young Wilfred or the Punishment of Falsehood (London, 1821). Described as a monster of deceit, fraud, falsehood, treachery and cunning, a disgrace to his unfortunate parents and to human nature, Wilfred is birched by every member of the school, confined in a dark room, hissed, stoned, and sent home ignominiously, a dreadful example to the reader.

It was not enough for model parents to punish misdoing, warn of danger, and develop in the child a scrupulous conscience. They must also avoid indulging the young by catering to whims and sensual desires. Idle Hours Employed (London: John Harris, 1826) contrasts the regimen of Mr. Beaufoy with that of Mr. Robinson. The sons of the former must rise early, wash in cold water, sleep in a bed, take daily exercise, and avoid rich food and wine. As a result, they are gay and happy. Mr. Robinson's children are allowed to have coffee, chocolate, wine, and tarts, and are protected from the cold. Their faces are yellow, their eyes dull, their teeth black and broken. They come to an early end as a result of catching pneumonia. Again, Mrs. Joe adheres admirably to the ideal. Pip's share of the Christmas feast is "the scaly tips of the drumsticks" and "those obscure corners of pork of which the pig, when living, had had the least reason to be vain." The "mortfying and penitential character" of the diet prescribed by his sister is apparent also in the watered milk and dry bread consumed in Mr. Pumblechook's parlor while the corn-chandler himself enjoys bacon and hot rolls.

Since Satan finds work for idle hands to do, the child must be kept occupied. Mrs. Joe avoids "pompeying" Pip by requiring him to work at the forge, frighten birds, pick up stones, and do other odd jobs, the remuneration for which is deposited in a money-box on the kitchen shelf. The child's character is strengthened by these exercises in industry, frugality, and self-denial.

Though prayers and church-going were part of a proper upbringing, a shift of emphasis from religion to pragmatic morality and good manners is apparent in much of the children's literature written in the first part of the nineteenth century. The Good Boy's Soliloquy (New York: Samuel Wood & Sons, 1822), for example, devotes most of its couplets to the kind of behavior which would cause the least trouble to adults.

> I must not bawl or make a noise,
> I must not throw about my toys;
>
> I must not quarrel with the maid
> When getting from or into bed;
>
> I must not dirty the clean stairs;
> I must not trample on the chairs . . .

And so on. For mnemonic purposes, many injunctions took the form of proverbs to be quoted by adults and embroidered on samplers by little girls—"Children should be seen and not heard"; "Waste not, want not"; "Cleanliness is next to Godliness."

The latter precept was given positive demonstration by Mrs. Joe who had "an exquisite art of making her cleanliness more uncomfortable and unacceptable than dirt itself." In preparation for his visit to Miss Havisham, Pip is squeezed, doused, soaped, kneaded, towelled, thumped, harrowed, rasped, put in clean linen of the stiffest character and trussed up in his stiffest suit. Both Pip and Joe are ejected from the house when Mrs. Joe, on the rampage, vents her wrath in an excess of scrubbing. A slave with her apron never off, she makes her passionate pursuit of cleanliness an effective weapon against her subservient males, a means of asserting not only her physical but also her moral superiority.

Diligence in study was another virtue upheld in children's literature. The Puritans believed that a child should learn his letters at an early age so that he could read his Scripture and Catechism. Though the presence in Mr. Wopsle's great-aunt's school of Bibles (defaced) suggests a vestige of Puritan influence, Pip's initial acquisition of learning is motivated less by religious inspiration than by the consciousness of social inferiority produced by his acquaintance with Estella. From the middle-class point of view, a sense of inferiority in the lower classes was commendable. For the reader of "Give with Prudence" and "Fanny Overkind," Estella's condescension would have been less remarkable than Pip's refusal to remain in the station to which God had called him.

In fact, the boy's sense of injustice at the way in which he is treated by Estella, his sister, and all the adults except Joe is explicable not in terms of the adult view expressed in didactic children's literature but rather in terms of actual experience. The young Dickens himself and the countless other children who were humiliated, bullied, repressed, and denigrated simply because they were children—"sixpennorth of halfpence"—must have rebelled against the servile role imposed on them by adults and by their social superiors. The fact that young Pip publicly exhibits the virtues of obedience, cleanliness, humility, frugality, industry, gratitude, and diligence in study provides ample evidence that he has, indeed, been properly brought up. But in the flush of prosperity and independence he repudiates these virtues which have been instilled by force and fear. He becomes proud, greedy, self-indulgent, lazy, self-satisfied and ungrateful. It is only when he has been frightened and physically punished as in the old days of his bringing up by hand that Pip returns to the virtues of his youth—industry, frugality, and above all, gratitude. What irony there is in the fact that the instrument of his restoration is Orlick, an archetypal parody of the stern, violent, pitiless, and irrational parents in much didactic literature for children!

Great Expectations is not the only work in which Dickens uses the methods and, at the same time, attacks, at least implicitly, the genre of the cautionary tale. Dombey and Son also contains satiric vignettes of child-rearing methods. Early in the book Susan Nipper expresses the view that "Childhood, like money, must be shaken and rattled and jostled about a good deal to keep it bright." Miss Pankey is assured by Mrs. Pipchin that nobody who sniffs before visitors ever goes to heaven, and the curious Paul is reminded of "the story of the little boy that was gored to death by a mad bull for asking questions." The Early

Readings assigned by the fearsome pedagogue conform admirably to the pattern of cautionary tale:

> The moral of these lessons was usually of a violent and stunning
> character: the hero—a naughty boy—seldom, in the mildest
> catastrophe, being finished off by anything less than a lion or a
> bear.

One would not conclude that Dickens disapproved of the virtues recommended in Georgian children's literature. But the horrendous tales of the nursemaid, Mary Weller, the mirthless lessons of the lady who kept the Dame school over a dyer's shop, the sermons of the Rev. William Gill at the Providence Baptist Chapel, his own readings of Watts and "Mother Bunch" as well as the "porings and blunderings over heavier themes" (referred to in David Copperfield) must have brought him to the conclusion that there were better texts from which morals for the young might be deduced. Ignoring the common prejudice against letting children read stories that were not true, he recommended the fairy tale as a source of instruction:

> Forbearance, courtesy, consideration for the poor and aged, kind
> treatment of animals, the love of nature, abhorence of tyranny and
> brute force—many such good things have been nourished in the
> child's heart by this powerful aid.

("Frauds on the Fairies" in Household Words, Oct. 1, 1853)

In Hard Times it is Sissy Jupe, brought up on stories of "the Fairies, sir, and the Dwarf, and the Hunchback, and the Genies," who embodies the virtues of compassion and imagination. The Coketown babies, on the other hand, with their "leaden little books . . . showing how the good grown-up baby invariably got to the Savings-bank, and the bad grown-up baby invariably got transported," are never permitted to wonder. Stuffed with the facts of the numerous ologies that make up the Gradgrind system of education, Louisa is not "impulsive," not "romantic," but "accustomed to view everything from the strong dispassionate ground of reason and calculation." Having made a "rational" marriage, she realizes that her proper education has resulted only in "the drying up of every spring and fountain in her young heart as it gushed out." Thorns and thistles symbolize the sterility of her life.

Equally disastrous has been the effect of the Gradgrind method on Tom who escapes from facts by means of self-indulgence. Drinking, gambling, and theft mark a downward path which ends in the lonely exile and death so characteristic of didactic children's literature. But Bitzer, he who had so factually defined "horse" in the Gradgrindian schoolroom, puts into practice the well-learned lesson that the whole social system is a question of self-interest, and gets to the Savings-bank from which the bad grown-up baby has been transported.

Though recommending the fairy tale as essential to "a childhood of the mind," Dickens would have nothing to do with imposed morality. When his friend,

George Cruikshank, rewrote familiar fairy tales as temperance tracts, (The Fairy Library, 1847-1864), Dickens indignantly depicted the artist as "Whole Hog of unwieldly dimensions" rooting among the roses of the fairy garden.

It is possible to see Great Expectations as an expanded moral tale of the improving kind recommended in A Father's Advice to his Son (London, ca. 1790). I prefer to see it as a rather wry fairy tale of the dümmlingkind pattern, in which the unpromising hero, unsatisfactorily equipped in the matter of parents, prospects, and possessions, nevertheless, against all expectations, achieves success and marries the beautiful princess.

---

1 James Janeway (1636?-1674) was a well-known English non-conformist minister whose Token for Children was published in London ca. 1671-2. An early American edition was entitled A Token for Children. Being An Exact Account of the Conversion, Holy and Exemplary Lives, and Joyful Deaths of several young Children. By James Janeway, Minister of the Gospel. To which is added, A Token for the Children of New-England. Or, Some Examples of Children, in whom the Fear of God was remarkably Budding before they died, in several Parts of New England. Preserved and published for the Encouragement of Piety in other children. With New Additions (Boston: Z. Fowle, 1771).

2 Re-issued London: Oxford University Press, 1971, with an introduction and bibliography by J. H. P. Pafford.

3 Leonard de Vries, ed. Little Wide-Awake—an Anthology from Victorian Children's Books and Periodicals in the collection of Anne and Fernand G. Renier (London: Arthur Barker Ltd., 1967), p. 18.

4 Boswell's Life of Johnson (London: Oxford, 1953), p. 487.

5 A number of these are included in Flowers of Delight, ed. Leonard de Vries (Toronto: McClelland and Stewart, 1965).

THE PUPPET IMMORTALS OF CHILDREN'S LITERATURE

Michael Michanczyk

An art form without a muse, puppetry, not unlike the Greek drama, is rooted in the religious tradition and folk literature of western and eastern cultures. From the medieval miracle plays to the English Punch and Judy show, to the other side of the globe and the epic tales of the Mahabharata and the Ramayana, puppet characters have portrayed man's anthropomorphic struggle with the restive questions of death, resurrection, and immortality. In this respect puppetry is like the great body of folk literature that we customarily classify as children's literature. But puppetry has the distinction of vividly enacting those curiously significant stories.

Puppetry in children's literature is of two types: (1) literature written about, or containing a puppet character or characters; and (2) literature written, or in the oral tradition, performed by puppets. In the former category there is only one classic of its kind, namely Pinocchio, while in the later category there are numerous examples. I shall restrict myself to a brief discussion of the significance of the puppet portrayal in the first, and in the second to a discussion of the religious overtones and philosophical implications of puppetry and children's literature.

While today in America puppetry is relegated to the category of mere children's entertainment, the puppet dramas of the past were an instructive and entertaining form of art, with religious and philosophical ideas conveyed through the symbolic stylizations of hand, rod, shadow, and string puppets. In fact, in at least India, Java, and Japan, these dramas antedated the theater of actors and actually determined the style of production in the later human theater. For example, the Japanese puppet theater, "ningyo shibai" (doll theater), or "ayatsuri shibai" (manipulation theater), today referred to as Bunraku, after the nineteenth-century puppeteer Bunrakuen, were responsible for the growth of the Kabuki "song-dance-skill" theater of people. [1] Human actors learned and improved their art from the puppet actors they imitated. Why the puppet theater preceded the human theater will be discussed later with respect to the shadow puppet dramas.

The puppeteer, too, like the plays and puppets, has been associated with the religious drama—with the early Greek priests and their automatic mechanisms to inspire wonder, no less than with the dalangs of Java, who are initiated into their vocation by a priest "who writes the mystic syllable 'Ongg' on the dalang's tongue with the stem of a flower dipped in honey." [2] Whether they are accorded as illustrious a birth as the first puppeteer of India, Adi Nat, who sprang from the lips of Brahma the Creator, or whether theirs is a more humble beginning among a troupe of itinerant Italian performers of the Commedia dell' arte, puppeteers have entertained in the sacred tradition of their art, inspiring laughter, tears, and awe. Theirs was, and still is, not just a miniature theater for children. The motto printed on the proscenium of the nineteenth-century toy theater of Benjamin West then read <u>Quibus minus facimus multum</u> ("We make much out of less"). [3]

The industrial revolution produced a diminished interest in the puppet, and substituted for it the automated figure, or robot, and subsequently the refined figures of the Disney audio-animatronics. What was once a popular theater of the people has, generally speaking, been trounced by technology and forced to stare into the corner as an immature form of "children's theater," usually with insipid scripts, shoddy or unimaginative staging, and less than expert manipulation. However, where there is still a tradition of the art, puppetry remains and grows despite condescension; that is reason enough for speculation and experimentation, and for puppetry to define its own artistic veracities, names, "abstraction, motion, and synthesis." [4]

Carl Jung's description of the term <u>individuation</u> might well serve to explain the vicissitudes and vacillations of character and attitude that lead to the transformation of the puppet Pinocchio into a boy after his initiation from dream into the reality of life. "Individuation means becoming a single, homogeneous being, and, in so far as individuality embraces our innermost, last, and incomparable uniqueness, it also implies being one's own self. We could therefore translate individuation as 'coming to selfhood' or 'self-realization'." [5]

Pinocchio's willfulness leads the puppet through many misadventures; tricked, cheated, exploited, and burlesqued, he is climactically devoured by the mammoth Dogfish. This same monster has ingested the vessel upon which the puppet's "little papa" has been searching for his prodigal creation. Gepetto and Pinocchio, reunited in the belly of the Dogfish, are contritely reconciled, and the puppet's cleverness is finally put to good use in the first act of manly heroism of his wayward career; the puppet plots their escape through the mouth of the sleeping gargantuan. The Dogfish snores as the escape marks the puppet's first step initiation into adulthood, and soon thereafter the puppet becomes a boy.

In his article about the marionette, "Das Übermarinetten," (obviously, Pinocchio is a string puppet), the set designer Gordon Craig advocates the puppet as the subliminal superior to the human actor. He credits this natural superiority to the fact that the puppets are "egoless," and because they impersonate no one; they are what they were created to be, and no more. As a puppet then, Pinocchio is the dupe of the strings of determinism. It is only after his initiation into manhood that he transcends his manipulation, and realizes the divine providence that has pulled the strings of self-realization. To quote again from Jung:

> But again and again I note that the individuation process is confused
> with coming of the ego into consciousness and that the ego is in con-
> sequence identified with the self, which naturally produces a hopeless
> conceptual muddle. Individuation is then nothing but egocentricness
> and autoeroticism. But the self comprises infinitely more than a mere

ego. It is as much one's self, and all other selves, as the ego. Individuation does not shut one out from the world, but gathers the world to oneself. [6]

A parallel to the swallowing of the puppet by the Dogfish is the Old Testament story of Jonah and the Whale, always a popular show for puppeteers. Jonah, through his faith in the omnipotence and omniscience of God, is delivered safely from the bowel of the whale. Both the prophet and the puppet undergo a period of trial, or initiation, and both survive the cosmic trauma of inevitable death, being swallowed whole by the macrocosm, and find rebirth in the discovery of the self or microcosm. For Jonah, the event reaffirmed God's will; the puppet's dream ends in his conversion to boyhood and consequently to humanity.

This puppet classic exemplifies many of man's quintessential emotions about puppets, dolls, and masks, namely that they are filled with "mana," possessed by psychic energy or even a "soul." The puppet probably stimulates this feeling more than the others because movement, the criterion which defines puppetry, particularly inspires the notion of animism. In India, for example, there is a quaint custom among the Rajasthani bhats, or puppeteers, that when a puppet has died (outlived its usefulness) it is sailed down a holy river. Kathputli, or puppets, were regarded as little celestial creatures sent to the earth by the gods for man's amusement. "The longer the figure floats, the more kindly are the gods in judging its actions and experiences on earth." [7]

To give another kind of historical example, Heinrich von Kleist, in his famous essay on the puppet theater, "Über das Marionetten theater," states that "only God and the marionette can be perfect." In what sense he means that these entities of antithetical planes of existence are both the epitome of perfection is not always expressly clear; however, it does indicate the author's notion of the almost subliminal life of the puppet.

Among the myths of puppetry, the creation of the string puppet is sometimes counted among the miracles of St. Francis of Assisi. Another story has it that the name "marionette," applied to the string puppet, derives from the fact that in the Middle Ages the Nativity was performed by puppets, or "little Marys," hence the name "marionette." However obscure the derivation of the term, puppet plays were an integral part of the church service in medieval times, beginning about the tenth century with moving puppets accompanying biblical recitations. These illustrated Bible lessons were an early attempt to educate the common people, adults and children alike, with a visual aid.

The Bible was the source of inspiration to the puppeteers, and they drew as well upon the most dramatic stories of the miracles of the Church of Rome. One production in the Church of St. James at Dieppe in 1443 celebrated the Assumption of the Blessed Virgin Mary. As Bil Baird relates in his history of the puppet theater,

> Four life-size angels beat their wings in time to the music of the organ
> and the voices of the choir. Two smaller ones sounded an Ave Maria

161

on little bells to signal the end of each office, accompanied by two huge angels blowing trumpets. Below and at either side were angels holding large chandeliers ablaze with wax candles to light the scene. When the service was over and priests came to snuff the candles, these angels would quickly dodge from side to side to prevent it, and bring a laugh from the congregation. [8]

Such a lively burlesque, during such a solemn feast day of the Church, while not inconsistent with the talents of the puppet, did not sit square with the priests and Pope, and eventually led to the puppet's expulsion from the churches. What had begun as an educational tool for manifesting the literature proved too delightful, distracting, ribald, risqué, and sacrilegious an entertainment.

Today in Poland there survives the remnant of these Miracle plays, the Polish szopka, or manger. At Christmas time, these cathedral-like theaters are set up in front of the churches. First made by the brickmakers' guild, they are still made by peasant brickmakers during the winter as a pastime while unemployed. Tiny figures are moved on the several levels of the theater (three levels might denote heaven, earth, and hell) through slots in the stage. Thus the religious connection between the puppet and the Church has survived to form a lasting impression, dramatizing with childlike simplicity the narratives of the Bible.

In the high Middle Ages, the friars took the puppets to the town square. Their scripts were likely improvised, perhaps loosely based on familiar stories, but more often than not with added local appeal and topical allusions. One such puppet play, modified and passed down from generation to generation among the folk was the familiar English Punch and Judy show.

In 1828 Payne Collier, dramatist and puppet enthusiast, along with George Cruikshank, the artist-illustrator, witnessed a Punch show performed at the King's Arm Tavern by the Italian showman, Giovanni Piccini, recognized as the best puppeteer of his kind. Collier copied the script as performed, and Cruikshank supplied the illustrations. Their book was published that same year.

Punch has numerous cousins throughout Europe and Asia—Karaghioz in Turkey, Karaguez in Greece, Punchinello in Italy, Polichinelle in France, Hanswurst to Kasperle in Germany, Kasparek in Czechoslovakia, Vitez Laszlo in Hungary, and Petrouchka in Russia. But it is the English Punch that has become the archetype of all antiheroes, delighting children and adults with his antics. It is Punch's final outrage that is of particular interest to our discussion. The events leading to this culminating act are the successive murders of his neighbor Scaramouche, his wife Judy, the baby, the constable and officer, the hangman Jack Ketch, and finally the duel with and defeat of the arch fiend.

Punch defiantly takes the name of the devil in vain, taunting,

> They're out! They're out! I've done the trick.
> Jack Ketch is dead—I'm free;
> I do not care, now, if old Nick
> Himself should come for me. [9]

Sure enough the devil pops up his horns at the mention of his name and after a few preliminary bouts of fisticuffs, Punch screams out in his squeaky voice,

> Oh, my head! What is that for?
> Pray, Mr. Devil let us be friends.

The Devil hits him again and Punch begins to grow angry.

> Why you must be one very stupid Devil not to know your best friend
> when you see him. Well, if you won't, we must try which is the
> best man, Punch, or the Devil. [10]

A life and death struggle ensues; Punch and the Devil score wins over each other with successive blows on the opponent's head. Punch deals the coup de grâce. Hoisting the devil upon his "physic stick," he exclaims,

> Hurrah! Hurrah! The Devil's dead. [11]

More eloquent times have echoed this cock's crow of the cuckolded common man against the motions of the devil, symbol of all evil in the world, author of death. As John Donne, addressing Death, had said before Punch, but might have said with more bathos if he were Punch confronted by a mere puppet-devil, [12]

> Why swell'st thou then?
> One short sleep past, we wake eternally
> And Death shall be no more; Death thou shalt die!

Although Donne's poem is certainly an affirmation of the faith of man and the power of the Deity, Punch's story, too, is an affirmation of earthly stubborness in the face of the unconquerable. The declaration is the same, the immortality of man, and by inference, the spirit of the puppet. What started as a marionette show turned into the fierce battle between hand puppets wielding clubs, violently fighting, amusing the crowds that gathered in front of the castelet. Brutal as the show they watched is the earnest struggle of life against death that the Punch show personifies.

Shadow puppetry was popular in the eastern countries of China, India, Java and Siam, and later in Egypt, Turkey, and Greece. But it is in India and Java that the great religious epics of the Ramayana and the Mahabharata are still performed much in the same way they were hundreds of years ago.

The effect of seeing gods which one can never truly see except in the mind's eye because of their spiritual effluvium is conjured up upon the lighted screen of the dalang. Rama, the god-man and his espoused wife Sinta, the mythic ancestors of the Javanese, moral exemplars of male and female archetypes, appear in silhouette. Princess Sinta remains pure when threatened by the ravaging Rawana; the flames of immolation refuse to touch this sacred woman. And Rama, the hero of the race of the gods, rescues his queen and honors his father's promise to his stepmother. Such are the puppets of the shadow world.

It is significant that Plato alludes to shadow puppets in his image of the "cave" in Book VII of the Republic, because it demonstrates that puppets existed and were well enough known to inspire such a metaphor. Yet the implied attitude toward the shadow world is very different:

> Imagine mankind as dwelling in an underground cave with a long entrance open to the light across the whole width of the cave; in this they have been from childhood, with necks and legs fettered, so they have to stay where they are. They cannot move their heads round because of the fetters, and they can only look forward, but light comes to them from fire burning behind them higher up at a distance. Between the fire and prisoners is a road above their level, and along it imagine a low wall has been built, as puppet showmen have screens in front of their people over which they work their puppets. [13]

Imagine the reality of a shadow world upon a mind unable to identify the true forms casting shadows in passing. A parable of ignorance needing enlightenment, the shadow puppet world is an illusion created in the viewer's mind. The myth of the Chinese emperor (shadow puppets in China go back to the seventh and ninth centuries A.D.) offers a revealing contrast. Unable to bear the grief of his wife's death, he offers a reward to anyone able to produce her likeness once again. Moving silhouettes stir his memory of things past and return his wife to him once more.

The Javanese shadow puppets, the wayang kulit, as far back as the eleventh century A.D., inspired a reflection akin to Plato's. The Meditation of Ardjuna— Ardjuna Wiwaka, composed by the court poet of King Airlangga (1035-1049) says: "There are people who weep, are sad and aroused watching the puppets, though they know they are merely carved pieces of leather manipulated and made to speak. These people are like men who, thirsting for sensuous pleasures, live in a world of illusion; they do not realize the magic hallucinations they see are not real." [14]

A combination of puppet theater, folk literature, and religion produced the puppet immortals of children's literature. It is interesting to note, in conclusion, that when Michel Fokine staged Igor Stravinsky's "Petrouchka," the body of the murdered puppet lies upon the stage. The showman tugs at the poor dead puppet when suddenly the ghost of Petrouchka appears over the tent shaking his fist, frightening the showman offstage, and reminding the audience of his immortality.

---

1 Faubion Baowes, Japanese Theatre (New York: Hill and Wang, 1959), pp. 31-35.

2 Bil Baird, The Art of the Puppet (New York: Macmillan, 1965), p. 56.

3 George Speaight, The History of the English Toy Theater (London: Studio Vista, 1969), p. 174. First published as Juvenile Drama (1946).

4 Basil Milovsoroff, "Toward a Better Puppet Theatre," The Puppetry Journal, 3 (January-February, 1971), 7.

5 Karl Jung, "Two Essays on Analytical Psychology," in <u>Collected Works</u>, ed. R. F. C. Hull (Princeton: Princeton University Press, 1926), VII, 171.

6 Karl Jung, "The Structure and Dynamics of the Psyche," <u>Works</u>, VIII, 226.

7 Baird, p. 47.

8 Baird, p. 64.

9 Diana John, <u>St. George and the Dragon, Punch and Judy</u>, (Baltimore: Penguin, 1966), p. 83.

10 John, p. 85.

11 John, p. 86.

12 Speaight, pp. 8-10.

13 Rex Warner, <u>The Greek Philosophers</u> (New York: New American Library, 1966), p. 78.

14 James R. Brandon, <u>On Thrones of Gold: Three Javanese Shadow Plays</u>, (Cambridge, Mass.: Harvard University Press, 1970), p. 3.

IDEOLOGIES IN CHILDREN'S LITERATURE:
SOME PRELIMINARY NOTES

Ruth B. Moynihan

Stories told or written for children are often indicators of the dominant values within a society. Various times and cultures reveal various attitudes, not only towards children but also toward life and society. As a Swedish specialist in children's literature recently said,

> Every age has felt the need to provide new instructions in its children's books on how life is to be lived. Thus children's books do not merely reflect the contemporary social scene and the problems of adult life; the simplified manner in which they treat their subjects also makes them something of magnifying glasses. [1]

The number of such magnifying glasses in our modern world is greater than ever before in history. An adequate discussion even of a particular era in one society could well be a major study. The purpose of this brief essay is merely to point out a few examples and to indicate some possibilities for further investigation.

The Wonderful Wizard of Oz, published in 1900 by Lyman Frank Baum, is one of the best known of American children's stories, but few have given much thought to the way in which its characters and plot reflect the political and social situation of the time. However, an article by Henry M. Littlefield recently described in detail the way the book serves as a populist parable. The Scarecrow, for example, represents Midwestern farmers, while the Tin Man represents the honest laborers bewitched by Eastern industrialists (personified in the Wicked Witch of the East). The Cowardly Lion is a parody of William Jennings Bryan. The Wizard, says Littlefield, "might be any President from Grant to McKinley. He come straight from the fair grounds in Omaha, Nebraska, and he symbolizes the American criterion for leadership—he is able to be everything to everybody." [2] But Dorothy's innocence and her loving kindness, along with the brains, heart, and courage of her friends (which were within them all along though they didn't know it), are sufficient to unmask even the formidable Wizard and to achieve Dorothy's goals—the freedom of her friends and her own return to reality among her hard-working relatives in Kansas.

If we compare The Wizard of Oz to the English classic for children, Winnie the Pooh, the contrast is startling. A. A. Milne's story takes place in a sheltered circumscribed world, the easy-going world of the English upper classes, where one lone child might live on a huge green estate with a dozen stuffed animals for playmates, and in a fantasy world where he himself was in complete control. Baum's book, on the other hand, reveals a world full of conflict and danger where the heroine lives in a harsh grey world with only a little dog for a playmate (but a live dog, not a stuffed one) and can only escape into fantasy by being hit on the head in a tornado. Furthermore, even the fantasy world is full of dangers and harrowing experiences. Dorothy and her friends must deal with events as they occur, while Milne's characters generally frame or manipulate events according to their own expectations.

Winnie the Pooh, published in England in 1926, has been tremendously popular in America as well, though perhaps not as influential as The Wizard of Oz. It is better known to the intelligentsia, probably, while Oz is better known to the "common man." Pooh reflects a disillusionment with the pre-World War I world and its leadership. It is a sustained low-key spoof on official bureaucracies, the adult world in general, and the adventure and travel tales of nineteenth century imperial Britain. Where many earlier fairy tales were full of seriousness and took pretentiousness for granted as necessary and good, A. A. Milne's tales are all humor—especially in regard to pretensions. The ideology is that of a bumbling imperfect world, though a generally kind-hearted and not at all dangerous one.

Let us look at one chapter as an illustration. Chapter VIII, called "In Which Christopher Robin Leads an Expotition to the North Pole," reveals even through its title its deliberate parody of such earlier literature as Robinson Crusoe or the works of Robert Louis Stevenson.

This particular story concerns an expedition to the North Pole which Christopher Robin is planning. When asked by Pooh Bear what it is, Christopher says, "It's just a thing you discover," since he isn't quite sure himself, and then goes on to explain that all his friends can come because "that's what an Expedition means. A long line of everybody." Pooh goes off to gather the friends and they set off. After passing a "dangerous" part of the river where Christopher claims there might be an "ambush," they settle down in the first grassy area to eat their provisions—the best part of the "expotition" to most of the participants. After Christopher takes Rabbit aside to check with him about just what the North Pole might look like, the crisis event occurs. Baby Roo falls in the water while washing his face. He thinks he's swimming, while everyone else tries desperately to rescue him. Finally Pooh rescues Roo with a long pole and is informed by Christopher Robin that he has also discovered the North Pole. They put a sign on the Pole to that effect and go home. Pooh, "feeling very proud of what he had done, had a little something to revive himself."

Within the story, each character carries a message, too. Eeyore, the donkey, is the complaining old, self-centered, hypocritical relative with whom society must be patient and forgiving. He doesn't ask things, he just tells people. He comes along only "to oblige" and everything is "all the same" to him, though when things start moving he says, "Don't Blame Me." He's a perennial wet blanket, full of self-pity, an eater of thistles who assumes that Pooh sits on them on purpose to keep them away from him. He preaches consideration, which he does not practice, and he "don't hold with all this washing" of Roo—"This modern Behind-the-ears nonsense." Finally, he's totally useless despite his painful efforts when it comes to rescuing Roo. The message is that the older generation is generally irrelevant, but well-meaning, and one must be nice to its members.

Owl is the intellectual who always knows about things, like the meaning of "ambush," and who tells "Interesting Anecdotes full of long words like Encyclopedia and Rhododendron" while his listeners fall asleep with boredom. In the emergency he explained that "in a case of Sudden and Temporary Immersion the Important Thing was to keep the Head Above Water," while the others hurried to the rescue. His knowledge is always either obvious or useless or both, but he is respected just for thinking and for his slightly mysterious potential usefulness.

Kanga is a spoof on motherhood. While she "explained to everybody proudly that this was the first time [Roo] had ever washed his face himself," he fell in the water and had a glorious time while she worried. The only female in the story, she represents a complacently sexist viewpoint—all women are mother figures and mothers are rather a nuisance most of the time. Piglet is a lovable coward in a world where there is nothing to be afraid of, while Rabbit has an unseemly number of relatives—message: fecundity is not really proper. Pooh is, of course, a "Bear of little brain"—the good and average person, and happily so. Presumably, the reader identifies with Christopher Robin, the paternalistic natural leader and protector simply by virtue of his superior birth, even though he is not much smarter or more capable.

It seems clear that this North Pole Expotition is intended to parody the great exploratory polar expeditions of the previous fifty years, especially those of Admiral Robert E. Peary. Peary had planned and provisioned several expeditions during the 1890's and even took his wife and new-born baby along. The Peary Arctic Club consisted of a few of his friends helping him towards his goal. Finally, on his sixth attempt in 1909, with much publicity, Peary succeeded in planting the American flag at the desolate site of the Pole. Milne's plot is debunking the imperial myth while preaching an easy-going, live-and-let-live myth. The leader doesn't know where he's going or what he's looking for, his friends and followers are mainly concerned with eating and enjoying themselves, the minor crisis as well as the major quest is resolved purely by accident by a bumbling good-natured hero, and everything is happy and okay because they all really love one another. The message is that goals don't matter so long as everyone enjoys himself and is kind to one another along the way. And in a way, the whole book suggests that reality itself, whatever that may be, doesn't matter much either if everyone is happy.

American books on the other hand, are usually firmly rooted in some aspect of reality and in the pursuit of specific goals. For example, The Little Engine That Could by Watty Piper, published in 1930 (and regularly reprinted ever since), clearly reflects the official optimism with which most of the nation entered the depression. Even though the "happy little engine," carrying all sorts of toys and good food to the children on the other side of the mountain, had broken down, apparently irreparably, and even though the shiny new Passenger Engine and the big strong Freight Engine and the Rusty Old Engine refused to help, the Little Blue Engine which had never been over the mountain at all was willing to try. And, of course, it succeeded. As Hoover told the nation at that time, it was the willingness of all the little people to make temporary sacrifices and work a little harder which would soon solve the problems of the depression. And Roosevelt too, after 1933, as most historians agree, set all the little engines to work without really changing the system for wealth and industry.

The American myth of innocence, goodness and determination which was so much a part of The Wizard of Oz is revealed again in this simple book. Furthermore, it implies that there is no need to be more than temporarily sad at the refusals of big business or wealth or the older generation (whose interest in toys and good food for children could not really be expected anyway), since there is bound to be a "little Blue Engine" who is equally capable and glad to help. The world of great passenger and freight engines is not really our concern. If we just keep hoping and trying, everything will be all right. There is nothing wrong with the system, only with small parts within it. "I think I can, I think I can" became the motto of a whole generation of depression parents and their children, while society's general structure remained unchanged.

A similar message shines out of The Little House by Virginia Lee Burton, winner of the Caldecott Award in 1942. An extremely simple, but endearing, story of the life history of a little house overwhelmed by urbanization and industrialization, the story is clearly a parable about the development of American society. This little house which had weathered the seasons for an untold number of years sees the beginning of the destruction of its country idyll with the coming of the first horseless carriage "down the winding country road." Inexorably, the car is followed by steam shovels, highways, houses, tenements, trolleys, subways, skyscrapers, and abandonment. "No one wanted to live in her and take care of her any more," but she remained because she was so well-built. Furthermore, her wise original builder had said, "This Little House shall never be sold for gold or silver and she will live to see our great-great-grandchildren's great-great-grandchildren living in her."

It is this stipulation which suggests that the house represents something more than just rural life. The house stands for a whole civilization and perhaps also for the American Constitution—the system of government which many conservatives felt was threatened by the New Deal as well as by increasing industrialization. The story preaches a nostalgia for the past and the rural innocence of snow and stars and apple trees and daisies. And when "the great-great-granddaughter of the man who built the Little House so well" recognized "the shabby Little House" in the midst of the hurly-burly city, there was an obvious solution —move it to the country. "Never again would she be curious about the city . . . A new moon was coming up . . . It was Spring . . . and all was quiet and peaceful in the country."

The flight to suburbia as a return to innocence and beauty is the message of
The Little House. The world of the past was better, while the city and all of
modern industrialization is evil and dirty. Nor is there any possible compromise
or evolution, only escape. Even the class element is quite blatant, for it is
only the well-to-do who can stop all the traffic to move a house out of the city.
In this case it is also an "old" family, a fifth-generation family in 1942, which
is thus representative of only a very small proportion of the population. (Interestingly enough, at approximately thirty years per generation, this also makes
the house the same age as the Constitution.)

Horton Hears a Who! by Dr. Seuss, published in 1956, is a fantasy in form,
but its ideology is very goal-oriented and socially concerned. While Winnie the
Pooh centered on the on-going happiness of a group of mutually respectful but
self-contained individuals, and The Little House on a nostalgic recreation of a
lost rural past, Horton is, above all, concerned with the individual's crucial
role as a member of society. And it is a society full of conflicts and antagonism,
with constant crises and dangers, and social pressures of every sort.

The plot of Horton is very simple. A benevolent elephant hears a voice from
a small speck of dust and immediately feels obligated to help and protect it "Because, after all, / A person's a person, no matter how small." This refrain is
repeated again and again as the elephant faces one crisis after another. First
some kangaroos mock him, then some monkeys steal the clover with the speck of
dust on it. They give it to Vlad Vlad-i-koff the "black-bottomed eagle" who ob-
ligingly flies off with it and drops it in a 100-mile wide field of clover. Horton
toils after it "with groans, over stones/ That tattered his toenails and battered
his bones" and then picks three million clovers before he discovers his speck of
dust. The people on the speck are in real trouble (like the dolls and toys on the
little train) because they had "landed so hard that our clocks have all stopped. /
Our tea-pots are broken. Our rocking-chairs smashed. / And our bicycle tires
all blew up when we crashed." Horton promises once again to "stick by you
small folks through thin and through thick!" But the kangeroos have decided to
rope and cage the elephant for "chatting with persons who've never existed" and
for "Such carryings-on in our peaceable jungle!" Furthermore, they are going
to boil the dust speck in Beezle-Nut oil. (How mild was the disdain of the big
Engines for the toys in comparison!)

The action now shifts to the people of Who-ville on the speck, since Horton
can no longer protect them. Their only hope, and his, lies in shouting enough to
make even the kangaroos hear. As Horton puts it, "you very small persons will
not have to die / If you make yourselves heard! So come on, now, and TRY!"
They do try—desperately—but without success, until the Mayor "discovered one
shirker," a very small one who "Was standing, just standing, and bouncing a
Yo-Yo!" He lectured the lad that this was the "town's darkest hour! The time
for all Whos who have blood that is red / To come to the aid of their country!"
Finally, "that one small, extra Yopp put it over" and the Whos "proved they ARE
persons, no matter how small. / And their whole world was saved by the Smallest
of ALL!"

The ideological message of this story is so blatant that one is tempted to interpret it almost too specifically. For example, it seems to reflect the Cold War mentality of the Fifties—especially in the name of its arch-villain, the Eagle. It also teaches the general virtue of responsible paternalism—the big should take care of the little, the comfortable should protect the oppressed, no matter how great the cost. And then it further preaches that an individual's value is determined not by his own pleasure (playing with Yo-Yo's), but only by his contribution to the whole, his active participation in achieving the goals of his society.

Horton is not a "middle-of-the-road" story. The preservers of the status quo are the kangaroos, and they are clearly evil. They also represent the pressures for social conformity and against "hearing voices." The ideal which Horton represents is that of the sensitive, spiritual, artistic, dedicated lone defender of humanity with all the world against him. There is a similarity to the Little Engine of 1930, but Horton is far less humble and the stakes are much higher. This is a life-and-death struggle, not just a matter of toys and good food. Horton's non-conformism is shown as right because it is in a good cause benefiting others—just playing and minding one's own business like the Who with the Yo-Yo is clearly immoral. (Winnie the Pooh characters would certainly be frowned upon in the Horton value system.)

One may suggest that Horton represents the messianic idealism which has been for so long a part of American tradition—with periodic eruptions on both the right and the left in internal affairs, and, in the twentieth century especially, on the international scene as well. Nixon, Johnson, and Kennedy could claim to be identified with Dr. Seuss's dedicated elephant just as well as Ellsberg, Dr. Spock, and Daniel Berrigan. Radical fighters for social justice come right out of the mainstream of American ideology, and violent confrontations are an accepted part of our world view.

In another way, Horton reveals the two main themes of a mass democratic society—the paradoxical importance of individual resistance to mass pressure for evil but cooperation with mass pressure for good. In such a society neither the large "elephant" nor the small "Who" is safe without the help of the other— and both are always in danger.

From the debunking of the Wizard in Oz and of the Empire in Pooh, America moved to an idealization of hopeful struggle in the face of difficulties in The Little Engine and of older rural values in the face of modernization in The Little House. And then in the Fifties we became newly aware of the irreconcilable conflicts of our mass modern society and also of the impossibility of escape. A study of our children's literature in its historical context might have forecast both a Viet Nam type encounter and the youthful upheaval of the Sixties. Both adults and students were acting out the values they had absorbed at an early age. And those values were taught by their own parents and in their own books. An analysis of the most popular children's literature indeed provides a magnifying glass for its society.

NOTES

1   Mary Orvig, "One World in Children's Books?" The May Hill Arbuthnot Honor Lecture, Top of the News, June, 1972, p. 40.

2   "The Wizard of Oz: Parable on Populism," American Quarterly, 16, (1964), 54.

"Maximilian Pfeiferling" (see page 182)

Sketch of a scene from a REICHSKABARETT play.

CHILDREN'S THEATER IN EAST AND WEST GERMANY:
THEORIES, PRACTICE, AND PROGRAMS

Jack Zipes

Germany has never been known as a children's paradise. In fact, if one wanted to be crass, one could argue that even dogs have received better treatment
than children in Germany. For years childhood has had a status similar to that
of the immigrant who is forced to suffer through a series of tests to prove his
"worthiness" as a good, loyal, obedient citizen before being recognized by the
state. Children have been drilled, groomed, manipulated, and processed to
serve the family and state so that they won't question these institutions and will
comply with ruling class strictures. Compulsion has been the main educational
experience. Children have been expected to take arbitrary authority seriously.
But they in turn have not been taken seriously, nor has children's play. The result of the authoritarian upbringing which has been common throughout Germany
is, as Wilhelm Reich has pointed out, "the individual who is forever afraid of life
and of authority and thus creates again and again the possibility that masses of
people can be governed by a handful of powerful individuals." [1]

Recently, German authoritarian attitudes toward children and children's education have undergone some changes. Here "recently" has two different meanings. In East Germany it is the period after 1945 when communist educators re-
vamped the traditional family structure and educational system to bring about
more equality for workers, women, and children. In West Germany it means
after 1968 when students and other progressive groups challenged the patriarchal
family structure and exclusive educational institutions and initiated all kinds of
anti-authoritarian programs which are still being developed. In both instances
positive gains have been made in respect to the general condition of children:
they are now being taken more seriously by groups of adults who are fighting for
the rights of children to determine their future and realize their full creative and
critical potential. Admittedly, the struggle for children's rights is being waged
by relatively small groups of progressive-minded adults, but these people have
carried the struggle into all spheres of social life—families, schools, youth centers, governmental agencies, and theaters. In particular, the recent development in children's theater is considered by some to be most significant, and they
argue, as did Walter Benjamin in his now famous essay Programm eines proletarischen Kindertheaters, that children's theater is the only place where children
can fulfill their childhood.

Of course, Benjamin wrote about a specific children's theater, a proletarian
theater for and by children which had been organized by the Latvian actress Asja
Lacis immediately after the Russian Revolution. This proletarian children's
theater is not the goal of most children's theaters in East and West Germany.

The majority of them insist upon having adults as directors and performers who set the policy and tone. These people profess a sincere concern for the welfare of children and seek to stimulate their minds and imaginations. In both East and West Germany they have aimed at making children's theater more popular, and indeed, its popularity has risen remarkably since 1945. However, West German leftists, who are adherents of Benjamin's program and are organizing radical theaters for and by children, are suspicious about the seriousness of those adults who have popularized children's theater, especially when they can prove that it has remained unpopular. According to these radical groups, a genuine, popular children's theater which responds to the real needs of the majority of children in both Germanies has yet to assume its proper form.

The German leftists may well have asked the right questions again. Why is it that great effort has been exerted to make children's theaters commercially and politically popular? Why are children, who have generally been excluded, now included as important cultural components in the domain of theater? These questions form the framework of my analysis of contemporary children's theater in East and West Germany. Underlying the framework are four premises which must be explained briefly if the total approach is to be understood.

First, I shall purposely deal with children's theater both in East and West Germany to counter the current one-sided approach to contemporary German literature in American Germanistik, which concerns itself almost exclusively with West German literature. This concern is indicative of the narrow-mindedness of scholars who tend to dismiss East German literature as vulgar, i.e. popular or trivial, and hence, not worth discussing. Contemporary German literature means literature in East and West Germany, and the only studies of it which can be fruitful are those that address themselves to (or at least take into account) the antagonisms, influences, and cross-currents between East and West Germany.

Second, negative and condescending attitudes toward children and children's art must be recognized for what they are—destructive for children and detrimental to adults. A serious concern in children's affairs keeps us in constant contact with our total experience as human beings. We are too often inclined not to take children's cultural activities seriously—as if children were an inferior species of the human race. However, a real respect for children's needs, ideas, and games can lead to a respect for differences among human beings as well as a respect for our spontaneous and creative energies which we tend to repress out of fear.

Third, it is absurd to consider children's theater inferior art. Children's theater demands as much if not more ingenuity and skill than adult theater. The shorter attention span of children and their greater imagination calls for more concentrated and lively plays and productions. It is also questionable whether adults should define children's theater. At present, its standards and requirements are in a state of transition, but like other popular genres, it is not an inferior art. It is different. It is only inferior insofar as it fails to interest and stimulate its audience, to raise consciousness, to shed new light on particular human situations and indicate ways in which man can become master of his destiny.

Four, the history of children's theater is inextricably linked to the total history of theater, and the total history of theater cannot be written without taking children's theater into account. This has recently been made explicit in two books: Kindertheater: Geschichte, Modelle, Projekte by Melchior Schedler,[2] and Theater in der Zeitenwende by an East German author collective.[3] This also holds true for general histories of literature which must sooner or later include comic books, science fiction, children's books, detective novels, and other popular forms if they want to be complete.

Since my analysis will focus on the history of the seriousness and popularity of children's theater in East and West Germany since 1945, it will be necessary to present some background material about the beginnings of children's theater before turning to the present scene. Ironically the origins of contemporary children's theater are to be found in the Soviet Union when Asja Lacis and Natalia Saz began their experiments in 1918. In particular, Saz's work eventually led to state-supported theaters which now serve as models for children's theaters throughout the world. In Germany during the 1920's attempts were made to develop a children's theater, and there were some agitprop groups like Die Roten Jungpioniere and Die Roten Trommler which were effective;[4] but because such groups lacked state subsidies, and because of the depression and the rise of fascism, the independent proletarian children's theater proposed by Lacis and Benjamin in 1928 could never get off the ground,[5] nor could other experiments be realized. What remained was the Christmas fairy tale play which was performed by state and private theaters mainly during the holiday season. This tradition had its beginnings in 1854 when, according to Schedler, two enterprising theater men, C. A. Görner and Baron von Klesheim, made the discovery that "theater at Christmas has to be presented in such a way that it attracts the entire family and at the same time gives them a sense of having experienced a unity of irrationality in keeping with the bourgeois Christmas ritual."[6] During the twentieth century, this tradition took on an added culinary aspect and was coordinated with the conservative policies of educators and the extravagant policies of the consumer industry. In all cases, the irrational and escapist features of children's theater were reinforced, and these features were maintained during the fascist period. In addition, Hitler youth festivals and propaganda plays were created for children with the intention of mystifying and exploiting them in order to make them into good Nazis.[7]

East Germany

It is against the Christmas fairy-tale tradition and the fascist educational programs that East Germany (using the Soviet Union as its model) began founding state-supported children's theaters and developing innovative programs which, according to Ilse Rodenberg, were geared toward bringing out the children's best qualities and making them into independent thinkers.[8] After a law was passed in

1945 which fostered the founding of children's theaters, East Germany manifested a tremendous concern in children by systematically organizing theaters in Leipzig (1946), Dresden (1949), Berlin (1950), Halle (1952), Erfurth (1953), Brandenburg (1967), Magdeburg (1969), and in several other smaller cities. With the gradual development of these theaters, whose work was always coordinated with the policies of the state theaters, general programs and guidelines were developed at conferences, and a special commission for children's theater was established. [9]

Children's plays in East Germany are performed by young adult actors who receive expert training in this field. The actors and directors work closely with educators and psychologists who are attached to the theater. There are constant discussions and programs instituted to assess and improve the methods of acting and the contents of the plays. Here schoolteachers and their pupils play an important role since they regularly attend these theaters and are solicited for advice and tested for reactions. As a result, East German children's theaters have found it best to divide their audiences into three groups according to stages of consciousness: (1) five- to eight-year-olds are offered plays based on fairy tales; (2) nine- to thirteen-year-olds are offered plays based on fairy tales, adventure stories, history, and contemporary events; (3) fourteen- to eighteen-year-olds are offered classical plays and also attend the regular theater. The plays themselves are written by actors, directors, and playwrights who have close contact with children's theater. Often well-known writers are commissioned to write a play. Such stimulation has led to a great repertory of high quality children's drama—including translations of Soviet, Czech, Polish, and Bulgarian plays.

Broadly speaking, there are two types of plays in children's theater for the ages five through thirteen, the two age groups which will be my major concern.[10] These are plays of socialist realism and plays based on fairy tales. Looked at chronologically, the development of the two types reflects changes in both the theater and educational system. As Ilse Rodenberg has remarked: "It is well known that theater for children and young people is educational theater in a special way, but not in the way of a continuation of school lessons. The educational must blend with the artistic and should not be an end in itself." [11] Despite this seemingly undoctrinaire statement, the main tendency in East Germany has been to utilize "art as a weapon," and children's theater (like the regular theater) has been employed to serve the state. This may be all right if the interests of the state further those of the people, in this case, the children. But do they? This is the question to be asked while analyzing the popularity and seriousness of children's plays in East Germany.

Let us begin with prominent examples from the theater of socialist realism: Du bist der Richtige (1950) by Gustav von Wagenheim, Schneeball (1950) by Vera A. Ljubimova, and Tinko (1969) by Hans-Dieter Schmidt. Du bist der Richtige has its setting in Berlin, 1950. Members of the Free German Youth have come to the city from Mecklenburg to help build the Walter-Ulbricht Stadium. Three of them, Waldi, Heinz, and Karl, discover some hoodlums from West Berlin stealing copper wire. Waldi runs off while Heinz and Karl force the hoodlums to flee. Waldi's concern is only for himself, and back in Mecklenburg, his individualistic ways are frowned upon by his comrades. On the other hand, Heinz and Karl give their utmost to help the collective, so that when a delegate is supposed to be sent to Berlin again to participate on a special committee, the members of the Free German Youth choose Heinz over Waldi. However, a functionary gets the names mixed up, and Waldi receives notification that he is the delegate. The others protest. But Heinz writes a letter to the minister asking that Waldi remain as the right one since this might move him to be less individualistic. Naturally, this is what happens: Waldi changes and even helps apprehend one of the hoodlums who was involved in the theft of the copper.

Like other plays of this period, Spiel ins Leben (1950) by Hedda Zinner, Kampf um Hegoland (1951) by Peter Martin Lampel, and Die Moorbande (1953) by Horst Beseler, Wagenheim's popular drama is overly didactic and was used by the government as a sort of agitprop play: it was taken on a tour throughout East Germany and used to commemorate the opening of Theater der Freundschaft in Berlin. The play's main emphasis is on the need for collective work to rebuild Germany. Here too a choice is required: the Free German Youth or a band of hoodlums from West Berlin, collectivism or egotism, socialism or capitalism. As a reflection of the conflicts of that time, the drama does mirror accurately the subversive acts from the West and the difficulties that young boys conditioned by bourgeois ideology had in overcoming their self-concern and transforming it into an objective concern for the socialist state. However, the ideal and idealistic resolution belies the real tendencies of the time. Essentially, the play remains a recruiting piece for the Free German Youth.

One of the dominant features about the early plays of socialist realism for both children and adults was the focus on the enemy outside the state. This led to a neglect of the internal conflicts and an obscuring of the real contradictions in the German Democratic Republic. Der Schneeball, like Tom Sawyers grosses Abenteur (1953) by Stefan Heym and Hanus Burger, is a case in point. The play is about racism in America. A millionaire's daughter enters a liberal school as a new pupil and objects to having two blacks, Betty and Dick, nicknamed Snowball, in the same class. She gets her father to apply pressure on the school to dismiss the blacks. However, the progressive forces at the school join together in a solidarity strike and defeat the reactionary forces. Despite its overly simplistic plot, there are many good things in this play: the attack on racism which would have been understood in Germany at that time as an attack on anti-semitism, the depiction of the connections between racism and the class struggle, and the picture of police used as tools by rich capitalists. However, the setting is America, and though the critique of American capitalism may be justified, the play does not help audiences understand similar problems in East Germany, where peculiar forms of racism, sexism, and exploitation should also be exposed and overcome. In this respect, Schneeball can be used for both positive and negative educational purposes. Recently it was produced throughout East Germany to show support for Angela Davis and to decry the racism in America. A good objective. But, in educating audiences about racism in America, East German plays often suggest that it does not exist in socialist countries, consequently blurring the issues in their own backyard. Where are the plays that deal with prejudice and privilege within East Germany? Why aren't plays produced about anti-semitism in Poland and the Soviet Union?

During the 1950's there was a noticeable lack of plays about contemporary problems, [12] and this became the subject of concern at the Bitterfelder Writers Conference in 1959 where Walter Ulbricht stressed the necessity for all writers to address themselves to the contemporary scene and to acquaint themselves more with the problems of workers. The result was a wave of plays which focused on contemporary affairs. For the most part, they were pseudo-critical or affirmed the goals of the state. Almost all of them taught self-sacrifice and demonstrated how an outsider can learn the value of collective work and find his or her place in socialism. One of the best examples of all the children's plays written in accord with the Bitterfelder policy during the 1960's is Schmidt's Tinko, based on the novel by Erwin Strittmatter.

Tinko begins in the late 1960's with Martin Kraske, president of a farm collective, taking the stage and recalling the past to explain how he became a socialist—a dominant theme in East German plays. We are then taken back in history through a series of flashbacks to the village of Märzbach from the summer of 1947 to 1949. Kraske, nicknamed Tinko, recalls how he was faced with a series of crucial decisions as a young boy. In short, he had to make a choice either for the reactionary past represented by his grandfather, who raised him during the war and continued to hold to traditional individualistic ways, or for the progressive future represented by his father, who returned from the war, remarried, and worked to organize small farmers into a collective. At first, Tinko rejects his father, who is a total stranger in his eyes and appears to want to upset the old harmony of the farm. However, as he sees how his grandfather and another reactionary farmer ruthlessly subvert the aims of the community and also curtail his own freedom, he joins the Young Pioneers and is reconciled with his father. Tinko is the subject and product of the vicious struggles between communist reformers and reactionary farmers, and Schmidt does not write a simple didactic play about how he waltzed through this period on his way to becoming a socialist. Tinko's grandfather is a dynamic, appealing figure, and Tinko's love for him makes it all the more difficult to make a choice. But as he sees how his grandfather defeats himself by clinging to the past and a harmful ideology, he realizes that he must be educated to the new way of doing things. Although the play deals primarily with the 1947-49 period, it is very much a contemporary play: the emphasis on new socialist education lends support to the 1965 and more recent educational reforms; [13] and the entire theme of arrival in socialism reinforces the general policy of the state which sees itself as developing its own peculiar type of socialism and working out non-antagonistic conflicts in this new stage of development.

Perhaps because they are so didactic, socialist realist plays about history, adventure, and contemporary events are not nearly so popular or effective as the fairy-tale plays. Here most German writers have been influenced by the Soviet authors Jevgeny Schwarz and Samuil Marschal. In fact, any discussion of the fairy-tale play in East Germany must include these authors, especially Schwarz, whose plays are produced for adults and children alike. His most significant play is Die verzauberten Brüder (1955), the most popular of all the children's plays in East Germany. The story concerns Vassilissa, a working woman, who goes in search of her two sons, who ran away from home at the age of thirteen to become heroes but were instead transformed into trees by the witch Baba-Yaga. Vassilissa is helped by Mischa the bear, Kotofei the cat, Sharik the dog, and her youngest son Ivanuschka in a battle of wits with Baba-Yaga. After several incidents in which Baba-Yaga shows how treacherous she is, Vassilissa manages to trap her, and in her triumph, she remarks:

> "Never in your life have you built a box, or woven a basket, or
> planted seeds. You've never thought up a fairy tale or sung a song.
> All you've ever done is break, beat, and destroy things. And you
> think you can hold your own with us, you good for nothing?" [14]

As the negative principle of life, Baba-Yaga is a parasite who not only lives off other people's work but leads young people astray and petrifies them. She is opposed by the working woman Vassilissa, who represents unsentimental love and wisdom. She depends on the collective efforts of the animals and Ivanuschka, who bring their skills, imagination, strength, and wit into play. Their mutual respect and recognition of what is evil in life enable them to overcome Baba-Yaga and free the two sons, who as trees witness the struggle and learn from it just as the audience does. What they learn is not only how to recognize and defeat parasitic evil but also not to run away from home. As Vassilissa says: "Whoever runs away from home without a reason won't grow and won't become any smarter. Those people remain thirteen years old." [15] This remark among others explains why the play is so popular and performed so often in East German children's theaters.

All of Schwarz's fairy-tale plays are ingenious socialist interpretations of Russian folktales. Though his plays have feudal settings, he endows the action with contemporary implications and subtly weaves socialist moral and ethical principles into the substance of the story. Schwarz's fairy-tale plays and those by other Soviet and East German dramatists differ from those by western writers in that they play down the motifs of marriage and the acquisition of wealth. They emphasize more the struggle against life-negating forces and take a stand for the emancipation of the oppressed. In contrast to the closed form of the traditional fairy tale which usually depicts a prosperous world intact at the end, the socialist fairy tale is open, [16] that is, the hero is not interested in preserving the status quo but in change, and the play usually ends on some note of change. Also important is the protagonist's recognition of his social obligation—his service to all of mankind, not to a monarch.

Most East German writers of children's plays have been encouraged to follow in Schwarz's footsteps, [17] and some of the most innovative work has been done in the field of fairy-tale plays: Anna Elisabeth Wiede's Das Untier von Samarkand (1956), Heinz Kahlau's Der gestiefelte Kater (1967), and Joachim Knauth's Wie der König zum Mond wollte (1969) are plays which are representative of the serious efforts of the East German children's theater to provide children with lively and educational fairy tales in the socialist tradition.

Das Untier von Samarkand is about the young baker Sinjar, who is transformed into a monster and then becomes so infuriated by the inhuman laws and acts of the Khan of Samarkand that he takes control of the city. At first, the people and the Khan live in dread of him. However, the people learn to love him because he abolishes slavery, lowers taxes, and treats the masses in a humane way while the monstrous Khan thinks of ways to eliminate the good monster. However, he is exposed by a common trader and turned into a frog while the monster is turned back into the baker Sinjar, who will rule in Samarkand with the collective help of the people. Wiede stresses the interdependence of the monster and the people. They learn to love him because of his sense of justice and humanity. He learns that he will not be able to maintain a good government without their support. As he declares in the end: "I also think that the minds of the common people are better suited for ruling than those of the great people. After all, they're more down to earth." [18]

A key concept in Das Untier von Samarkand is change. Sinjar becomes a monster who changes things and is changed back into a human being because of his humane behavior. He and his compatriots will continue to make changes in society. This concept of changing for the better is also emphasized in Kahlau's Der gestiefelte Kater. Written in verse, the play concentrates on changes made by the cat who causes other people to overcome their fear of an oppressive magician and make great changes. For instance, the cat uses his brains to help Stefan, the miller's son, break down class barriers so that Stefan and the princess can love each other freely. In his service to Stefan, the cat also serves the farmers and natural elements by giving them the courage to turn against the parasitical magician who exploits them. Then, with their help and his own ingenuity, he tricks the magician into transforming himself into a mouse. Naturally, the cat gobbles up the mouse, and the rule of the land is restored to the rightful rulers—the people. Man's struggle to change and gain power over his destiny becomes the central theme in a traditional fairy tale which used to focus on how the miller's son used trickery to become an aristocrat and marry a princess.

Das Untier von Samarkand and Der gestiefelte Kater rarely make direct references to the contemporary scene. In some of the more recent fairy-tale plays like Knauth's Wie der König zum Mond wollte, there are clear parallels to be drawn with present-day events and problems. Knauth depicts a king as a spoiled brat who demands to go to the moon. He orders a carpenter to build him a tower that will reach the moon within three days. The carpenter suggests a wooden

bird instead, but the king insists on a tower and threatens the carpenter with
death. In the meantime, the king's uncle intrigues against him and orders a
blacksmith to build a canon that will shoot him to the moon. In the end, both projects fail. The king and his uncle go bankrupt. Without money and hired bullies
to push the people around, they are weak, and the people rebel. As they prepare
for general elections, the carpenter flies above them on his wooden bird heading
for the moon, and his last words to the people are: "Make good use of the works
of your own hands, and of your own brains, too." [19] Knauth's critique of tyran-
nical rule is conveyed through the contemporary songs, games, and acrobatics in
the play. [20] Also the competition to be the first one on the moon is an obvious
reference to the present-day competition in space research. In general,
Knauth's play advances Schwarz's technique of reshaping fairy tales in a socialist manner by giving the symbols a more concrete bearing on the present-day
lives of children.

Most of the fairy-tale plays in East Germany demonstrate the evil of exploitation and the necessity to combat this evil in all its forms. At the same time, the
fairy-tale plays have little to do with real situations in East Germany, nor do
they talk about the real ways in which children are raised. Those plays of socialist realism which profess to be more actual tend to stress the importance of
self-sacrifice and adaptation if not conformity to the socialist code of ethics and
work. Certainly very few plays deal with children assuming command over their
destiny. In fact, many of the fairy tales end with some benevolent ruler taking
command of the government. To be sure, he will rule with the support of the
people. But will he really? Is that socialism? Is that the way to stimulate children to become socialists? There is no doubt that the popular children's plays in
East Germany take children seriously, but to what purpose? This question cannot be answered without a thorough investigation of the educational system. However, considering the planned economy, the lack of manpower, and the revisionist policies of an authoritarian government, it is safe to say that children represent an important investment in East Germany—potential manpower; and one has
the sneaking suspicion that the children's plays, despite their critique of exploitation and portrayal of struggles for liberation, are intended to bring about heavy
returns on this investment. By diverting children from the real dragons in East
Germany, as Wolf Biermann has explained in his fairy-tale play for adults, [21]
they will lose sight of the real contradictions and struggles in their own country.

West Germany

In West Germany, the situation with regard to dragons is less confusing but
more contradictory. In fact, there are so many obvious dragons that it is difficult to determine which one to slay first. While radical **groups** develop various
theories about the cause of "dragonism," conservative groups maintain that there
can be no such thing as dragons in this day and age. This contradiction is a key
issue in the children's theater movement.

Unlike West Germany, there was no consistent state policy or system of children's theater developed in the West after the war. [22] Only a few theaters managed to sprout: Theater der Jugend (1950) in Nürnberg, Die Jugendvormiete (1952) in Dortmund, and Theater der Jugend (1953) in Munich. Essentially, these theaters continued the tradition of the Christmas fairy tale on a more regular basis, and this tradition was also celebrated by the state theaters during the Yuletide season. Up until 1968, there was very little experimentation in these children's theaters. Most of them were not supported by the state. The acting was done by adults, and the audiences were divided into two large age groups: six to twelve and thirteen to fifteen. Writers were not commissioned to write plays. There was a great reliance on the traditional repertory of fairy-tale plays in their original form and other infantile best-sellers such as Peter Pan and Peterchens Mondfahrt, always in lavish productions. Cooperation with educators and psychologists, if any, was superficial. Children's theater was largely an extension of the school program, an inferior theater which was to serve only sweet, harmless doses of middle-class educational ideals to sensitive young souls. No plays were written about the brutal treatment children received in homes. No plays were concerned about the lack of playing space and youth centers. Nothing was written about the elitist social system. In fact, only the more privileged children went to or experienced theater. There they were compelled to enjoy fantastic performances which affirmed the status quo in society, conjured vague evil forces which were readily defeated, and encouraged the acquisition of women, money, and status.

By 1968, signs of change in West German children's theaters became noticeable. Already in 1966, the Reichskabarett in West Berlin had begun producing children's plays on political themes, and three years later, attracted national attention with its production of Maximilian Pfeiferling. Attention was drawn to the Reichskabarett largely because of the radical movement which pushed for anti-authoritarian educational reforms on all levels. This resulted in programs for day care centers, socialist collectives, and the re-publication of important socialist texts on education and the family by Edwin Hoernle, Vera Schmidt, Wilhelm Reich, members of the Frankfurt Institute for Social Research, and other Marxist thinkers. The most important for children's theater was Walter Benjamin's Programm eines proletarischen Kindertheaters, which was rediscovered along with Asja Lacis' innovative work in 1968.

These essentially positive developments reflect a serious interest in the situation of children on the part of radicals. At the same time, attempts have been made to distort their work by making the seriousness of their concern in children's theater popular in a commercial sense. The wealthy state theaters have decided to cash in on the rise of interest in children. Because of the continuing drop in adult attendance, enterprising Intendanten have expanded their programs for children. The bourgeois Christmas ritual for the entire family is being replaced by a bourgeois shopping ritual: cultural commodities are to be consumed, with the parents enjoying an infantile regression spree and the children enjoying technical gadgets and mod designs which are intended to increase their lust to consume. Obviously, since they have more money and are in the majority, the state theaters and conservative children's theaters hold an advantage over the more radical children's theaters. Nevertheless, the radical groups are more vital and may ultimately cause great changes in both East and West German children's theater. This will become clearer as we review some of the programs of the Reichskabarett, Theater im Märkischen Viertel, and Arbeitsgruppe Spielumwelt.

It is not by chance that most of the more serious projects involving children's theater and theater in general emanate from West Berlin. Ever since it was made into an island and stamped by the political tensions between East and West, the city has become a center of radical activity. Its special situation has clearly made it into the pulse of German capitalism and socialism alike. It is there that all contradictions are most evident, and there that most attempts have been made to provide alternatives to the rigid bourgeois and socialist institutions.

The Reichskabarett, which now calls itself Grips, [23] is one such alternative. Set in the middle of West Berlin, the small theater makes maximum use of its space to give children a sense of free play. Performances run about an hour and a half for children from six to twelve. There is usually music, and the plays are performed by adults who have worked collectively with educators and psychologists to study children's needs and problems. Most of the plays are written by Rainer Hachfeld, his brother Eckhardt (who goes under the name Volker Ludwig) and members of the ensemble.

Reichskabarett began with two plays that depended heavily on fairy tale motifs. Die Reise nach Pitschepatsch (1967) and Stokerlok und Millipilli (1968) tended to be too abstract and irrational, and the ensemble decided to make their plays more realistic, hoping for more effect. The result was Maximilian Pfeiferling (1969) by Carsten Krüger. The drama concerns little Max, who as the youngest in a lower class family is constantly being exploited by his sister and parents. He resorts to using the only weapon he has: a shrill whistle which he produces through the gap between his two front teeth. The whistle embarrasses everyone, and by using it strategically, Max manages to defeat his oppressors.

Almost all the plays performed by the Reichskabarett manifest a concern for the different ways children are exploited, and they demonstrate ways to overcome the exploitation. Hachfeld's Mungnog Kinder! (1971) is about two children who drag a box named Mugnog with them wherever they go. The box, symbolizing the imaginative energies of the children, makes adults anxious, and they try to destroy it. But the children ultimately force the adults to respect their creativeness by replacing the box with a stove-pipe named Mugnog, too. Balle, Malle, Hupe und Artur (1971), written by the ensemble, reveals how children are compelled to play in the streets and how they change their situation around by occupying an abandoned building. Trummi Kaputt (1971) by Ludwig concerns a toy manufacturer and his son who are constantly making a profit off other children with their toys until the children invent games with their imagination and no longer depend on the toys of the manufacturer. By far the most important and most realistic play to date is Mannomann! (1972) by Ludwig and Reiner Lücker. The story involves a single working woman with her two children, harrassed by a landlord who is forcing them to move to a new building. The mother decides that she should marry again largely because she feels the need for protection. The new lord of the house, a factory worker, upsets the harmonious working conditions at home with his male chauvinism and bossy ways. Consequently, the children run away. As they hunt for crates at their new father's factory, they accidentally see how he is bossed around on his job without standing up to the foreman. They add two and two together and decide to return home. They explain the reason why in a song:

> If you don't fight back, you feel mighty low—man oh man!
> So you pick on others to feel big again,
> It's the same old story, you know,
> Until someone stands up and says No!
>
> Stand up, fight for your rights,
> Stand up, fight for your rights,
> and keep on asking things
> that make the others think. [24]

So the children return home, incite the mother to stand up for her rights, and convince the father that he will not lose respect or manliness in doing collective work. In the end, they join together in mutual support and defeat the landlord. Mannomann! is a remarkable play in that it provides a succinct class analysis of the exploitation of children, women, and workers, and it also shows a workable way to cope with the different forms of oppression. What's more, the Reichskabarett appears to be on its way toward realizing Brecht's idea of a naive theater: the pleasant productions bring out how pleasurable it can be to change working conditions and oneself to improve human relations. The only difficulty with the Reichskabarett is that its audience is largely composed of children from progressive families who do not have the same problems as the children in the plays. Despite occasional performances in lower class districts, Reichskabarett has not managed to reach the audience it wants to reach: the proletarian children.

This cannot be said about the Kindertheater im Märkischen Viertel which follows the Benjamin program of a proletarian children's theater more closely than any other theater in East or West Germany. Located in a low-income housing development in Berlin, the theater was begun by Helme Ebert and Volkhardt Paris in 1969. [25] They meet with two different groups of children ranging from eight to eleven in a school twice a week. Their basic purpose is to create a theater for and by proletarian children, and they are aided in their work by two psychologists and an educator. The work has three phases involving (1) the development of children's skills of observation and expression; (2) the use of improvisation to raise the class consciousness of the children and bring about an understanding of social conflicts; (3) experiments with possible solutions to the conflicts worked out in performances. By dealing with incidents from the daily lives of the children, Ebert and Paris have guided them so that they can build and act out scenes which concern drunken fathers, cruel housing officials, nasty landlords, oppressive educators, and neglectful parents. The scenes have led children to recognize various ways they have been oppressed and to search for solutions. Here Ebert and Paris are cautious since they see a danger in stimulating children to work out a new way of behavior with parents who might react negatively toward them. Since the parents are products of certain social contitions which shape their parents' behavior so that they do not mistakenly condemn or hate them: "It is important to take the burden off the parents and to illuminate the background factors. In this way the children will learn to comprehend their parents much better. Whatever they can understand can no longer cause them anxiety. Their self-confidence will grow. Self-confident children are no longer so totally dependent on the affection and consent of grown-ups. We want to use stories and work with children in such a way that they will gradually reach the point where they can view their entire surroundings and themselves and make distinctions in a discerning way." [26] Unlike the Benjamin program, Ebert and Paris believe that performances are significant because the children learn to communicate their experiences in an artistic form to other children and adults, and because they also strengthen the group feeling. Thus far, the success of the theater has been limited—limited to small groups of children in their working class district of West Berlin. However, both Ebert and Paris are patient and realize that building a proletarian children's theater without the mass support of the proletariat will be a gradual process.

Another way of organizing proletarian children's theater has been developed by Arbeitsgruppe Spielumwelt, [27] and it is unique. In October of 1970, several former members of Hofmann's Comic Teater opened the Spielclub Kulmerstrasse in which they built a miniature city that had stalls for a bank, courthouse, newspaper, shops, businesses, etc. They distributed leaflets in the working class district inviting children ranging from eight to twelve to come to the club and play after school hours. Generally between thirty and forty children came regularly in the next seven months. The adults explained the rules of the game and stayed in the background as the play commenced. The children were financed by the bank which gave them money. Some became employers and others employees, and the city gradually organized itself according to the rules of the capitalist system. Soon conflicts arose. The workers complained about exploitation, and they protested to the court individually without results. Then some decided to form a commune to oppose the capitalists in the club. By the seventh month, they had organized a commune class which divided and shared things according to collective principles and took a united stand against the capitalists. The intentions of the adults were thereby realized: "This game had to be set up in such a way that the children could find the lure and attraction of the system reflected in it and feel themselves affected by the contradictions of the lure and attraction; and so that they could have a chance in this game to become successful and to develop an active social action in relation to the complex capitalist reality." [28]

In June of 1971, the Gruppe Spielumwelt took the game to the Märkisches Viertel and invited neighborhood children as well as those from their own Spielclub and Theater im Märkischen Viertel to build and run an outdoor city for ten days. The climax of the game was a storming of the fort by the workers who protested exploitation by the military and capitalists. The game was repeated by other groups in West Germany and again by the Gruppe Spielumwelt in August. The results have been positive. However—and this is obviously due to the success of this unique children's theater—funds have been taken away from the Gruppe Speilumwelt, and in March 1972, the ensemble was evicted from the Spielclub. Shortly thereafter, 300 children and several adults occupied an abandoned factory in the same neighborhood where it was hoped that a new Spielclub could be built. During bargaining sessions with district officials and senators, Berlin tactical police invaded the factory and cleaned out the occupants. Barbed wire and police dogs were then installed to "protect" the factory until it could be demolished at the cost of 180,000 DM to the city. This was absurd theater at its best, and it has, for the time being, only strengthened the resolve of the Gruppe Speilumwelt to continue its work in tighter cooperation with other leftist theaters in Berlin by forming a cooperative with them.[29]

There is another experiment in Berlin, which was based on the work on the Theater im Märkischen Viertel, [30] and a project in Kassel developed by Wolfram Frommlet, who organized a theater with children from five to eight who tried traditional fairy tale motifs against their daily experience and negative examples from children's literature in order to develop new roles and modes of behavior. [31] Other children's theaters in West Germany are more moderate. The most progressive is not a children's theater, but a regular one, Theater am Turm in Frankfurt, which now has a regular program of three children's plays a season and wants to develop popular socialist forms and ideas in such productions as Das Untier von Samarkand, Die Ostindienfahrer, and an adaptation of Nestroy's Der Talisman by Wolfgang Deichsel. Most of the other large state theaters in West Germany have gone into the business of producing plays for children mainly as a stop-gap measure to offset the losses in the adult theater. The majority of the plays produced are adaptations of traditional fairy tales by such distinguished writers as Thelka and Guido von Kaulla, Hermann Wanderscheck, Wolf Dieter Pahlke, and Hermann Stelter, who have these words of wisdom to say to children: "Whoever is rich is not always happy . . . There are many evil people in this world . . . My two daughters are now going to become princesses. Who would ever have imagined that! . . . Good always triumphs over evil . . . It's never too late to learn . . . You have to work in order to eat and have a roof over your head . . . A clear conscience is like a soft pillow."[32] Even when a state theater does decide to produce a play like Balle, Malle, Hupe und Artur (as in Dortmund), [33] it generally waters down the radical implications of the play.

The tendency to rewrite and produce fairy-tale plays for children is just as pronounced in West Germany as in the East. But, the emphasis is totally different. Whereas East Germans revise and reinterpret the fairy tales according to Marxist theory and their own socialist system of education, the West Germans retain feudal features and merely reshape the story to make it more fashionable, cute, charming, and delectable according to bourgeois taste; which is to say, they make the play into harmless fun which is in essence harmful to children. Of course, there are some exceptions. Gerhard Kelling has written an amusing political fairy-tale play, Der Bär geht auf den Försterball, based on a story by Peter Hacks. It deals subtly with the racism of dumb drunken foresters who actually go on a bear hunt led by the bear himself dressed as head forester. The hunters make all sorts of bigoted remarks about bears and apprentices, and when the bear finally reveals his true identity, they are unwilling to deal with this. But the bear forces them to face up to the destructive nature of their racism by ordering them to shoot him. As they close their eyes to shoot, the bear disappears in triumph.

Unfortunately, this play by Kelling and those produced by Theater am Turm (TAT) are more the exception to the rule in West Germany. Even the experimental version of Der gestiefelte Kater by Alice Toen (which can be likened to much of the pseudo-progressive work being done at the Munich and Nürnberg children's theaters) breaks down in comparison to the solid socialist fairy-tale plays in East Germany. 34 Toen employs five actors who decide to put on a play for children. They distribute the roles in front of the audience, play many different roles, and often interrupt the plot to step out of the roles. The story-line of the traditional Puss 'n Boots remains the same. The emphasis is on the meaning of the play and on role-playing, and the alienation technique is used to stimulate the critical thinking of the children. However, in no way do children learn how difficult it is to break down roles and why there are roles such as the oppressed and the oppressor. The children in the audience are encouraged to free themselves from set roles and become creative, but the play can only have meaning for privileged children who have the real possibilities to try out different roles and experiment. Progressive bourgeois plays like Toen's are mainly concerned with children who already have social advantages and well-developed skills. In effect, the needs of these children are different from the majority of children, and they can afford to forego orthodox schooling. But working-class children need schooling desperately just as they need theater—but schooling and theater which are in their interests, not those which serve to keep them in their place or make them upwardly mobile tools of the ruling class.

Tentative Conclusions

Though the educational systems are different in East and West Germany, they are both geared to making children into upwardly mobile, functional servants of the state. In West Germany, mobility is more limited. The system is elitist. The attitude toward proletarian children is one of neglect. In East Germany, the mobility is controlled. The attitude toward working-class children is one of paternalism. The West German state masks the inhumanity of its system in a welfare posture bent on keeping workers in a humble and humiliating position. Proletarian children (and others as well) are educated to feel their unworthiness and dispensability, for they must learn how dispensable they are in the capitalist system of planned obsolescence. The East German state masks its authoritarianism and revisionism in a paternal posture and socialist slogans bent on raising the

187

productivity of the workers to benefit a new class society. Proletarian children (and others) are educated to feel the importance of self-sacrifice in a revisionist socialist system of planned economy which places a great investment in each individual worker with whom it cannot dispense.

The educational systems and the ideologies of the states determine the condition of children's theaters. In East Germany, the children's theaters are uniform and popular to the extent that every child is exposed to the theater, and it becomes a part of his or her moral and aesthetic experience. Essentially though, children are taken seriously mainly in terms of their usefulness to the state so that the moral and aesthetic experience does not open up new possibilities for them to develop their creative and critical faculties. In West Germany, there are relatively few children's theaters. Their tendencies vary, and for the most part, they are not popular in a positive sense, i.e. they do not reach the masses of children. They are more for the privileged classes and play upon their sentimental attitudes. Children are taken seriously insofar as they are potential consumers. Otherwise, there is no overwhelming concern on the part of the state to build children's theaters to serve the needs and interest of most children.

In opposition to the standard children's theaters in East and West Germany, the radical children's theaters (primarily in West Berlin) have sought to raise the class consciousness of proletarian children (and others) and are building theaters which can be used as instruments for the children's own self-development. They base their work on Marxist theories of children's education and on the practice of leftist day care centers and schools. Their support in the theater comes from the socialist publishing house Verlag der Autoren and the Westberliner Volkstheaterkooperative. Thus far, their most outspoken proponents have been Wolfram Frommlet and Melchior Schedler. Frommlet has been active in the KEKS-Gruppe (Kunst/Erziehung/Kybernetik/Soziologie), which has promoted radical children's theater and literature in Munich and Nurnberg. He was also one of the organizers of the important Children's Theater Conference in Marl during October, 1970,[35] and continues to push for changes throught his activities as writer and director. This is also the case with Schedler, who adheres more closely to a strict interpretation of the Benjamin program. Schedler not only supports the concept of theater for and by children, but he also attacks the fairy-tale play as being too feudal, escapist, and vague to be of help to children who must learn to come to terms with their immediate environment.[36] Despite his incisive argument, Schedler is too categorical in dismissing fairy-tale plays and theaters with adults as performers. Such plays and productions can serve to clarify issues for children in the youngest age groups who have difficulty in conceptualizing, and here adults as performers can serve as exemplary figures. No doubt, the ideal children's theater is a type of proletarian children's theater as Benjamin outlined it and as it is being developed today in West Berlin. However, without the mass support of the wage-earning class, radical children's theaters are subject to the antagonistic social conditions that define their room for play, their margin of effect, and their course for the future. Their historical role in the development of children's theaters is a limited one—limited but most important. They are presently pushing the standard theaters in East and West Germany into a new historical phase. By taking children seriously and developing alternate popular forms of theater in the interests of most children—against the pop commercial forms that support the interests of the ruling class—they have forced the standard theaters in the East and West to make certain alterations. Even though these changes in the seriousness and popularity may be artificial and co-optive, the more genuine forms being developed by radical theaters will continue to expose these defects and help shape the future proletarian children's theater. Naturally, this theater can only find expression in a society that permits children to take themselves seriously and fulfill their childhood, without constraint and compulsion, in play.

---

1 The Sexual Revolution, rev. ed. (New York, 1969), p. 79.

2 Kindertheater, edition suhrkamp 520 (Frankfurt/M, 1972).

3 Manfred Berger, Manfred Nössig, Fritz Rödel und Liane Pfelling, Volker Kurzweg, Inge Münz-Koenen, Christel Hoffmann, Theater in der Zeitenwende, 2 vols. (E. Berlin, 1972).

4 See "Asja Lacis, Walter Benjamin und ihr 'Programm eines proletarischen Kindertheaters,'" in Schedler, Kindertheater, pp. 209-255.

5 Ibid. Not only that, but their work was neglected for forty years. In this regard, the contemporary radical children's theaters are making a connection with the raical tradition of the 1920's.

6 Ibid., p. 44.

7 Some interesting work has been done on children's literature during the Nazi period. See Peter Aley, Jugend Literatur im Dritten Reich (Hamburg, 1967). At present there have been no studies of children's theater during the fascist period to my knowledge. Neither Schedler nor the East Germans deal with this historical phase which must be understood if we are to develop complete histories of theater.

8 In 1971, Ilse Rodenberg, a leading official and policy-maker in children's theater, made a programmatic statement which sums up the communist position with regard to children's theater: "Wir sehen die Aufgabe des Theaters darin, der Jugend durch alle unsere Aufführungen, ob durch Märchen oder Zeitstücke, Musicals oder Schauspiele, Beispiele menschlicher Selbstverwirklichung zu geben, d.h. solche Kunst zu machen, die den Kindern Aufgaben stellt, Aufgaben zum selbständigen Denken und Handeln, die Impulse gibt, die uber das Theatererlebnis hinausweisen, als die Wirklichkeit indirekt beeinflussendes Element. Das Theater ist ein Teil der Anregungen und Einflüsse, die auf das Kind einwirken, wobei das Theater zu der gesellschaftlich bewußt einwirkenden Einflußsphare gehört." See "Der Beitrag des Theaters zur Selbstverwirklichung der kindlichen Persönlichkeit," Theater der Zeit, 3 (1971), p. 28.

9 See Theater der Zeitenwende, p. 370.

10 Most of the more innovative work is done for the first two age groups. The fourteen- to eighteen-year-olds attend both the Jugendtheater and the regular theater where plays such as Horst Salomon's Ein Lorbass, Paul Gratzik's Umwege, and Arnim Müller's Franziska Lesser are produced for them.

11 Theater für Kinder und Jugendliche in der Deutschen Demokratischen Republik, Referat, (E. Berlin, 1963). Cited in Elke Bauer, Theater für Kinder (Stuttgart, 1970), p. 44.

12 This lack is also criticized in Theater der Zeitenwende, p. 387.

13 For a good discussion of East Germany's educational system, see Nigel Grant, Society, Schools and Progress in Eastern Europe (New York, 1969), pp. 203-231.

14 Jewgeni Schwarz, Stücke (E. Berlin, 1970), p. 378.

15 Schwarz, p. 340.

16 Cf. Bauer, Theater für Kinder, pp. 58-90.

17 During the early 1950's there was some debate about the relevance of fairy tales to the policy of socialist realism in East Germany. However, it was decided that the fairy-tale plays could help demonstrate class contradictions in clear linear forms. See Theater in der Zeitenwende, pp. 398-402. Also important is Ilse Rodenberg's statement in "Der Beitrag des Theaters zur Selbstverwirklichung der kindlichen Persönlichkeit," p. 28. "Die Märchen lenken also nicht von der Gegenwart ab, sondern sie sind auf sie gerichtet. . . . wir spielen Märchen, weil es die Kinder an die realen Widersprüche und deren Lösungen heranführt."

18 Das Untier von Samarkand, manuscript (E. Berlin: Henschel Verlag, n.d.), p. 48.

19 Wie der König zum Mond wollte, manuscript (E. Berlin: Henschel Verlag, n.d.), p. 48.

20 Ibid., Vorbemerkung: "Zirkus und Feuerwerk, Clownerie, Spiel und Liedforen alter, folkloristischer Kinderliteratur sind zum mixtum compositum vereint, weil ich auf der Strasse, auf jedem Spielplatz sehe, welches Vergnügen der bunte Wechsel ihrer Phantasie-Inhalte und Formen bereitet, und weil ich den Versuch für lohnend halte, ihnen dieses Phantasie und Intellekt bildende Vergnügen im Theater zu vermitteln."

21 See Der Dra-Dra, W. Berlin, 1970.

22 Cf. Bauer, Theater für Kinder, pp. 36-40.

23 For information on the Reichskabarett, which was formerly one of the leading political cabarets in the West, see Schedler, Kindertheater, pp. 256-260; Volker Ludwig, "Über die Anmassung, Theater für Kinder zu machen,"

Theater heute, 11 (April, 1970), 27-28; Rainer Hachfeld, "Über das Schreiben von Szenen für Kinder," in Kindertheater und Interaktionspadagogik (Stuttgart, 1972), pp. 117-123; Bernard Marinier, "Théatre Anti-Autoritaire," Travail théatral, 8 (July/September, 1972), 146-152.

24 Mannomann! manuscript (Frankfurt/M: Verlag der Autoren, 1972), p. 81.

25 See Helme Ebert and Volkhardt Paris, "Theater mit Kindern im Markischen Viertel," Theater heute, 11 (April, 1970), 28-29.

26 Ibid., p. 29.

27 For a history of Hofmann's Cosmic Teater, see Schedler, Kindertheater, pp. 275-282. Also Arbeitsgruppe Spielumwelt publishes its own magazine which has important information in it. See Heft 1 and 2 of Fest's Magazin, which appeared in June 1971 and June 1972 in Berlin.

28 Fest im M. V. ein Gesellschaftsspiel, Heft 1, W. Berlin, 1971 (A report on the game in the Markisches Viertel published by Arbeitsgruppe Spielumwelt).

29 The name of this cooperative is the Westberliner Volkstheaterkooperative, and its members are Reichskabarett, Theaterkollektiv die Zentrifuge, das Lehrlingstheater Rote Steine, das Theater für Kinder im Märkischen Viertel, das Puppentheater Bränli, and Arbeitsgruppe Spielumwelt.

30 See Arno Paul, "Theaterspiel mit Arbeiterkindern," in Kindertheater und Interaktionspädagogik (Stuttgart, 1972), pp. 95-116.

31 See Heike Mundzeck "Zwischen Märchen und Agitprop," Die Welt, October 22, 1970.

32 These quotations were collected by Hermann Beil in his short, but important article "Über Kinder dagegen haben Phrasen keine Gewalt," Theater heute, 8 (August, 1969), 42-43.

33 Schedler, Kindertheater, pp. 259-260.

34 Toen is Dutch, and her play was translated by Rahel Elisabeth Feilchenfeldt. Like the Soviet plays in East Germany, there are various western plays which become part and parcel of the West German repertory. Toen's Der gestiefelte Kater has not reached that stage yet, but it is representative of West German progressive plays which have recently become popular but really do not speak to the majority of children.

35 See Protokolle der Kindertheatertagung in Marl, (Marl, 1971). Frommlet has also written an interesting Handbuch für Spielaktioner with H. Mayerhofer and W. Zacharias—Eltern Spielen, Kinder Lernen (Munich, 1972).

36 See "Sieben Thesen zum Theater fur sehr junge Zuschauer," Theater heute, 10 (August, 1969), 30-33.

BUNGALOWS AND BAZAARS:
INDIA IN VICTORIAN CHILDREN'S FICTION

Clarissa M. Rowland

In 1815, The Indian Pilgrim, Mrs. Sherwood's adaptation of Pilgrim's Progress for converts to Christianity, was published in England. In 1901 one of E.
Nesbit's families, the Would-Be-Goods, act out scenes from Kipling's Jungle
Book in their garden. In the years between, the theme of India is used in English books and stories for children. Besides directly inspiring several superb
tales for children, we can surely say that India served as a source of plot and
situation, and that Indian settings reflect changes in travel and education which
were taking place during the nineteenth century.

Conversion was Mrs. Sherwood's obsession, and it dictated the shape of those
tracts written by her for young people which have an Indian background. But she
had spent more than ten years in India with her husband's regiment, and her tales
also illustrate something of the life led by European children there, at a time
when the voyage out from England took four or five months by sailing boat. In
Little Lucy and her Dhaye, written in 1816, for instance, Mrs. Sherwood tells us
all about the household which Mr. Grenville, Lucy's father, set up for his daughter in the town where he was a merchant, after her mother's death. She records
for us the names and duties of all the attendants employed in looking after the infant, from the beheistie, or water-carrier, to the garry-waun who drove her bul-
lock-coach. She describes the daily routine, from the early-morning airing, to
the cool of evening when Lucy would finally fall asleep on her nurse's lap in the
jasmine-scented air outside their bungalow. Little Henry and his Bearer (1819),
Mrs. Sherwood's best-known tale, gives an account of the short life of an orphaned English child, taken into the house of a wealthy English lady living in India and
tended there, until his early death, by Boosey, the devoted bearer and nurse.
Here is a lively picture of him:

> Henry could not speak English but he could talk with Boosey in his
> language as fast as possible; and he knew every word, good or bad,
> which the natives spoke. He used to sit on the verandah between his
> bearer's knees and chew paun and eat bazar sweetmeats. He wore
> no shoes or stockings; but was dressed in panjammahs and had sil-
> ver bangles on his ancles (sic).

In The Memoirs of Sergeant Dale, written in 1816, we are introduced to the
routine of a regiment serving in India, at the Cawnpore barracks, a life punctua-
ted by daily parades and the guns fired off morning and evening. Some of the
problems of raising a baby in the tropics are touched on here, when Sergeant
Dale and his young daughter Sarah discuss whether between them they can take in

and care for the orphaned baby, Mary; what she is to be fed, how Sarah will manage to cook and get the baby's washing done. It comes as no surprise to learn that during Mrs. Sherwood's years in India her great interest was the founding of schools and homes for soldiers' orphans. She established an orphanage near Calcutta, wrote a book on the subject, [1] and brought three regimental orphans home, together with her own five children, when in 1816 she and her husband left India for good.

Mrs. Sherwood could pick out scenes which would touch a parent, and which have often been used in later stories. She mentions little Lucy's despair after the final parting from her dhaye, who "probably until these few hours had been ready to attend to her every call"; she even notes the dilemma of Lucy's father starting on the voyage home—totally unused to the care or company of his daughter, but convinced that it would be highly improper to bring any female attendant into his cabin to help him with the child. (This particular problem was solved by the timely and tactful help of the lady who was to become Lucy's stepmother.) Perhaps she remembered from her own experiences the quandary of a parent returning with a child who has been born in India and who now wants to know what England is going to look like. Sergeant Dale handles this problem by explaining to orphan Mary that "A village is a little bazar and a town is a great bazar" and that a church is not to be confused with a pagoda. Eternity and Judgment Day were indeed the grand themes of Mrs. Sherwood's writing but she gladly teaches her readers something about India when she can, by embodying native words and phrases in her text, and by instinctively adding details of the scenes she knew so well.

Mrs. Ewing's Six to Sixteen appeared in 1872. By this time steamship travel to India had become well-established, and the Suez Canal had been open for three years. It is a tale of two girls growing up together, their education and miseducation. India is for Mrs. Ewing both the starting-point of the story and the vantage-point from which to comment on girlhood and girls' schools in England. Christabel Maxwell, Mrs. Ewing's biographer, suggests that she picked up the Indian details for the early chapters from her husband, who had served there in the army, and Six to Sixteen was written during the years that the Ewings spent at the Aldershot barracks among families many of whom must have come back from India too. Perhaps the Indian scenes do not have quite the sharpness with which she describes army life in England, which she herself had learned to love —as we see in The Story of a Short Life. But if Mrs. Sherwood could pick out moving episodes from a child's experience in India, Mrs. Ewing certainly knows how to make us share them, and there is much truth of feeling in the Indian setting of Six to Sixteen. The heroine, Margery, tells the story, which begins when her parents die suddenly in India, one of cholera and one of fever. She is taken in by a brother-officer and his family, and comes back to England with them, on a troop-ship, when she is six, after an idyllic nursery life with a gentle ayah. All Margery's memories of this Indian episode are full of scent and color and certainly the dramatic account of her parents' death reads as though it were based on a story heard first-hand. There follow scenes from regimental life, first on the troop-ship, with all the stresses and strains of a long voyage, and then at the new station in the south of England, where Mrs. Ewing comments observantly on the plight of returning Anglo-Indian families. When Kipling praised Six to Sixteen as "a history of real people and real things" (as he did in Something of Myself) I believe that he was remembering not only its Indian setting, but Mrs. Ewing's sketches of officers and more especially, their wives; the feuds and social rituals, the all-absorbing gossip about fashions and friendships. The live-ly chit-chat of Margery, her cousins and aunt may have stayed at the back of his mind to suggest the portraits of spirited army ladies which first began to appear in his Plain Tales from the Hills (1888).

India as a situation or plight was to become, of course, a handy resource for writers of childrens' books who needed a convincing way to get rid of parents, when the story was to focus on a certain child, or on the life and play together of a group of children. This need grew as writers began to take an interest in chil-dren for their own sake, and started writing to please as well as to teach or con-vert them. The nine Tudor children live with their mother in the Welsh country-side, but the adventures we hear about in The Children of Hermitage [2] happen after their mother has left to go out to Afghanistan when news has reached her that her husband has been wounded. The houseful of children which Flora Shaw describes in Castle Blair (1878) is another example. They had been sent back from India and turned loose to run wild in the Irish countryside, under a stalwart housekeeper's eye. Their father, we are told, has had enough of watching them grow pale and quiet in India, and his ambition is that for a few years they should be left on their own to grow up as healthy and ignorant as the neighboring village children. The Blair children are only a few of many others who will be described alternatively as "wizened and yellow with fever" when they come back from liv-ing in India, and the roll includes of course Mrs. Hodgson-Burnett's famous pair of heroines Sarah of The Little Princess (1887) and Mary of The Secret Garden (1910). The opening chapters of both these books show Mrs. Hodgson-Burnett making great dramatic effect with disaster in a bungalow; frivolous mother, de-voted brother officers and scared native servants in the background. We should perhaps remember that scenes of violent death were at this period as common in Yorkshire cottages and London slums as in Indian bungalows. Another theme be-gan to appear, too, directly connected with the plight of an orphan child or one separated from parents, and that is specifically the course of the child's adapta-tion to English life and ways. Both Mrs. Ewing and Mrs. Hodgson-Burnett could see that this was an interesting and complex situation, and they made a firm con-nection in their stories between the child who is naughty and the child who is also bewildered and unhappy. Rumer Godden is a writer of our own times who has not only recorded her own memories of a childhood in India (in Two Under the Noon-day Sun) but has interpreted for children in Miss Happiness and Miss Flower the special agonies of a little girl sent back to England to live with her cousins, and her adjustment both to them and to school.

Kipling's life and stories span the Indian experience of children in his day. He was born at Bombay in 1865, and his first trip back to England came in 1871,

during the period from 1857 to 1869 when the voyage between England and India
was made by steamship, with an overland trek from Alexandria to Suez. This he
mentions in Something of Myself:

> There was a train across the desert (the Suez Canal was not yet
> opened) and a halt in it, and a small girl wrapped in a shawl on the
> seat opposite whose face stands out still. There was next a dark
> land, and a darker room full of cold, in one wall of which a white
> woman made naked fire, and I cried aloud with dread, for I had
> never before seen a grate.

Kipling's parents went back to India after their leave was over, leaving him
and his sister in charge of a foster-family, and the six years of separation that
followed are described in his story Baa Baa Black Sheep. The household at
Southsea was ruled by threats of damnation, much as Mrs. Sherwood would have
prescribed, and it is no wonder that when Kipling mentions Mrs. Ewing's Six to
Sixteen he does it with real affection, for its glowing picture of Indian days may
have helped to keep up his courage. It is interesting, too, that one sentence in
his story William the Conqueror[3] is an explicit link with Mrs. Sherwood's India.
Two army officers are sent out to find and feed starving children during a famine,
and as they traveled, Kipling writes, " . . . they came to an India more strange
to them than to the untraveled Englishman—the flat, red India of palm-tree,
palmyra-palm and rice, the India of the picture-books of Little Harry and his
Bearer—all dead and dry in the baking heat."

Kipling also sketches, in Wee-Willie-Winkie Stories and Tod's Amendment,
for instance—the Anglo-Indian army child in an Indian setting, a child who is
both pet of the regiment and terror of the nursery but sturdy and honorable and
devoted both to his Indian friends and to the officers' mess. These army brats,
the babalog, Kiping made the acquaintance of as an adult, after his years at boarding-school were over. Increasingly boarding-schools became the solution first
for boys and then girls whose parents were committed to careers in India. Kipling's account of his school-life at the United Services College, which followed
the incarceration at Southsea, appears in Stalky and Co. When Mrs. Ewing describes a boarding-school for girls in Six to Sixteen (a school from which Margery and her cousin are soon rescued) it is a place where the teaching is so
rigorous that health and sports are entirely neglected—a far cry from the cliffs
and sea-breezes and paper-chases which play such a large part in the Stalky
stories.

In Kim India explodes in all its variety and color, as it perhaps dazzled Kipling when he went to live and work there after he had left school at the age of
seventeen. Here for the first time—though it was not written until he had left
India for good—is a book for children in which India is not a background or a device, but a wonder-house, an endless bazaar. We go out on the road with Kim,
and share the lives of travelers and villagers, jostled by religions, food, dress
and caste of every variety. Mowgli, the hero of The Jungle Book eventually returns to live with men again, and in these tales Kipling is insisting on the theme

195

of obedience to the laws of the pack and the jungle. But Kim remains a free
spirit, and it is of his own desire that he binds himself to the Lama, the Great
Game and even for some years to a boarding-school in India—a school for which
he may have been in Mrs. Sherwood's debt. Kim's India is packed with the detail of real, observed life; it is the landscape of an Indian boy where British ad-
ministrators and officers are interlopers, powerful and alien ones.

It was in 1899 that Helen Bannerman left her little girls at school in Scotland
and wrote them a picture-letter on the boat going back to India, where she was
rejoining her husband, a surgeon. She may simply have wanted to remind the
children of Indian scenes and villagers. At any rate, in Little Black Sambo an
Indian family is described for the youngest children, with an affection to equal
Kipling's and a humor of Mrs. Bannerman's own. The illustrations distress us
today, but the story remains a masterly one. Not a word is wasted, the pattern
of the plot satisfies both reader and listener, and the hero overcomes the tigers
not by magic but by his own wits.

Indian folklore had been collected from 1866 on, when Mary Frere compiled
Old Deccan Days, tales which an ayah had heard from her grandmother and hand-
ed on to the children in her care. And Henty used the history of India as the
source of five tales, written between 1884 and 1902, which chronicle the wars
and fortunes of the British in India. It was for him only one of the countries he
traveled through and wrote up, always through the eyes of young men of action
and forthright courage. But neither he nor any of the other writers whose stories we have mentioned ever used India simply as a quick solution or a stage-de-
vice, as sloppier or less inventive story-tellers have done since. To each of
them it was a place which had touched their lives in a special way and which they
chose to pass on to us through their books, for no other reason than that it had
meant something special to them.

---

1 Indian Orphans. Berwick, 1836.

2 The Children of Hermitage. Frances E. Crompton. First published in serial
form in Little Folks, 1903, first published in book form Macmillan, London,
1970.

CHILDREN'S VERSE AND THE HALLE-KEYSER THEORY OF PROSODY

Jacqueline Guéron

In this paper I should like to show how a recent development in linguistics, namely the Halle-Keyser theory of prosody, has advanced the general theory of poetic forms.

Applying this theory to the study of English and French children's verse, I shall show how it permits us to state the rules governing individual meters, and, what is even more interesting, to reveal similarities between different meters.

In what follows I first state and illustrate the Halle-Keyser theory of prosody. I then give the rules,governing the meter of English Nursery Rhymes and that of French comptines. Finally, I show how the theory allows us to treat these two meters as variants of a single underlying metrical pattern.

I. THE HALLE-KEYSER THEORY OF PROSODY. [1]

According to Morris Halle and Samuel Jay Keyser, a poetic meter can be considered as consisting of a simple abstract pattern plus a body of realization rules which determine what sequences of a language can be considered as realizations of the underlying pattern.

Here, for example, is the Abstract Metrical Pattern of iambic pentameter verse: [2]

$$V \rightarrow (w) \ S \ w \ S \ w \ S \ w \ S \ (w) \ (w)$$

where V symbolizes "verse," $\rightarrow$ may be read "consists of" or "is rewritten as," w is a weak metrical position, S a strong metrical position, and the elements in parentheses may be omitted. And here are the Realization Rules which determine which segments of English discourse may be considered realizations of the underlying pattern:

1. A metric position corresponds to a single syllable, OR

   to a sonorant sequence incorporating at most two vowels (either immediately adjoining or separated by a sonorant consonant).

DEFINITION: When a fully stressed syllable occurs between two unstressed syllables within a line of verse, this syllable is called a "stress maximum." [3]

2. Fully stressed syllables occur in S positions only and in all S positions, OR

   fully stressed syllables occur in S positions only but not in all S positions, OR

   stress maxima occur in S positions only but not in all S positions.

The first alternative of each rule defines the most simple realization of the pattern. Thus the simplest possible iambic pentameter line consists of a ten-syllable sequence in which every strong position (S) is occupied by a stressed syllable in a segment of English discourse, and every weak position (w) is occupied by an unstressed syllable, as in the following example:

(1) The cúrfew tólls the knéll of párting day.
    w S w S   w S   wS   w S

Such a line contains the maximum number of stress maxima (stressed syllables surrounded on either side by unstressed syllables). These are marked / above.

Whereas the first alternatives of Rules 1 and 2 give a simple iambic pentameter line, later alternatives of these rules give more complex realizations:

(2) And leáves the wórld to dárkness <u>and</u> to <u>me</u>.
    w S   w S   w S   w S   w S

Here two S-positions do not contain stressed syllables: position 8 (<u>and</u>) and position 10 (<u>me</u>). Accordingly, there are only three stress maxima in this line and not four.

(3) <u>Batter</u> my heart, <u>three</u>-personed God, for <u>you</u>
    w S w S   w   S w   S   w S

The underlined syllables above represent complex realizations of metrical positions. The first weak position is occupied by a stressed syllable, while the first strong position contains an unstressed syllable. We recognize an example of an "inverted foot." Whereas former theories of iambic pentameter could only consider this metrical figure as an "allowable exception" to the "rule," the Halle-Keyser theory gives a principled explanation for its occurrence. The reason the first weak position can contain a stressed syllable is that there is no other syllable preceding it. There is therefore no possibility of having a "stress maximum" in this position. (The rules of iambic pentameter permit a stress maximum in <u>even</u> position only.)

Similarly, the third weak position contains a stressed syllable (<u>three</u>). However, here it is the stressed syllable in the adjoining strong position (<u>per</u>) which prevents the occurrence of an unmetrical stress maximum in weak position. Line (3) is therefore a <u>complex</u> but <u>metrical</u> iambic pentameter.

The concept of the "stress maximum" is thus the principal criterion distinguishing metrical from unmetrical iambic pentameter lines. While the norm for this meter is an alternation of stressed and unstressed syllables, a certain deviation from the norm is accepted, up to a precise point: there must not be a stress maximum, a figure consisting of a stressed syllable surrounded on either side by an unstressed syllable, in a weak position. Whereas (3) above is a metrical line, the construct (3') is unmetrical:

(3') God in three persons will bátter my heart.

w S w S w S wS w S

In this line, there is a stress maximum in a <u>weak</u> position; this rules the line out as a metrical realization of iambic pentameter. [4]

The Halle-Keyser theory expresses in a precise and formal way our 'intuition' that iambic pentameter consists of an alternation of stressed and unstressed syllables, with stressed syllables occupying even positions.

To further justify this theory we must ask: (a) Is this theory empirically adequate? Does it allow us to account for all the iambic pentameters in the English tradition, and to distinguish between metrical and unmetrical lines as well as say, a poet or a trained scholar of English verse? (b) Is this theory explanitorily adequate? [5] Does it permit us to study other meters than iambic pentameter and to advance the general theory of meter?

I have tried to answer the first of these questions in another study in which I propose certain modifications to make the Halle-Keyser theory even more empirically adequate than it is. [6] Here I should like to take up the second question and show how the Halle-Keyser theory enables us not only to describe different types of children's verse but to lay the foundations for a general theory describing <u>all</u> children's verse forms.

II. THE METER OF ENGLISH NURSERY RHYMES. [7]

The English Nursery Rhyme consists of one or more stanzas, each containing (normally) four lines. The line is a syllabo-tonic sequence consisting of four stressed syllables with from one to three unstressed syllables between the stressed ones.

<u>Abstract Metrical Pattern</u>: V $\longrightarrow$ (w) S w S (w) S w S (w)

<u>Realization Rules</u>:

1. <u>S-position</u>: a. An S-position corresponds to a single metrical syllable.

<u>Definition</u>: A metrical syllable contains either a single vowel or a sonorant sequence consisting of two vowels which immediately adjoin or are separated by a sonorant consonant.

b. The syllable which occupies the S-position is the stressed syllable of a major category word: Noun, Verb, Adjective, Adverb, or Exclamation, OR

the secondary stressed syllable of a plurisyllabic word, OR

an unstressed syllable.

<u>Definition</u>: When a stressed syllable is located between two unstressed syllables within a verse, such a syllable is called a "stress maximum."

c. Stress maxima occur in strong positions only.

199

2. <u>w-position</u>: a. A w-position is realized by one to three syllables, OR

by a major syntactic pause. [8]

b. The syllables which occupy the w-position are the un-stressed syllables of major category words or any syllable of minor category words: Pronoun, Preposition, Auxiliary Verb, Conjunction, etc., OR

one of the syllables occupying <u>w</u> may be a stressed syllable provided that it is immediately adjacent to another stressed syllable in S-position. Such a syllable is "neutralized" by the adjacent stressed syllable.

Illustration of the rules: (I number S-positions for convenience of reference.)

(4) <u>Humpty Dúmpty sát</u> on a <u>wall</u>.
   S_1 w S_2 w S_3 w S_4

In line (4) every S-position is occupied by a stressed syllable. The obligatory w-positions, between S_1 and S_2 and between S_3 and S_4 are filled with either one or two unstressed syllables. Of the optional w-positions in the pattern, the one between S_2 and S_3 is realized by an unstressed syllable, but the ones preceding S_1 and following S_4 are empty.

(5) <u>Wee</u> Willie <u>Winkle rúns</u> through the <u>town</u>.
   S_1 w S_2 w S_3 w S_4

Here all S-positions are filled by stressed syllables. The w-position between S_1 and S_2 is occupied by a single metrical syllable consisting of two vowels separated by a sonorant consonant <u>1</u> (<u>Willie</u>). This syllable is neutralized by the stressed syllable in S_2 (<u>Wink</u>) as described by the last alternative of Rule 2. The w-position between S_3 and S_4 is realized by two unstressed syllables.

<u>The Nursery Rhyme stanza</u> consists of four lines, with paired rhyme (aabb), as in the example below:

(6) 1. <u>Ride</u> a cock-<u>horse</u> to <u>Bánbury Cross</u>
    S_1 w S_2 w S_3 w S_4

    2. To <u>sée</u> a fine <u>lady</u> up<u>on</u> a white <u>horse</u>
    w S_1 w S_2 w S_3 w S_4

    3. <u>Rings</u> on her <u>fíngers</u> and <u>bélls</u> on her <u>toes</u>
    S_1 w S_2 w S_3 w S_4

    4. <u>She</u> shall have <u>músic</u> wher<u>év</u>er she <u>goes</u>.
    S_1 w S_2 w S_3 w S_4

All obligatory S and w positions are correctly realized in this Nursery Rhyme. Fourteen of the sixteen S-positions in the stanza are realized by stressed syllables while two are filled by unstressed syllables (<u>on</u> in line 2 and the pronoun <u>she</u> in line 4). There are three cases where a "neutralized" stressed syllable occu-

pies a weak position: cock-<u>horse</u>, fine <u>la</u>dy, and white <u>horse</u>. In each case it is
           w   S   w   S   w   S

the presence of a stressed syllable to its right which permits a stressed syllable
to occupy a weak position. [9]

The Halle-Keyser theory, by distinguishing between the 'deep' structure of a
meter, identified with an abstract metrical pattern, and a 'superficial' structure,
resulting from the application of a series of realization rules, permits us to differentiate in a precise way between metrical and unmetrical lines. While (4)
above is a metrical Nursery Rhyme line, (7) is unmetrical:

(7) <u>Hum</u>pty is a very nice <u>dump</u>ty when he <u>síts</u> on a <u>wall</u>.
    S_1 w S_2 w S_3 w S_4

In this line, the w-position between S_1 and S_2 is incorrectly filled. For one
thing, it contains too many syllables: no more than three are allowed. For another, it contains two stressed syllables, whereas the last alternative of Rule 2
allows but one "neutralized" stressed syllable in a weak position.

Line (8) below is also unmetrical, but for a different reason:

(8) <u>Once</u> up<u>on</u> a <u>time</u>
    S_1 w S_2 w S_3

Here there are simply not enough syllables to complete the line. [10]

There is an important aspect of the Halle-Keyser theory of meter which we
have not yet considered. And that is, that this theory links poetic meter to the
prosodic rules of the language.

In both iambic pentameter and in Nursery Rhymes, this theory links <u>strong</u>
<u>metrical positions</u> to <u>stressed syllables</u> in English, and <u>weak metrical positions</u>
to <u>unstressed syllables</u>.

Such metrical rules are in conformity with a general principle proposed by
Halle and Keyser that poetic meter does not violate the stress laws of a language.
One cannot shift word stress around for the sake of the meter.

This principle implies, for example, that the following scansion of a line from
"Sing a song of sixpence" is unmetrical:

(9) <u>When</u> the <u>píe</u> was <u>opened</u>
    S_1 w S_2 w S_3 S_4

This scansion is already unmetrical because there is no unstressed syllable between S_3 and S_4, but also because it violates the stress laws of English by giving
equal metrical status to the two syllables of <u>opened</u>.

(9) can therefore not be a Nursery Rhyme line. It can only be a half-line:

(9') When the <u>píe</u> was <u>ópened</u>. [11]
     w S_1 w S_2 w

III. THE FRENCH COMPTINE.

We have all learned that in French it is the final syllable of a word, or a group of words, which receives stress. [12]

Yet when French children (or adults) scan a <u>comptine</u>, what one actually hears are not groupings of words with final stress but groupings containing an <u>alternation</u> of stressed and unstressed syllables, in fact, Nursery Rhymes!

Here is an example:

(10) Une poule sur un mur
    Qui picote du pain dur
    Picoti, Picota,
    Lève la queue et puis s'en va. [13]

As we see in the following example, this <u>comptine</u> scans just like "Humpty Dumpty." (I chose "Humpty Dumpty" as an analog to "Une poule sur un mur" because it suggests the interesting—if unanswerable—question, 'Which came first the <u>poule</u> or the egg?').

(11)	(w)	$\underline{S}$	w	$\underline{S}$	(w)	$\underline{S}$	w	$\underline{S}$	(w)
1.		<u>Hump</u>	ty	<u>Dump</u>	ty	<u>sat</u>	on a	<u>wall</u>	
		<u>U</u>	ne	<u>pou</u>	le	<u>sur</u>	un	<u>mur</u>	
2.		<u>Hump</u>	ty	<u>Dump</u>	ty	<u>had</u>	a great	<u>fall</u>,	
		<u>Qui</u>	pi	<u>co</u>	te	<u>du</u>	pain	<u>dur</u>.	
3.		<u>All</u>	the king's <u>hor</u>	ses and	<u>all</u>	the king's	<u>men</u>		
		<u>Pi</u>	co	<u>ti</u>	,	<u>Pi</u>	co	<u>ta</u>,	
4.		<u>Could</u>	n't put	<u>Hump</u>	ty to	<u>geth</u>	er a	<u>gain</u>.	
		<u>Lèv</u>	e la	<u>queue</u>	et	<u>puis</u>	s'en	<u>va</u>.	

The <u>comptine</u> line, like the Nursery Rhyme line, is a segment of discourse consisting of four stressed syllables separated by from one to three unstressed syllables.

Here is a second example:

(12) <u>Pampanipole</u>, un <u>jour</u> du temps pas<u>sé</u>,
    S_1 w S_2 w S_3 w S_4

    Pass<u>ant</u> par la <u>ville</u> ren<u>contre</u> les gens du <u>Roy</u>,
    w S_1 w S_2 w S_3 w S_4

    <u>Beau</u> pigeon <u>d'or</u>, les <u>gens</u> des allumettes,
    S_1 w S_2 w S_3 w S_4

    <u>Beau</u> pigeon <u>d'or</u>, le p'tit cochon de<u>hors</u>! [14]
    S_1 w S_2 w S_3 w S_4

An alternative to scanning the comptine as I have done is to say that each comptine line has two stresses, and not four. One might want to argue that each comptine line contains two "word groupings," each of which has stress on the final syllable, in accord with the phrasal stress rule of French as described by Grévisse.

(13) Une poúle sur un múr
    w   S   w   S

    Qui picóte du pain dúr
    w   S   w   S

    Picotí Picotá
    w   S w   S

    Lève la quéue et puis s'en vá.
    w   S   w   S

Then to explain the fact that in performance the comptine is scanned with four major stressed syllables, as in (11) above, and not with two, as in (13), we might want to say that superimposed upon this two-stress meter is a four-stress rhythm. (There is some serious documentation to support a claim that all children's verse has a four-beat rhythm. [15])

One might also want to say that the French comptine is ambiguous between a two-stress and four-stress line, or that the choice of a two-stress or four-stress line is optional.

However, within the framework of the Halle-Keyser theory of prosody, the decision one makes concerning metrical pattern is not without consequence for the theory of the stress rules of the language itself. Halle and Keyser claim that metrical rules do not violate the stress rules of the language. I should like to strengthen this principle and say that the metrical rules always reflect the stress laws of the language. Meter has a metalinguistic function: it calls attention to the prosodic facts of a language.

It would follow then that if the comptine line has but two strong stresses, one for each "word grouping," then French is correctly described as a language with a single final stress on each word grouping. But if the comptine line has four strong stresses, two in each word grouping, and if the meter reflects the prosodic laws of the language, then it would follow that a word grouping in French has, in addition to a strong final stress, a second "initial" stress. [16]

Adopting the second alternative, I should like to offer the following rules for the French comptine:

Abstract Metrical Pattern: Same as for Nursery Rhyme line.

Realization Rules:

203

1. S-position: Same as for Nursery Rhymes except that the syllable which occupies S_2 and S_4 is the major stressed syllable of a word grouping, while the syllable which occupies S_1 and S_3 is the secondary stressed syllable of a word grouping. [17]

2. w-position: Same as for Nursery Rhymes.

Rules for the stanza: Same as for Nursery Rhymes.

Thus, the Nursery Rhyme and the French comptine have essentially the same meter. The difference between them can be expressed by means of a single Realization Rule. This rule in turn reflects the difference in the manner in which the respective languages assign stress.

In English, phrasal stress is superimposed upon but does not obliterate the inherent stress carried by the words within the phrase. But in French, stress seems to be assigned solely in terms of word groupings. In fact there seems to be no inherent word stress in French, only phrasal stress. The reason an isolated word is accented on the last syllable is then because it constitutes a phrase consisting of a single word.

As an example of the difference between English and French stress, as reflected in children's verse, let us consider the last half-line example (12) above:

(14) le p'tit cochon dehors!

This word grouping, if stressed according to English principles, would have three strong stresses, as in the equivalent grouping below:

(15) the small canoe outside.

Accoringly, in a Nursery Rhyme, it would count for three S-positions:

(16) the small canoe outside.
      w   S   w S   w S

There is no way to fit (15) into the two-stress pattern corresponding to a Nursery Rhyme half-line (w) S w S.

In French however, the equivalent segment (14) is scanned as a half-line, with two strong positions:

(17) le p'tit cochon dehors!
      w S   w   S

While (15) is a word grouping consisting of three words, each with its inherent stress, (14) is a word grouping without word stress, but with two phrasal stresses, a major stress on the final syllable and a secondary stress on the first stressable syllable.

IV. CONCLUSION.

The Halle-Keyser theory offers a formal apparatus which permits us not only to describe the meter of Nursery Rhymes and that of French <u>comptines</u> but also to compare the two and thus to discover that the two forms have the same 'deep' meter. Both are based on the Abstract Metrical Pattern:

$$V \longrightarrow (w) \ S \ w \ S \ (w) \ S \ w \ S \ (w).$$

In addition, the Realization Rules for both forms are the same, the only difference being that the strong position in a Nursery Rhyme corresponds to a syllable receiving <u>word stress</u> while the strong position in a French <u>comptine</u> corresponds to a syllable receiving major or secondary <u>phrasal stress</u>.

Further study will show whether it is the case that <u>all</u> children's meters (or many children's meters) have the same underlying pattern, their only difference lying, as for the Nursery Rhyme and the <u>comptine,</u> in the realization rules, which in turn reflect differences in the prosodic laws of the languages involved.

There is of course no reason to limit the search for metrical generalizations to children's verse. There are, for example, obvious similarities between the rules for iambic pentameter and those of children's verse. No doubt a general theory of meter, or at least of accentual meter, is now available, awaiting only more scholarly work. Such work will owe a great debt to Halle and Keyser (and to their forerunners, such Russian formalists as for example V. Bryussov) for developing a theory of meter which, in distinguishing between underlying abstract pattern and superficial realizations, enables us to describe and compare metrical forms in a general and interesting way.

---

1 Halle and Keyser have published a number of articles explaining their theory of prosody. The most important of these are probably the first article, "Chaucer and the Study of Prosody" <u>College English,</u> 28 (1966), 187-219, and the latest, "A Theory of Meter," Chapter III of <u>English Stress</u> (New York: Harper & Row, 1971). Also see Halle, "On Meter and Prosody," <u>Progress in Linguistics,</u> ed. Manfred Bierwisch and Karl Erich Heidolph (The Hague: Mouton, 1970).
The theory is discussed, criticized, and defended in volumes 31 (1970) and 33 (1971) of <u>College English</u> (articles by Magnuson and Ryder, Beaver, Halle and Keyser, etc.).

I am grateful to Professor William Robert McMunn for his critical reading of this article and for suggesting a number of improvements in form and substance.

2 This pattern is a slightly simplified version of the one given in <u>English Stress,</u> p. 169.

3 I have modified the definition of stress maximum given in <u>English Stress,</u> p. 169. My reasons for so doing are discussed in "Une théorie du pentamètre iambique" (unpublished manuscript).

For Halle and Keyser a "fully-stressed" syllable is the tonic syllable of a major category word: Noun, Verb, Adjective, Adverb, or Exclamation, but not, for example, the tonic syllable of a Pronoun like we or us, or of a Preposition like after or about.

4 Though unmetrical, such lines exist, of course, in poetic practice. In Keats, for example, we find,

    (1) How many bards gild the lapses of time.
       w   S w S   w   S w S   w S

    (2) And other spirits there are standing apart
       w   S w S   w   S   w   S w S

in Donne,

    (3) For those whom thou thinkst thou dost overthrow
       w   S   w   S   w   S   w   S w S

in Milton,

    (4) Fallen Cherub, to be weak is miserable.
       w   S w   S   w   S   w S w S w

5 For the distinction between empirical adequacy and explanatory adequacy, see Noam Chomsky, Aspects of the Theory of Syntax, M. I. T. Press, 1965, pp. 26–27.

6 "Une théorie du pentamètre iambique."

7 For detailed rules, with justification and illustration, see my "The Meter of Nursery Rhymes" to appear in Poetics (The Hague: Mouton).

8 The pause corresponds generally to a syntactic constituent which is separated from what follows in writing by a comma or period, and in speech by a pause.

9 A second type of Nursery Rhyme exists, which I am not dealing with here, consisting of an alternation within the stanza of four-stress and three-stress lines. An example:

    (5) Little Miss Muffet sat on a tuffet
       S_1 w S_2 w S_3 w S_4

    Eating her curds and whey.
    S_1 w S_2 w S_3

    Along came a spider and sat down beside her
    w S_1 w S_2 w S_3 w S_4 w

    And frightened Miss Muffet away.
    w S_1 w S_2 w S_3

[10] The construct (8) can only be the second or fourth line in the kind of stanza described in the preceding note, as in the following construct:

(6) A líttle gírl did ríde her horse
    w S$_1$ w S$_2$ w S$_3$ w S$_4$

Once upon a time
S$_1$ w S$_2$ w S$_3$

[11] The Nursery Rhyme line can be defined in terms of two half-lines or hemistiches. I have not included the discussion of this point here in order not to complicate the presentation.

[12] "Accent de mot. Dans les mots français considérés isolément, l'accent d'intensité frappe la dernière syllabe articulée . . . :

Vérité, sentiment, indifférenc(e) . . .

Accent de groupe. Dans la phrase, l'accent d'intensité frappe la dernière syllabe articulée, non pas de chaque mot, mais de chaque groupe de mots unis par le sens et prononcés sans aucun repos de la voix (chaque groupe est un seul mot phonétique, un groupe rythmique):

Prenez votre livre(e).

Comme vous le savez, / je pars demain . . . " —

Maurice Grévisse, Précis de Grammaire Française (Gembloux: Duculot, 1957), p. 11.

[13] Translation: A chicken on a wall
                Who is pecking at some dry bread
                Peckaroo-Peckarah,
                Lifts his tail and off he goes.

For a lovely collection of comptines, complete with variants and geographical sources, see Comptines de langue française (Paris: Seghers, 1961 and 1970).

[14] Translation: Pampanipole, once long ago
                Passing through the city, met the King's men.
                Beautiful gold pigeon, match people,
                Beautiful gold pigeon, out little pig!

[15] See, in particular, Robbins Burling, "The Metrics of Children's Verse; A Cross Linguistic Study," American Anthropologist, 68, pp. 1418-1441; and Constantin Brailoiu, La rythmique enfantine, notions liminaires, Elsevier, 1956.

[16] When emphasized expressively in discourse, this stress is known as the accent d'insistence, as in "C'est détestable," "C'est un spectacle épouvantable" (Grévisse, op. cit., p. 11). The accent d'insistence falls on the same syllable as that which fills an S$_1$ or S$_3$ position in a comptine line. It thus

seems to be the case that a word group in French has two main accents, a primary accent on the last syllable, and a secondary accent on the first stressable syllable. This secondary accent can in turn be emphasized and raised to primary status in at least two situations: (1) in a comptine, where "stressed syllable" includes both primary and secondary stressed syllables, all other syllables in the word group being unstressed; and (2) in discourse, for expressive contrast.

17 While the major stressed syllable of the word grouping is the last articulated syllable of the grouping (this excludes a syllable whose vowel is "e muet"), I am not sure how to qualify the secondary stressed syllable of the grouping. Often this is the initial syllable, as in

(7) Une poule sur un mur,

but it can also be the second syllable, as in

(8) Sinon le loup te mangera

or in example (17) in the text.

However, whatever rule it is necessary to invoke to predict on what syllable the secondary stress in a comptine (S_1 and S_3) will fall is independently necessary to determine where the accent d'insistence will fall in a discourse word grouping.

THE CHILD IN SHAKESPEARE

Letters and Comments to the Editor by Shakespeareans

Boys in Shakespeare

. . . I found myself at the recent meeting of the Shakespeare Association talking about boys in Shakespeare. My presumable subject was Shakespeare's women, but I found I could not discuss the one subject without touching on the other, especially since Shakespeare's women were boys after all; and children, especially male children, still were for him as in the Hellenistic world, available sexual subjects. Thinking of the offstage boy who causes all the trouble in A Midsummer Night's Dream together with Hermione, brought to my mind Blake's little poem:

It was the Greek's love of war
Turned Love into a boy,
And woman into a statue of stone
And away flew every joy.

—Leslie A. Fiedler
(Author of The Stranger in Shakespeare)

In Praise of Herod

The children in Shakespeare's plays are a rum lot: but they would not have seemed so strange in the sixteenth century when boys were dressed, and treated, as little adults. The young princes in Richard III, emblems of innocence, seem in their horrible pertness almost to deserve the fate in store for them. The laments of Constance, prolonged as they are, are thought to have been inspired by the early death of the poet's only son; but Arthur indulges in frigid conceits. Macduff's son is redeemed by his bravery. The boy Marcius is a savage. Perhaps the only child a modern parent would not be ashamed to own is Mamillius, though the schoolboy in The Merry Wives of Windsor is natural and lively. Apart from him the children are introduced, as Dickens introduces most of his, so that they can be liquidated as innocent victims. One suspects that they were played more naturally by the sons of Shakespeare's fellows than by the well-drilled child-actors of today who make one sympathize with King Herod.

—Kenneth Muir
(Editor of Shakespeare Survey)

Regarding Shakespeare's use and depiction of children: to my mind what is interesting is the number of them that appear in the plays in comparison with other Elizabethan dramas. I mean authentic young children too, not adolescents like Juliet, Perdita, Marina and Miranda, or Guiderius and Arviragus, those young adults. Casual reflection brings to mind the following characters: The royal princes in Richard III, Lady Macduff's children (I exclude Fleance, his age being unclear), little Caius Marcius in <u>Coriolanus</u>, young Mamillius in <u>The Winter's Tale</u>, and his baby sister, and possibly Lucius in <u>Julius Caesar</u>. In addition, there are references to Cleopatra's children by Antony and by Julius Caesar, and there is the little "changeling boy" in <u>Midsummer Night's Dream</u>.

The number here accounted for would, I hope, scarcely make for a catalog of the blessed; but it is not completely negligible either. The <u>dramatic</u> role of children in Shakespeare may not be a commanding one; but their <u>symbolic</u> role is in some cases of striking importance. Witness the murder of the princes in <u>Richard III</u>, or the destruction of Lady Macduff and her children. Note further the "banishment" of Perdita and the death of Mamillius. In each of these instances, violence done to youthful innocence is an indicator of the deepest perversion of the hero's human sensibility, and the signal of "Nature" and conscience to turn against him, manifest the power of the universe, and shift the tide of events—for worse, as in the two former illustrations, and, miraculously, for the better in the last.

In Shakespeare, children mean human possibility, and in this sense their role is often symbolically crucial.

—Matthew N. Proser
(Author, <u>The Heroic Image in Five Shakespearean Tragedies</u>)

Shakespeare's Children

Shakespeare's children are far too articulate for their own good. Though we can accept a stage convention of blank verse and heightened prose from adults, and children in real life use language very much as their parents do, we still seem to feel that children must proclaim their innocence by some well-rehearsed lisping and stumbling.

Shakespeare's children (every one male) are all within the convention of competence in speech, yet they are all different. Young Macduff, a calm, clever child, is as persistent as a mosquito in questioning his mother and traps her delightedly with his logic. Little York (<u>Richard III</u>) is highly-strung, over-excited by company, showing off disastrously. Young Marcius Coriolanus is the spoiled, aggressive center of a female household. Mamillius in <u>The Winter's Tale</u>, frail and affectionate, loves to scare his mother with ghost stories; his few lines are more moving than all the calculated pathos of Arthur in <u>King John</u>. <u>Titus Andronicus</u>, Shakespeare's bloodiest play, has an effective part for Lucius' son, terrified of the mutilated Lavinia, and overwhelmed by grief for his grandfather Titus; and in the oddest, most compelling image of all, we see the villain Aaron clinging fiercely to his black bastard son, desperately bartering confession for his life.

No Shakespeare child, with the possible exception of Arthur, is cute or sweet or intended to make us nostalgic of past innocence; the emotions evoked by each in those around him are far more basic and authentic. Played gravely and straight, as unfinished human beings rather than angels or puppies, these children come off well. What other major playwright, of Shakespeare's century or another, has chosen to represent children and parental emotion on stage so frequently?

—Barbara Rosen
(Co-editor, Signet edition of <u>Julius Caesar</u>)

Shakespeare portrayed his child characters as little adults because he, like many of his contemporaries, recognized that they <u>are</u> little adults.

—Francelia Butler
(Author, <u>The Strange Critical Fortunes of Shakespleare's Timon of Athens</u>)

I first recall those striking victims of violence or sudden death—the Princes in <u>Richard III</u>, young Macduff, and Mamillius in <u>The Winter's Tale</u>. And somehow Coriolanus' son Marcius seems to belong with these other boys, although he survives and is himself a violent attacker who "did so set his teeth and tear" the "gilded butterfly." The implied attitude of the dramatist tends to overshadow the extreme pathos of his mimetic representation of children. I am disturbed to discover that one of Leslie Fiedler's favorite questions, "Why did Shakespeare kill Cordelia?"—which has always struck me as inappropriate to <u>King Lear</u>—echoes more tellingly if we think of these children as a group or a class.

But to look so directly at Shakespeare's treatment of young boys is to reduce their creator to that persona of Ogden Nash who, you recall, finished his "To a Small Boy Standing On My Shoes While I Am Wearing Them" with the lines:

Or sonny boy I'll wring your neck
and a happier man today I'd be
If someone had wrung it
ahead of me.

Coriolanus' impassioned anger at being called "Boy!" and Cleopatra's disparaging allusion to the squeaking child-actor "boy[ing] my greatness i' the posture of a whore" might seem to reinforce such a cynical attitude. But I doubt that these examples indicate any deep-seated psychological resentment or obsession. In each case the characterization or personality of the child is sacrificed to the role in the melodramatic narrative or thematic action. While it always seems sensible to resist and test any assertion that Shakespeare's overall design justifies incidental superficiality, we can see in my cluster of children from his late plays that he never makes an effort to present a rich, complex, or full portrait. Mamillius especially seems invented only to die in such a striking way. Far more than his line to his highly jealous father, "I am like you, they say" (I. ii. 208), we remember him for the unrealistic, hyperbolic description in the repartee of the opening scene: "It is a gentleman of the greatest promise that ever came into

211

my note . . . it is a gallant child; one that makes old hearts fresh. They that
went on crutches ere he was born desire yet their life to see him a man." Whatever Shakespeare was up to here, he did not attempt a mimetic portrait. We
never doubt his compassion for his characters when this is what he wants to
express.

—Herbert Weil
(Editor of <u>Discussion of Shakespeare's Romantic Comedy</u>)

Review Articles

TERTIARY WORLDS

Jabberwocky: The Journal of the Lewis Carroll Society. Published four times yearly by the Society. Subscription rate (as of winter 1972) $6.00 per year. All correspondence to: The Secretary, The Lewis Carroll Society, Room 16, South Block, The County Hall, London, S.E. 1. 7PB.

The Baum Bugle. Published three times yearly by the International Wizard of Oz Club, Inc. Subscription, including Club membership, $2.50 per year. All correspondence to: Fred M. Meyer, 220 North Eleventh Street, Escanaba, Michigan.

"The natural world has its laws, and no man must interfere with them in the way of presentment any more than in the way of use; but they themselves may suggest laws of other kinds, and man may, if he pleases, invent a little world of his own, with its own laws . . . " Thus George MacDonald in the course of an essay on "The Fantastic Imagination." Clearly Professor Tolkien had this essay in mind when he came in 1938 (in "On Fairy-Stories") to make his own discrimination between Primary and Secondary Worlds.

The Primary World is the one we can't help inhabiting—the given, objective world, study of scientist and historian, that exists whether we do or will or not. The Secondary World is that ideal one willed or imagined or (anyhow) fabricated by what Tolkien calls—with a deferential bow to God—the "sub-creator," i.e. the poet or storyteller. His master MacDonald felt that man "pleases" to make a little world because "there is that in him which delights in calling up new forms —which is the nearest, perhaps, he can come to creation." Tolkien more plaintively stresses the agency of sorrow and longing in such a making; he views the Secondary World as a sort of counterpointing of the Primary in terms of compensation or consolation, rectification or attempted escape. For both men the invented world must be predicated upon an harmonious system of laws. When these laws are forgotten or flouted credibility gapes and the structure collapses. "Suppose," says MacDonald, "the gracious creatures of some childlike region of Fairyland talking either cockney or Gascon!" Enough said perhaps.

As one just returned from browsing through recent issues of Jabberwocky and The Baum Bugle I can offer a corollary: the sign of a thriving Secondary World lies in its ability to breed and maintain a Tertiary. A Tertiary World is an enclave or more or less secret society existing in the heart of the Primary World and composed of real Primates who have, in Frost's phrase, "taken an immortal wound" from a specific Secondary World. Your true Tertiate is loyalist to, scholar and curator and professor of, the Secondary World that, like a bolt from the blue, hit him; he seeks out and writes for his fellows. Unlike Don Quixote the Tertiate is under no illusions as to the Primariness of the object of his cult. His passion is purely platonic and he cannot be doublecrossed by reality. Sharp-

eyed, he is a strict constructionist and is not at all amused at what he conceives
to be liberties taken with the Secondary World of his calling. Traditionally Tertiates have been professional people (professors, colonels, bishops and the like)
though this is less certain today. Usually they are over thirty and looking forward to retirement. They keep a certain distance and their humor is likely to
strike an outsider as "donnish." They publish journals.

Jabberwocky is the organ of British Tertiates devoted to the Secondary Worlds
(chiefly Wonder- and Looking-Glass Lands—I think I noted a coolness about the
phantasmagoria of the Sylvie and Bruno stories) of Lewis Carroll. It is small
and purple, with a reproduction of Tenniel's White Knight on the cover. It offers
reviews of theatricals based on the canon (one seated an audience of 200 "placed
on a turntable which was turned by hand with the assistance of Boy Scouts and
their fathers"), of books about either Carroll or his Worlds (the Norton Alice
comes off well, Robert Phillips' Aspects of Alice gets a rather frigid Tertiate
stare), much bibliographical and bibliophile material, manic lists of things like
Alice imitations and parodies from special collections (Malice in Blunderland,
Alice in the Delighted States, Alice in Acidland, Rose in Squanderland, etc.), a
seductive crossword puzzle (17: 6 letters across: "Did the Walrus and the Carpenter spit them out or were they cultured?"; answer: "Pearls"), and a pro-
foundly Tertiate Letters to the Editor feature about matters like the shape and
number of bends in the mouse's "tale" ("moves from the bizarrely spiky to the
horridly socklike"). In all, highly recommended to lonely American Tertiates
and all Tertiate-watchers (Quadlings).

The Baum Bugle is the established journal dedicated to the life and works of
L. Frank Baum and his successors (Ruth Plumly Thompson and Rachel R. Cos-
grove); the Secondary World in view of course is Oz, with side-glances at other
Baumy lands such as Oz and wherever the Boy Fortune Hunters hung their hats.
The Bugle has been around long enough to have published two anthologies, viz.
The Best of the Baum Bugle: 1957-1961 and The Best of the Baum Bugle: 1961-
1962 ("reprints everything except a few obsolete announcements") and is also behind the International Wizard of Oz Club's Maps of Oz and the Countries Surrounding which Tertiates will find sine qua non. The journal is lavishly illustrated (cover in color) with old Oz drawings. Its features range from a column called "Oz in the News" ("Ray Bolger a Light Step in Front of Father Time"), a
series on the little-known other writings of Baum, much Baum correspondence
with publishers giving insight into the gestation of, say, The Patchwork Girl of
Oz, book reviews on related matters, and a hard-hitting discussion of the virtues
and limitations of Baum's brand of sub-creativity which blew up a storm of impassioned Tertiate riposte. Basic reading for Baumite Tertiates.

One final word to Quadlings. Tertiate organs like Jabberwocky and The Bugle
can be of considerable interest to the non-addicted and one could do far worse
than take out a trial subscription to one or the other. One feels at first a little
like Stella Dallas standing in the rain and looking through the window at Lolly's
wedding—which is to say, a bit wistful. But beyond this there is something about

the scrupulous devotion of Tertiates which is heartening . . . examples of joy
in service the likes of which this Primary World does not often afford.

—Joseph Cary

P.S. Late word from The Baum Bugle is that both the International Wizard of Oz
Club and The Baum Bugle were founded in 1957 by a thirteen-year-old boy, Justin
B. Schiller. The Baum Bugle has been edited by adults since 1961, Justin having
to resign because of school pressures; David Greene has been editor since 1968.
Each issue contains a little-known Baum story and a bibliography of a Baum book.

RECENT BOOKS ABOUT BLACK AMERICA,
AFRICA, AND THE CARRIBEAN

Izzard by Lonzo Anderson. Illustrated by Adrienne Adams. 35 pp. (Charles
Scribner's Sons. $5.95).
Josephine's 'magination. Written and illustrated by Arnold Dobrin. 48 pp.
(Four Winds Press. $5.95).
Bisha of Burundi by Mary Louise Clifford. Illustrated by Trevor Stubley. 140
pp. (Thomas Y. Crowell Co. $4.50).
Sunrise Tomorrow by Naomi Mitchison. 120 pp. (Farrar, Straus and Giroux.
$4.50).
Mukasa by John Nagenda. Illustrated by Charles Lilly. 120 pp. (Macmillan.
$4.95).
Poems from Africa. Selected by Samuel Allen. Illustrated by Romare Bearden.
205 pp. (Thomas Y. Crowell Co. $4.50).
Barney Ford, Black Baron by Marian Talmadge and Iris Gilmore. 237 pp.
(Dodd, Mead and Co. $4.50).
Guests in the Promised Land by Kristin Hunter. 133 pp. (Charles Scribner's
Sons. $4.95).
Time-Ago Lost: More Tales of Jahdu by Virginia Hamilton. Illustrated by Ray
Prother. 85 pp. (Macmillan Publishing Co. $4.95).

Most children's books are not very good books for essentially two reasons:
(1) they too often sentimentalize the facts of life; (2) (a not wholly separate res-
son) they are often condescending toward their intended audience. Having the
former fault, they make the truly ugly beautiful, challenging not the imagination
so much as the reader's sense of reality. Having the latter fault, they oversimp-
lify to such an extent as to insult the intelligence. They are commonplace in conception and execution and they give the impression that their authors neither know
nor respect the intelligence and imaginative capacities of children.

Two books which seem to me to fail for the reasons suggested above are
Lonzo Anderson's Izzard and Arnold Dobrin's Josephine's 'magination, whose
scenes are respectively the Virgin Islands and Haiti. Izzard tells a very unreal
tale about a lizard, unreal, because it attributes human characteristics to an inhuman creature in a context so realistic otherwise as to call into question the

imaginative reality of the tale. That is to say that there is no distinction between the real and the imagined in the lizard's mind, the chief human character's mind, the minds of the other characters in the story, nor the author's mind. The reader is asked to grant too much. He is asked to believe that the apparently sane people around the chief character, Jamie, in actuality participate in Jamie's fantasy. The reader is intended to participate too, but nothing, other than his goodwill, encourages him to suspend disbelief. The characters are black with the exception of the green lizard—but that fact is not relevant to the tale.

Josephine's 'magination is a brightly illustrated book whose author reflects in his tale something of his sense of its exotic setting. It is clearly a book written from a perspective outside of the events and scenes it describes. It colors Haitian peasant life in such a way as to make it charming and beautiful. Some facts are there—the implication of hardship in peasant life, the poverty and difficulty of general living conditions—yet the whole is so treated as to distort. I would be most unhappy if any child's sense of the life of peasants in Haiti were inferred from this book or books like it. The intention of the book is to indicate the commonality of childhood experience, but the implication that happiness stems from the exercise of the imagination despite socio-economic conditions seems at best a distortion.

Three novels about Africa, Bisha of Birundi by Mary Louise Clifford, Sunrise Tomorrow by Naomi Mitchison, and Mukasa by John Nagenda all deal essentially with the same problem, the conflict between traditional and more modern values. The focus in each of these novels is on the younger generation and describes their conflict, especially with parents and grandparents, about tradition and modernity. In each case the younger characters decide that though modern ways are most desirable, one's preference must be tempered by reverence for the past. These novels are interesting to a reader who knows little or nothing about Africa. Once one has read one, however, he has the essentials of many, many others which are within the narrow bonds of this very common theme superficially treated.

Poems from Africa, edited by Samuel Allen, is a different case altogether. It is a broad collection containing works of the best known African poets along with some lesser known ones. The collection is for young readers, but neither its introduction nor the poems themselves suggest condescension on the editor's part. The anthology would have limitations as an anthology for general readers because it has so few poems by each of its poets. But as a general introduction to African poetry it works well.

Three recent books by or about black Americans for younger readers are Barney Ford, Black Baron by Marian Talmadge and Iris Gilmore, Guests in the Promised Land by Kristin Hunter, and Time-Ago Lost: More Tales of Jahdu by Virginia Hamilton. Barney Ford is among those biographies whose subjects are intended to serve as examples to young people of what is possible in life. There may be a bit of condescension involved insofar as Ford is called a "black" baron. One wonders whether a white whose bank account at his death totaled fourteen

thousand dollars and who died shovelling snow from a walk would have been referred to as a "baron." It seems to say that a "black baron" may be a man of
less achievement than a "white baron." Underneath the surface glitter it seems
to me that Mr. Ford led a very sad life, a sadness glossed over by the authors'
desire to write an uplift book. Mr. Ford may be in the eyes of the authors a successful man—and he certainly made significant accomplishments—but I hope my
own children don't grow up so entirely committed to monetary success. I would
say the authors' commitment to individualism and its possibilities blinds them to
the limitations of success as so defined.

Guests in the Promised Land is a book of short stories which everyone should
read who feels he has some sense of what blackness is about. Kristin Hunter is
one of the few writers who is able to see it in terms of its character, who sees
distinctions that many, in their haste to simplify, do not see. She has the understanding to differentiate among black people, to see them in their complexity, and
to recognize the effects on black life and character of socio-economic influences.
Any expert on soul should read in this book Ms. Hunter's "Two's Enough of a
Crowd."

Time-Ago Lost is one of those truly fantastic books whose quality is attested
to by its depth and simplicity. Virginia Hamilton is a myth maker, the Jahdu
Tales seeming akin to ancient mythology about basic elements of nature. They
are simple, yet they deal with matters ultimately philosophical and theological.
Trouble, the concept, is personified as a giant who is benign as long as darkness
prevails, for without light he has no memory and no sense of time, since time,
the book says, depends upon light. Jahdu encounters him while running to the
east to be reborn and to recover his magic. The language alone of these tales is
remarkable for its suggestion of black speech, a suggestion only faintly reminiscent of black speech and at the same time possessing enough disjointedness to
indicate a certain remove from ordinary reality.

There is far more to be said about this book than space permits but the significant thing in this context is the great possibilities it suggests for children's
literature. Time-Ago Lost is a great book—truly above the usual run of such
literature, and suffering neither from sentimentality nor condescension.

—Donald B. Gibson

THE FEMINIST IN FAIRY TALES:
TWO BOOKS FROM THE JUNG INSTITUTE, ZURICH

An Introduction to the Interpretation of Fairy Tales (1970; $3.50) and Problems
of the Feminine in Fairy Tales (1972; $6.00) by Marie Louise von Franz.
(Spring Publications, Suite 306, 130 East 39th Street, New York, N.Y. 10016)

The earlier of these two books, Interpretation of Fairy Tales, is an excellent
short exposition of the Jungian view of fairy tales and myths. Dr. von Franz lu-

cidly explains why fairy tales are a source of attraction for Jungian analysts. Jung considered myths, as products of particular cultures, to have national character. He believed that a myth expresses the cultural collective consciousness of the nation in which it originated, but that fairy tales mirror the basic structure of the human psyche, and thus transcend racial and cultural differences. Jung held that in fairy tales one can best study the comparative anatomy of the psyche, because the tales contain less specific cultural conscious material than is found in myths. Dr. von Franz explains the Jungian method of psychological interpretation of tales, and applies it to several stories.

Her more recent book, The Problems of the Feminine in Fairy Tales, analyzes the situation of women in fairy tales in order to explore the Jungian point of view further. While the book contains a good deal of interesting cross-cultural material, and illuminating discussions of certain images and symbols, the Jungian premise underlies the entire study, and the fairy tales are analyzed rather to show how they reflect the Jungian view than to see what else they might yield. Psychological presuppositions are applied to the tales. This will be interesting to someone who wishes to explore Jung's theories, and to the reader who seeks discussion of some of the mysteries we find in the tales. Feminists, however, will have difficulty with Dr. von Franz's approach. She believes that the minds of men and women work differently, and that they have distinct personality principles, not only as individuals but also collectively, by sex.

She makes certain categorical statements about women: they love to be unclear, they vegetate more easily than men, they have more of a herd instinct, and are more interested in love and personal relationships. She notices that the heroines in fairy tales are generally more passive than the heroes, but assumes that this reflects the essential nature of feminine personality. After analyzing an early version of Cinderella, in which the heroine must sort out mildewed corn from good seed, Dr. von Franz remarks that "the Cinderella task would be the task of the woman": if she can penetrate her hidden nature and there separate bad from good, "she does something which corresponds to the hero's deeds of slaying the dragon, or building the new town, or freeing the people from terror" (p. 162). In referring to stories in which curious women are punished, she observes that "curious inquisitiveness, as far as I have seen, is not so often punished in myths about heroes, though it often attracts destruction onto the heroine" (p. 168). A feminist would ask whether the tale was not intended to support a patriarchal cultural view that rebukes women for being curious.

Most feminists would deny Dr. von Franz's whole set of assumptions, although they would share the Jungian interest in the tales. Feminists do not recognize themselves in fairy tales, and do not believe that they depict women accurately. Rather, they believe that the tales serve to influence children and women, and to acculturate them to accept an externally imposed view of what is innately or properly feminine. What is lacking in Dr. von Franz's work is any consideration of the socializing effect that the tales have had upon readers.

—Marcia R. Lieberman

THE SPRING LIST *

Tinker and the Medicine Man by Bernard Wolf. (Random House, $4.95). Illustrated.

The "Snoopy Come Home" Movie Book by Charles Schulz (Holt, Rinehart, & Winston, $6.95). Illustrated.

Firegirl by Gibson Rich. (Old Westbury, New York: Feminist Press, $1.95). Illustrated.

Nothing But a Dog by Bobbi Kutz. (Old Westbury, New York: Feminist Press, $1.50). Illustrated.

Where Do Babies Come From: A Book for Children and Their Parents by Margaret Sheffield (New York: Alfred A. Knopf, $3.95). Illustrated.

Twist, Wiggle, and Squirm: A Book About Earthworms by Laurence Pringle. (Thomas Y. Crowell, $3.75). Illustrated.

If what a culture really cares about is what it tries to pass on to its children, then our culture is even more shallow and mindless than many have feared.

At least this seems true if this Spring's crop of new children's books is anything to go by. There are scads of sappy biographies, writ clean, presumably to protect their readers from human excess, weakness, misery and depth. And phony nostalgias about that grand old Pennsylvania Dutch farm we all used to know full of cheerful, simple chubby folk, overeating, and bland, thigh-slapping good humor. And slick books of heroic proportions about clean-living sports heroes we all of course worship. What we really care about, apparently, is today's gladiators, yesterday's lies, and colorless, plastic living.

There are exceptions, though. Tinker and the Medicine Man, by Bernard Wolf, is a notable one. Not only does it not condescend about the miseries and nobility of the lives of a Navajo family, but it is about the passing on of meaningful tradition—in this case the secrets of a Peyote religion medicine man—to a younger generation taken seriously enough to be entrusted with it. Wolf's text is meaningful and simple as well as direct; his story, a true one of a six-year old boy's initiation into the Peyote rituals of his culture, is rich in detail and interest; his photographs, fully half the space of the book, are stark and magnificent as the wild Arizona landscape and people they record.

Another good sort of exception is a new Peanuts book by Charles Schulz, The "Snoopy Come Home" Movie Book. And hereby hangs a tale: my children saw my review copy of the book before they saw the movie it is from. After the movie my four-year old offered this unsolicited opinion: "The book was better." And it was. Without even venturing into the possibilities this suggests—among them the cliché that this is a post-literary generation—I can't help feeling that

* Mr. Miner, Managing Editor of Children's Literature, also reviews children's books for The Hartford Courant, where this review appeared Sunday, June 10, 1973.

the "Movie Book" may herald a new trend. Instead of the book-to-movie progression of the past decades, T V, ironically enough, may have made the moving picture commonplace for today's children and the moving word intriguingly new. Schultz's book is graced with the laconic humor and pointed jabs of pure feeling that already have made Peanuts a staple for adults of all ages. The book also offers some startling double-page illustrations that share, in their unconventional focus and perspective, some of the unnerving aptness of perception about small people's relationship to the full-size world that marks the works of all great writers of children's literature.

From moving pictures to moving words to Movement pictures and Movement words. Two books for children from the Feminist Press demand mention not because they are great literature—they are not—or even just because they are socially responsible—which they are. Firegirl by Gibson Rich and Nothing But a Dog by Bobbi Katz are important because of what they demonstrate about the whole problem of books for children.

While most children's books have been social propaganda of one kind or another, they have to almost precisely the same extent been undistinguished in quality. These two books from the Feminist Press suffer the same failing. Laudably lofty in consciousness, scrupulous in detail (there is a dignified representative of almost every major minority in Firegirl, for example), and commendable in intent, they just fail to prove what they assert. Yes, we agree a girl ought to be able to be a fireperson (fireman, in sexist parlance), and yes, we agree, girls as well as boys ought to be able to have a dog of their own instead of the traditional cat, but neither book is ornery, complex, contradictory or even whimsical enough to offer any reader the experience of that truth. In society one can insist on the logic of quotas and tokens as a means to an end, but in literature you have to make that logic live.

Speaking of living logic, one other major type of good exception to the Spring crop of children's books is the book of facts. Not batting averages or believe-it-or-nots, but commonly accepted facts about things commonly kept from children. Two of the most taboo facts in children's lives, worms and sex, are frankly faced in two interesting new books for children and their fastidious parents. Twist, Wiggle, and Squirm, A Book About Earthworms by Laurence Pringle, is the naked, earthy truth about those fascinating bilateral invertebrates we were never supposed to eat or take to Sunday school. Full of detailed and aptly dynamic illustrations of everything from worm love (they lie side by side and exchange rings—just like people) and worm death (at the hands—or, rather, mouths—of birds, toads, moles, shrews, skunks, and owls), the book also explains why after rain there are worms lying all over the place (their holes fill up and they have to surface) and the numbers of worms in your average backyard (50,000).

As if the life cycle of worms weren't already shocking enough, Alfred A. Knopf has dared to bring out a book about the life cycle of the people who read books about worms to their children. Where do Babies Come From, A Book for Children and Their Parents by Margaret Sheffield, is adapted from the award-winning B.B.C. program of the same name and deserves some awards of its own. Answering the basic question of man—"Where do I come from?"—in terms delicate enough for the adults who will hopefully have the sense to read it to their children and direct enough for the curious minds of the young, the book offers beautifully illustrated explanations of that basic question with relaxed candor and warmth.

If the overall offering of children's books is vapid and misleading, one thing that has improved over the last few years is the variety of good exceptions to the rule. Whereas before the twentieth century the best offerings were usually of a healthy subversive nature (like Alice in Wonderland or Lear's limericks), now there are other options—from worms to Peyote this Spring, for example.

—Robert G. Miner, Jr.

A NOTE ON THREE CONTEMPORARY SOVIET CHILDREN'S STORIES

Unlike much Soviet children's literature in former years, several recent Soviet stories for children contain no economic propaganda. Examples are "He is alive and glows"[1] by Viktor Dragunskij, "Monster mushroom"[2] by Kazimira Poljakova, and "Girl on the ball,"[3] also by Viktor Dragunskij.

"He is alive and glows" describes one episode in the life of a small boy. He sits near the sandbox waiting for his mother to take him home after work. The story moves from his feelings of self pity to the unfolding of how this one little boy, alone in the falling darkness, finds one way to fill up the hungry time of waiting for the comforts of home, family and food.

He feels miserable and neglected: " . . . if I knew my mommy wanted to eat and was waiting for me somewhere at the edge of the world, I would run to her immediately and wouldn't be late and wouldn't make her sit by a sandbox and be bored."[4] He is joined by another child who tries to borrow his new dump truck. The other child doesn't count as company or comfort. He is barely tolerated; his questions are curtly answered. Our miserable boy has thoughts only of his mother's arrival. He sits and stares at the gate. The other child makes several offers of trades for the dump truck and finally offers his firefly. The trade is made and the other child leaves. The firefly is alive and glows, and the little boy is so charmed by the wonder of it that he forgets to watch the gate for his mother.

A bunny hears about "Monster mushroom" as he hops by a scout leader reading to children at a young pioneer camp. He is so excited by the news that he hops on before hearing the rest of the story. He tells his neighbors, the skeptical squirrels, about it. He tells them that in the tundra there are monster mushtooms bigger than birch or willow trees. They don't believe it, so he decides to go there and bring back a sample.

He makes a basket three times as big as himself. With the help of the Old Man of the Woods he is transported to and from the tundra just by wishing it.

There he discovers that mushrooms are bigger than birch and willow trees, but only because the trees are stunted by the severity of the weather. He first experiences a feeling of disappointment. Then he is cheered by the thought that he has learned something new. He brings back samples to show those sassy squirrels that mushrooms do indeed grow bigger than birch or willow trees in the tundra.

The fantastic and the magical interact with the real world in the happy way of pure fantasy. The magic bunny finds the life of the children at the pioneer camp intriguing and informative, but what could a magic bunny learn from mere mortals? The Old Man of the Woods has magic gifts to bestow and words of wisdom for all seekers. One would think that he himself would be much more interesting than information concerning the size of birch trees in the tundra: "The Old Man of the Woods appeared in a green caftan made from furry moss and wearing acorn slippers. His beard came down to the very ground."[5] However, the real problem of the moment is to ascertain certain perhaps useful facts concerning arctic vegetation. But the bunny finds a talking birch tree up in the tundra, no less! This story can be considered didactic only in the most extended sense of the term. It is a chase after reality for the sheer fun of it.

"The girl on a ball" is a simple story, beautifully told. Its theme is not simple or childish, however, or even limited to childhood. It is about one of the few very moving experiences of life. In every life there are the inevitable tragedies of death and loss as well as the rare emotional glories which are usually called love but which might more appropriately be called enthusiasms in the old religious sense. The child-narrator relates his enthusiasm for the girl on the ball with its attendant agony and predictable frustration. The child lives and suffers, but we nevertheless would not deny him his enthusiasm.

The narrator is a boy almost eight years old. The story is told entirely from his point of view. He begins by telling how he really didn't understand what a circus was all about his first time at the circus when he was six years old. Then he watched the orchestra instead of the performers. He noted how the conductor waved his baton and how the musicians ignored him and played as they wished. This time he is at the circus with all his classmates.

The girl on the blue ball is the second act. She is a beautiful child with blue eyes and long lashes. She dances on the ball, making it go forwards, backwards, to the right and to the left. She appears to be very tiny on the enormous ball, and he thinks of her as Thumbelina. The lights dim, the orchestra plays softly, and the tinkling of the golden bells on her wrists and ankles can be heard. He feels that this is out of a fairy tale. He finds himself enchanted. The act occupies a very brief span of time, but at the end his enthusiasm is upon him.

He thinks the girl looks only at him and smiles only at him and waves only at him. The clowns, lions, and other acts following the girl on the ball do not interest him. She exits through the curtain never to be seen again, but she will remain with him forever. His enthusiasm attaches to the miraculous, enchanted few minutes of her performance. He wants his father to see her and invite her to their home. However, the girl on the ball can never be his guest. She exists only tinkling in the dim light atop the ball as the orchestra plays softly and she shimmers in her silver dress. She is very real, nevertheless, in the enthusiasm she evokes.

He returns to the circus after two weeks to find that she has moved away to Vladivostok with her parents. He knows where Vladivostok is and proposes going there by train and by plane. His father suggests going to the ice cream parlor instead.

The story is a simple presentation of one small boy's enthusiasm and how he encounters loss and frustration. He is angry that his father can enjoy the circus when he can not. He feels alone with his grief. At the end of the story, his father squeezes his hand as they walk home together. He understands that he is not alone with his grief, but that his grief remains.

These three stories show contemporary Soviet children's stories concerned with the wonder of the world and meeting life's problems. There is nothing about them which is peculiarly Soviet. They are simply good stories, well told.

—Shirley Petrich

1 Viktor Dragunskij, "He is alive and glows," pp. 3-8 in He is alive and glows (Moscow: Children's Literature Press, 1971).

2 Kazimira Poljakova, "Monster mushroom," pp. 23-27 in The Old Man of the Woods (Kharkov: PRAPOR Press, 1970).

3 Viktor Dragunskij, Girl on the Ball (Moscow: Children's Literature Press, 1969).

4 Dragunskij, He is alive and glows, p. 3.

5 Poljakova, p. 24.

TEN BOOKS

Snow-White and the Seven Dwarfs: A Tale from the Brothers Grimm. Translated by Randall Jarrell. Illustrated by Nancy Ekholm Burkert. (Farrar, Straus and Giroux, $5.95).
The Fantastic Story of King Brioche the First by Anne Jenny. Illustrated by Jocelyn Pache. Ages 5 to 8. (Lothrop, Lee & Shepard Co., $4.25).
Sati the Rastifarian by Edgar White. Illustrated by Dindga McCannon. Ages 6 to 9. (Lothrop, Lee & Shepard Co., $3.95).
Away Went the Balloons by Carolyn Haywood. Illustrated by the Author. Ages 6 to 10. (William Morrow & Company, Inc., $4.75).

Books designed for teenagers become more sombrely adult every year, thereby perhaps contributing to the eventual disappearance of the market. It would be interesting to know how many teenagers who read for pleasure already skip straight from Lloyd Alexander to Tolkien, from horse and nursing stories to pulp romance, from Lois Lenski to Brautigan and Vonnegut.

Books for small children are still geared to the uncertain tastes of the parents who buy them; it is the pictures, we are told, rather than the few lines of print that sell the book. In the small amount of space allowed for print, the author's chief concern is not to bore tots brought up on the Electric Company; and even those books which try to extend the material in accordance with Women's Lib. or Third World concerns seldom escape the spoon-feed syndrome—dollop after dollop of incident ladled into a passive open mouth—pabulum spiced with paint.

For teenagers, a story is a way of extending and translating experience they already have; for toddlers, a story is life-experience itself, and they want to know where they begin and end. This is why the traditional fairy tales (however bowdlerised and Disneyed up) provide satisfaction. Everything has a cause and effect, with a comfortable explanation called magic for anything which a child doesn't understand, or anything which has beginnings outside the frame of the story.

But too often these stories appear only in collections or large anthologies, daunting to a beginning reader. A recognition of the need for new formats in the re-issue of classics must lie behind the latest edition of Snow-White. A Caldecott Honor Book, it is outstanding on many counts.

Product-testers Seven and Eleven were united in their praise of it. They took turns in reading the text aloud and studied the pictures together, exclaiming over and over at the details that gradually revealed themselves. (It seems to me that even much younger children enjoy sorting out a detailed, traditional illustration, long after they grow bored by splashy, colorful pictures that make their point at the first glance).

The illustrations to Snow-White depart from the usual format of children's books (picture accompanying text on the same or an opposing page); all the pictures but the first are double page spreads linked in subject to the last paragraph of the page before. Yet each picture is valid in its own terms, extending the world of the story by symbol and suggestion. For instance, when the wicked Queen laces Snow-White so tightly that she falls unconscious, the incident is shown as an insert in a landscape like an old map, stiff with trees, mountains and castles, dotted with overscaled knights and hunters, and made sinister by a crimson Celtic dragon capturing a plump white rabbit.

The printed pages, themselves beautiful, are set out with a variable number of lines, enticingly paragraphed and broken by conversations and verse. Randall Jarrell's traslation is simple and straightforward; while it is not pedantic, it does seem to be what he hoped—"as much like the real German story as I could make it." He retains without softening the cannibalism and cruelty that were so frequently omitted in earlier versions. (The effect of these on the product-testers was inconclusive; the passage where the wicked Queen is forced to don red-hot iron slippers and dance until she dies was received with appalled silence by Eleven and with shrieks of "Goody, goody" from Seven.)

In this matter too the illustrations developed a satisfactory balance, forestalling possible nightmares. The final page shows on the left the empty shoes and a crouching white hound gazing down a dark winding stairway, where a ghost of smoke hovers; on the right is a gentle, golden wedding scene, where stairs ascend under banners to a throne, and a window shows growing fruit and flowers.

True, the story ends with a wedding; is it damaging to little girls, instructing them that to be active is wicked, that social success lies in passivity? The story seems much more obviously to equate evil with the jealous rage of a woman whose only value for herself lies in her looks. The Queen has only one role available to her, that of beauty-queen; denied that, she turns murderess. Snow-White can play many parts with success and does not demand social approval; she meets threats with counter-suggestions, works hard to support herself in a new way of life, and never thinks about her appearance at all (till the wicked Queen tempts her with ribbons and combs for hair-styling, a lapse that is almost fatal). Glass coffin or not, hasn't she more autonomy than the Queen burning out her life with envy?

Whatever one's feelings, this edition puts Grimm back in the market on equal terms with other books for young children, and it will be interesting to see how he fares.

Two other books designed to reach lower on the age scale are less satisfactory. Illustrations to The Fantastic Story of King Brioche the First are colorful, if a bit formless, but there are too many characters of nearly equal importance in this brief story, and no inner logic to the fantasy. The splendidly irritating little bird who bounces about singing "I can fly and you can't! I can fly and you can't!" disappoints when he is turned by magic into giant size, and meekly flies King Brioche (the former object of his taunts) on a tour of his kingdom. Seven didn't buy this bit of sweetness and light, and neither did the reviewer.

Sati the Rastifarian has unusual stylized block prints in prevailing tones of black, brown and blue. They fit the sombre mood of Sati's journey from his idyllic West Indian island to a New York ghetto, yet they seem a little too static for a child's story; and children in general aren't inspired by closeup portrait heads of children (the pale face of Snow-White that occupies the whole front cover of that book is the one picture that readers have reservations about). Many details of Sati's life are sharply observed and effective, but co-exist uneasily with attacks of elevated style in the first few pages of the book. "The gift of memory and of dreams" doesn't seem a strong enough organizing principle for the story as it stands; it may be that we simply learn too little about Sati as a person. This is a pity, because the author is working in an area that has been little explored. His story stops without ending, as though it were the beginning of a series, and perhaps it should be.

A book for slightly older children, <u>Away Went the Balloons</u>, is a simple, rather conventional story about Balloon Day as it affects the first graders at Blue Bell School. Eleven said "Each chapter of the book was a different story, but all the chapters related to one thing." Seven explained "It was a very good book, the pictures were not as good as the story. It kept me wondering what would happen next." There doesn't seem anything to add to these comments, which were a little more enthusiastic than those of the reviewer.

<u>Last Horse on the Sands</u> by Arthur Catherall. Illustrated by David Farris. Ages 8 to 12. (Lothrop, Lee & Shepard Co., $4.25).
<u>Red Rock over the River</u> by Patricia Beatty. Ages 10 to 14. (William Morrow & Company, Inc., $5.50).
<u>Jockin the Jester</u> by Ursula Moray Williams. (Thomas Nelson, Inc., $5.95).
<u>Devil's Nob</u> by Philip Turner. (Thomas Nelson, Inc., $4.95).
<u>The Curse of Laguna Grande</u> by S. R. Van Iterson. Translated by Hilda van Stockum. (William Morrow & Company, Inc., $4.95).
<u>The War on William Street</u> by Reginald Ottley. (Thomas Nelson, Inc., $4.95).

The books for children over 10 are mostly of foreign origin, and they lay considerable stress on out-of-the-ordinary settings. Those which are not historical develop interest in an unusual or exotic way of life; two at least give considerable detail about rare or outdated occupations. The main characters in all of them are sharply cut off from the lives of most grown-ups, leading an existence of their own which simply does not impinge upon the consciousness of their parents or relatives. Aid and comfort comes from surrogate parents—friendly outsiders or others of the same age. By comparison with the heroes of books for younger children, these have almost complete autonomy.

Another striking thing is the open-ended nature of the plots. All but one end in a way which is not inconclusive, but which leaves open a door to possible developments in the future; there is still much more to be done by the main characters in the story. Teenagers dreaming roles find a spur to imagination in this way of writing; they need neither the slick "happy ending" nor the modish cut-off in despair. They need the assurance that people can learn to cope, and go on coping, even if it is only with defeat or their own feelings (the Zindel formula). On the way, they are willing to accept a great deal of harshness and disillusion, perhaps more than teenagers for decades before them.

The most conventional of the stories, <u>Last Horse on the Sands</u>, is still fairly bracing in its circumstances. The story is set in a seaside village where people live by inshore fishing and digging for shellfish. A plane crashes among the quicksands and passengers need rescue. There's a healthy poverty about everyone which makes it convincing that the children are expected to pull their weight as adults when occasion demands. The usual flummery which lets the brother and sister risk death by refusing to abandon the horse is marginally less irritating than usual because of their general competence and common sense. The local color is perhaps the best thing about this one.

Red Rock over the River has an unusual setting—Fort Yuma in 1881—and a promising character in Hattie Lou "half Indian, abnormally tall and a crack shot." There's good local color and detail and a lot of plot, but everything is rather too cursorily treated to be fully satisfying. Perhaps the vocabulary and outlook of the tough thirteen-year old girl who narrates are emotionally limiting; somehow there is too little feeling for the events described, and the story remains an affair of surfaces.

Jockin the Jester originally published in 1951, is a historical novel set in fourteenth-century England. The author seems a little uncertain of the sort of novel she is aiming for; sometimes she shows curiosity about the tangled roots of feeling, sometimes she settles for contrivance. She presents a wicked dwarf and a slow, almost saintly jester who can't make jokes; the tomboy daughter of an aristocrat creates trouble for everyone. There is the obligatory contrived flight across England by daughter, jester, donkey and washerwoman's baby, false imprisonment, and a happy resolution of troubles. Details of the jester's life are well imagined, however, and Eleven enjoyed the book.

Devil's Nob makes a commendable effort to deal with the history that isn't taught in school—the life of poor working people in nineteenth-century England. Grown-up emotions are handled with reticence but without dishonesty, and the economic pressures of a life where one dared not marry because one's wages would not support a family are fairly shown, as are the contrivances by which one achieved a new dress or a good meal. There is a rather schizophrenic attempt to show the local landowner as both wickedly frivolous and romantically brave, strong, sensitive, etc. In his person, the romantic genre itself betrays the more serious intentions of the author. The sudden change into romanticized psychology which brings about the happy ending weakens the painstaking realism of the earlier scenes. There is perhaps a little too much technical detail about the machinery of a slate quarry and a railway and, despite a lot of event, there isn't much suspense, but this is a good read for older teenagers.

The Curse of Laguna Grande is a mystery translated from the Dutch in a style occasionally and unhappily reminiscent of Cold Comfort Farm. There is a great deal of gloom and foreboding and a plot full of twins, illegitimate heirs, secret passages and lost inheritances. For a grown-up taste, there's too much exposition, too many characters who remain mere names, and too little movement in the plot till the last third of the book. But the setting—a decaying plantation in Colombia—is both original and exotic. Brief conversations and comments show the self-defeating, ingrained habits and superstitions of the country people in their full awesome strength, and the young man who had wished to challenge them and restore his inheritance becomes aware that he can hope for no more than some imperfect but possibly useful accommodation to a hopeless situation. In this sober conclusion, the way is left open for courage, and Eleven liked the book very much.

The War on William Street comes from Australia, and is set in that country in the 1930's, just after the Great Depression. Of the three main characters, one is comfortably off, one comes from a poor and half-aboriginal family, and one lives with a drunken old woman who looks after him for an absentee father. When the latter gets hurt, his friends take his place selling papers, and so get drawn into the dangerous battle between 'Gran' and her brutal rival Greasy. It is a rather clumsily plotted book, sometimes stilted and awkward in the conversations, but it somehow conveys the desperate importance of hero-worship and group loyalty, the strangled emotions and embarrassments of intense friendship. There is an honorable attempt to play fair with hardship, pain, and hopeless poverty; the hard-luck child has hard luck to the end and we finish with no more than a faint hope of good will from an adult benefactor who descends, like Jove, for brief visits between business trips. Sentimentality and all, this one sticks in the mind.

—Barbara Rosen

Book Reviews

YOUNG DRAMA

P. O. Box 2, Stroud, Glos., England. GLS 5 BE. February, June, October. $5.50 annually.

There is a new publication dealing specifically with children's drama, appropriately named Young Drama. Young Drama is published by the Thimble Press, England, in association with Heinemann Educational Books, under the editorship of Nancy Chambers. The purpose and scope of the publication are explained in the editorial of the first edition (February, 1973): to provide a vehicle for the exchange of ideas and experiences of various people in the field of children's theater and creative dramatics. The first edition contains a wide and varied series of articles.

David Adland's article, "A Room Full of Shylocks," is of particular interest as it presents an account of a class using creative dramatics for the study of Shakespeare in a classroom situation. It demonstrates what can be accomplished by a group approach in the interpretation of The Merchant of Venice.

There are additional articles discussing the use and aim of documentary material in creative drama. This is followed by a Workshop Section featuring stories and poems suitable for development through creative dramatics, including suggestions for music, mime, and movement.

In addition, there are articles exploring several fallacies in contemporary theories of young drama, especially as approached from the educational point of view, and how one person established, maintained, and improved drama classes for less than privileged children. These articles, plus a section of reviews on current youth scripts and additional drama publications, complete the material included in the first issue.

The magazine promises to accomplish its purpose as set forth by Ms. Chambers. It presents a varied choice of subject matter and valuable information for the follower of current thoughts and trends in young drama.

—Daniel L. Ater

CRICKET

Volume 1, Number 1, January, 1973 (Pilot issue: regular publication commences September 1973). To be published monthly except June, July and August. Annual subscription, $10.00; single copy, $1.50. Open Court Publishing Company, 1058 Eighth Street, La Salle, Illinois 61301.

A man recommending this magazine to me said it was the first high-standard magazine for children since St. Nicholas dwindled away in the 1930's. Having been reared on St. Nicholas in its great pre-1920 phase, I had some misgivings when beginning to make Cricket's acquaintance. I lost them halfway through. The thing is downright enjoyable.

As it happens, research for my own work has recently taken me through a run of St. Nicholas in representative good years. For my money, Cricket assays considerably better—level of quality better sustained, art work handling a wider variety of idioms, editorial imagination expertly eclectic and cordially amusing without too much cuteness, as in the little drawings-with-dialogue at the bottoms of pages in which crickets and assorted fellow insects discuss what goes on in the matter printed above.

Comparison must allow for the age levels of Cricket's intended audience not going beyond twelve, I should judge, whereas St. Nicholas aimed at youngsters well into their teens. Ordinarily that difference would have been to Cricket's disadvantage, dooming its content to easy-steps-for-little-feet mawkishness. Actually zest and thump and stimulating reachings toward growth-experience come through on a most gratifying number of pages.

Difference in editorial policy is diametric. St. Nicholas relied on previously unpublished material. One reason for Cricket's high quality and a good omen for its future is that most of its content consists of extracts from very good books for children published over the past few decades. Such cream-skimming can be very rewarding, and works out as well here for children as it did in good reading for adults in the old Golden Book magazine of pre-World War II days. A child nibbling at this first Cricket will find friends in T. S. Eliot, Isaac Bashevis Singer . . . and feel them as friends with the same spontaneities as the less augustly renowned but mostly admirable writers of the rest of the content.

Another good omen is the harkback to St. Nicholas in "The Cricket League" department asking readers to do stories or poems on . . . well, this month on "anything spooky or scary: ghosts, skeletons, witches, bats . . . hoots, boos, sighs, grins . . . " or drawings in that same mood in any color so long as it's black. The St. Nicholas League of my day was print-proving ground for Edna St. Vincent Millay, Stephen Vincent Benét, Rachel Carson, and so on. Could be this time, too.

—J. C. Furnas

RED POWER ON THE RIO GRANDE

The Native American Revolution of 1680, by Franklin Folsom. 144 pp. (Follett Publishing Company, Chicago. $5.95).

Native Americans living on the land and off the land, for countless generations, can not easily adjust to foreign cultures and slavery without a great deal of discomfort.

The Pueblo people were a peace loving, religious people, and by no means ignorant. If the Spaniards had settled near them and not disturbed their way of life, the Pueblos would never have rebelled.

The Spaniards were cruel, greedy, and unjust in their treatment of a people they found living in the valley of the Rio Grande. They enslaved and killed unnecessarily the Pueblos, who took all they could stand of this unjust treatment, then planned carefully their revolt. And they succeeded in their attempt to free themselves and live again as they chose. The thesis of the book is that this is a big country and all people who want to live peacefully with their neighbors, with nature and with their God should be left to work out their own destiny. Disturbing them causes unhappiness on both sides, for you cannot keep someone in a ditch without staying in the ditch yourself to keep him there, either in 1680 or in 1980.

—Princess Redwing
Wampanoag Nation

THE ANNOTATED WIZARD OF OZ

Michael Patrick Hearn. Many photographs and line illustrations; 24 illustrations in three colors, eight illustrations in four colors. 400 pp. (Clarkson N. Potter, $12.50).

L(yman) Frank Baum (1856-1919) is probably America's most important author of juvenile fantasies, but his work has been generally neglected;[1] only recently has his Wonderful Wizard of Oz (1900) begun to attain scholarly and critical recognition. There has been some significant material published about Baum: Edward Wagenknecht's Utopia Americana (1929), Fred Erisman's "L. Frank Baum and the Progressive Dilemma" (American Quarterly, 20[1968]), Marius Bewley's "Oz Country" (in his recent Masks and Mirrors), Roger Sale's "L. Frank Baum, and Oz" (The Hudson Review, 25 [1972-1973]) come to mind and there are others. Two book-length studies of general interest have appeared: Martin Gardner and Russel B. Nye, The Wizard of Oz and Who He Was (East Lansing, 1957) and Frank Joslyn Baum and Russell P. MacFall, To Please a Child, a Biography of L. Frank Baum . . . (Chicago, 1961). In 1957, The International Wizard of Oz Club was formed and in that year began its journal The Baum Bugle, which has published much material of critical and historical interest.[2] But the attitude of many scholars toward Baum remains negative.

By far the most ambitious attempt to present Baum to both the general and the scholarly public is the forthcoming Annotated Wizard of Oz, scheduled for publication in August, 1973. Clarkson Potter's annotated editions are well-known, but this volume is somewhat different from the others in the series. It is probably the most lavishly produced of them all, with the possible exception of the large quarto two-volume Annotated Sherlock Holmes (which, however, has no color illustrations). The illustrative matter in Annotated Wizard is the most striking portion of the volume. All W. W. Denslow's color plates for the book are reproduced in their original colors; all his text illustrations from the first

edition are used, plus many other Denslow Oz illustrations. These other illustrations include those he drew especially for the second edition of 1903, several
from his own Oz projects (his 1904 Scarecrow and the Tin-Man pamphlet and
newspaper comic page), and a number which were discovered by Mr. Hearn and
which seem never to have been printed before. Also included are photographs of
Baum, photographs from several of his theatrical and silent movie ventures, and
much more. The many drawings and photographs in The Annotated Wizard of Oz
make it a treasurehouse for Oz enthusiasts and for anyone interested in popular
culture of the 1895-1915 period.

I have seen various drafts of Mr. Hearn's manuscript during its composition,
and I am not an unprejudiced reviewer of the work. I believe, however, that a
less biased observer would agree that all future scholars will have to consult Annotated Wizard for its vast collection of factual material about Baum. Mr.
Hearn has assiduously searched out contemporary sources and added much to our
knowledge of Baum's life and the circumstances in which he wrote. In addition to
the textual notes (which will be discussed below), Mr. Hearn's own contributions
to the volume consist of an introduction, a bibliography, and an appendix on W.
W. Denslow.

I do not know how many pages his introduction fills (this review is based on
galley proofs), but I believe that it is longer than any other in the Potter series.
It tries quite successfully to see the Wizard within Baum's total output. The bibliography is fifteen pages long and consists of a complete listing of all Baum's
published works that have been discovered and all his known unpublished writings, a list of published material about Baum and Denslow, and a full summary of
foreign editions of the Wizard and of notable English language editions. The
Denslow appendix (eight pages) discusses the relationship between Baum and
Denslow, the disagreement between the two over which was more responsible for
the success of their books, and Denslow's own publications which used characters
from the Wizard without mention of Baum.

Mr. Hearn's critical comments are significant and should cause considerable
controversy. Unlike several of the other Potter annotated books, this volume
does not attempt to be a critical variorum. The annotater has tried rather to develop his own critical interpretations in both his introduction and notes, sometimes to the exclusion of other views. This means he is able to ignore such articles as Osmond Beckwith's Freudian "The Oddness of Oz" (Kulchur, Issue 4
[1961]), which finds in Baum an interest in prepubescent girls, sexual transfer-
ence, and castration.

Recently Professor C. Warren Hollister ("Oz and the Fifth Criterion," The
Baum Bugle, 15[Christmas, 1971]) has argued that the Wizard lacks stylistic
distinction, an identifiable theme, well-individualized characters, and an organized plot, but despite this staggering catalogue of faults, Hollister finds greatness in Baum's work because of its "three-dimensionality," which creates in
the young reader an overwhelming "compulsion to believe" in its fantasy world.
Mr. Hearn, on the other hand, sees in the Wizard a universal theme: the dis-

covery of self. While Dorothy is trying to find a way to return to Kansas, the Scarecrow, Tin Woodman, and Cowardly Lion sense that they are incomplete and they are seeking that which they believe will make them whole. The reader soon realizes that each already possesses what he is looking for. The Cowardly Lion has always been brave, the Scarecrow intelligent, the Tin Woodman kind. The humbug Wizard merely gives each of them visible signs of what he already had. The second half of the book, after the climactic scene in which the Wizard leaves in his balloon, shows the three testing their newly found qualities, as they journey to the Quadling Country to seek the assistance of the Good Witch of the South to return Dorothy to Kansas.

This thematic view of the Wizard is not entirely original with Mr. Hearn, but nowhere else has it been so completely and convincingly developed. His explanation of the trip to the South goes far to explain the structural problem that many readers sense: that the second half of the book is drawn out and anti-climactic. But a thematic explanation cannot change the fact that an anti-climax is a structural flaw.

Many of Mr. Hearn's other comments are provocative. He suggests, for example, that the episode in the China Country is a later addition. This episode has little relation to the rest of the book, but this speculation is not yet proven. Mr. Hearn indicates that the famous color scheme of Oz is based logically upon the spectrum, and proves, surprisingly, that Baum used Theosophy and Rosicrucianism as sources for some of his supernatural figures and devices. His comments on the naturalistic background of the Kansas scenes are acute and indicate that Baum's fantasy was not entirely escape, for it is a naturalistic world to which Dorothy wishes to return.

Occasionally, Mr. Hearn's writing style is unclear, but this is a minor flaw in a book that is a considerable contribution to our understanding of L. Frank Baum and his works.

—David L. Greene

---

1 All fourteen of Baum's Oz books are in print through Reilly & Lee (a division of Henry Regnery Company) in editions that include all or almost all of the original black and white illustrations, but not the color plates. Dover Publications has paperback editions of The Wonderful Wizard of Oz and its sequel The Marvelous Land of Oz reproduced photographically from the first editions, with the color plates included.

Several non-Oz fantasies by L. Frank Baum are currently available. Dover has paperback editions of The Magical Monarch of Mo (1900-1903) and Queen Zixi of Ix (1905). The International Wizard of Oz Club has published the first and only book edition of Baum's 1905 Animal Fairy Tales. Exposition has a new edition of The Life and Adventures of Santa Claus (1902). Several years ago, Opium Books of Hong Kong published paperback editions of Queen Zixi of

Ix and (with new illustrations) <u>John Dough and the Cherub</u> (1906). The two Opium Books are currently available at $5.00 each from Lois Newman Books, P. O. Box 24560, Los Angeles, California 90024.

Reilly & Lee recently reprinted <u>The Sea Fairies</u> (1911) and <u>Sky Island</u> (1912). Dover plans to issue <u>John Dough and the Cherub</u> photographically from the first edition, with an introduction by Martin Gardner.

2   Membership in The International Wizard of Oz Club ($2.50 a year) includes a year's subscription—three issues—to <u>The Baum Bugle</u>. Address: Fred M. Meyer, 220 North Eleventh Street, Escanaba, Michigan 49829.

LETITIA RABBIT'S STRING SONG

Russell Hoban. Illustrated by Mary Chalmers. (Coward, McCann & Geohegan, $3.64).

<u>String</u> song? Yes. The Birch Hollow rabbits call spring string, an identity confusion based on their discovery of a strange ball of string, years ago—a discovery that naturally enough triggered off an annual festival. But this year Letitia Rabbit horses around with the string, and it leads her to its owner, Miss Green.

Miss G. is involved in an awkwardly unregularized relationship with the frigid Mr. Brumus, for whom she must draw snowflake patterns (in this world each flake isn't unique) and frost flowers until with her magic ball of string, which rolls to places where songs are being sung under the ground, she finds the song that puts Mr. B. to sleep for a while. "I do all kinds of things I like to do," she tells Letitia, "but I can't do any of them until Mr. Brumus goes to sleep, and sometimes he's just so stubborn I don't know what to do." Now, <u>we</u> know what would warm Mr. B. and put him to sleep, but Miss G. —despite her common-law situation—hasn't figured it out. So she and Letitia go to work; but Miss G.'s on the verge of a nervous breakdown ("I'm so far behind and anxious by now that the harder I try the less good it does"), so her young surrogate ("Well," said Letitia, "I am this year's Miss Green in Birch Hollow") must cut the mustard for her.

A delayed climax is a serious matter, of course, but by dealing with a fox and singing about honey—easily interpretable matters—Letitia, whose name means happiness, brings sleep to Mr. B., evokes "a big sigh of relief" from Miss G., and wins many hugs and kisses for herself (from Miss G., of course) and an invitation to come again.

What will children think of all this? The more sophisticated will just yawn knowingly, I suppose, while the more naive will focus on the "string song" and snicker at those dumb rabbits who can't tell tea from pee.

—J. Donald O'Hara

THE OTHER WORLD: MYTHS OF THE CELTS

Margaret Hodges. Illustrated by Eros Keith. (Farrar, Straus and Giroux, $5.95).

If you scratch deep enough, W. B. Yeats once observed, everyone is a visionary; he quickly added that "the Celt is a visionary without scratching." Margaret Hodges' delightful collection, The Other World: Myths of the Celts, is an invitation to scratch. The ten stories she has "retold" are for children, to be sure, but—in Yeats' terms again—for "children of light," for those who are hospitable to visitors from magic worlds. Those visitors include Cuchulain, Dermot, and Finn MacCool of Ireland, the Scottish Tam Lin, Dahut of Brittany, and Bran of Wales. Of course, there are also some of the familiar faces of Arthur's court, along with one not so familiar but just as heroic, Gareth of Orkney. "How Finn MacCool Got His Wisdom Tooth" and "The Lad of Luck and the Monster of the Loch" are the most engaging of the stories, all of which are set in that mythical world of the shadowy past, where the pressures of the present workaday world are given meaning by the presence of something divine. "The well-loved heroes are part of ourselves," Ms. Hodges announces in her Introduction, "but the light is from the Other World."

The oral literature of the Celtic peoples—represented in this book by stories from Ireland, Scotland, Wales, Cornwall, and Brittany—is a treasure hoard of bardic legends, fairy tales, and heroic sagas. For the most part, this primal stuff has been submerged in the folklore of the dominant, English-speaking culture, especially in the Arthurian matter. But the important thing is not to vindicate its antiquity but to give it life in the present. On that alone, Margaret Hodges' book is a success. The magic is in the stories, and her telling doesn't detract from it. The style is simple but not simplistic, direct but not prosaic. The teller neither condescends nor exaggerates. It is regrettable that the same can't be said of the illustrations.

Frank O'Connor, himself a masterful teller of tales and a preserver of the Irish past, once summarized the Celtic gleam in this way: "From magic we come,/ To magic we go." This book captures the gleam.

—James H. Matthews

MISTRESSES OF MYSTERY:
TWO CENTURIES OF SUSPENSE STORIES BY THE GENTLE SEX

Edited by Seon Manley and Gogo Lewis. 220 pp. (Lothrop, Lee & Shepard, $4.95).

Mistresses of Mystery is a sequel to a recent volume called Ladies of Horror, also compiled by the sisters Manley and Lewis. The Edward Gorey dust jacket features a candelabra clutched in a male fist glimpsed through a doorway, a man on the carpet suffering from the dagger in his chest, a skeleton ascending (?) to heaven with a bunch of roses, its pelvis modestly draped, and a primly pensive lady seated at a desk writing with a quill pen; her cool is one of the scariest things in the volume.

A few of the stories, Dorothy Sayers' fine "The Leopard Lady" and "Madame Sara," by L. T. Meade and R. Eustace, bump off unwelcome heirs. The Sayers story is superior precisely because it is not mysterious: its fulfillment of our expectation is what delights us, along with the wittiness of a "removals" company that specializes in removing people.

Edith Wharton's "All Souls" is another gem, again not because of its suspense (i.e., the pace of the movement towards resolution) but because of the terror of the protagonist who wakes in the night to discover her house is mysteriously empty. The revelation of witchcraft appears rational and trivial when compared with her distress.

Wit and psychological accuracy, then, are the hallmarks of the best of these stories. Even the play "Good-bye, Miss Lizzie Borden," by Lillian de la Torre, is absorbing less for the imposing figure of Lizzie Borden swinging her axe around than for the revelation that she's all along been shielding her neurotic sister Emma.

Most of the violence in these nine stories occurs off stage, with the possible exception of E. Nesbit's "The Head," a faintly silly story about vengeance accomplished through a waxworks dummy. The cleverest offstage violence is done in Jane Rice's science fiction "The Willow Tree," the most recent tale in the collection (which actually spans less than a century). It features a future civilization in which "pooskats" are extinct, except at Aunt Harriet's, who lives in the "past" where four children are relocated because the "present" has gotten too crowded. The violence has been done in a loop of time both before and after the story itself. Quite sinister, that one.

In other words, in the best of these stories scenes of violence on the one hand and the steps towards rational explanation seem irrelevant—as they always are in good fiction. The sex of the writers probably has little bearing on the fact that in most of the stories it is women who perform the nefarious deeds, for women have accepted stereotypes of their own deviousness. More important, sex bears no particular relationship to wit and psychological accuracy. Teenagers of both sexes would enjoy the collection.

—Joan Joffe Hall

POEMS FROM THE HEBREW

Selected by Robert Mezey. Etching by Moishe Smith. 159 pp. (Thomas Y. Crowell, $4.50).

This anthology for children aged 12 and up is one of a series; other volumes assemble translated poems from the German, and from Africa, France, India, Ireland, and Italy.

Is there a distinctly Hebrew spirit, vision, and sensibility? one is likely to ask after reading through this collection. It is a question Uri Zvi Greenberg poses in an excerpt that introduces "The Modern Poets," the longest section of the book: "And is our nervous system in any way like that of the Gentiles?" And he replies: "The Hebrew mouth is more like a wound; behind the Hebrew forehead an eagle screams."

In reading these poems, one becomes aware of historical patterns that have helped shape both a consciousness and a literary sensibility. The Biblical selections, with their songs, psalms, and prophecies are more than personal celebrations and laments; they record the joy and sense of obligation of a people who believe in a special covenant with God. An individual is of supreme importance because God watches each; whatever happens to one person may therefore represent the experiences of many and even represent the destiny of a nation.

To celebrate life is to praise the wonders of God, not as abstractions, for the Hebrew language is uncomfortable with such things, but with concrete images and sharply defined details. The beauty of the world is to be enjoyed fully in this life:

> How fair and how pleasant art thou, O love, for delights!
> This thy stature is like to a palm tree, and thy breasts to clusters of
> grapes.

But when adversity comes, the anguish is particularly sharp because of the feeling of a broken covenant, of personal betrayal. Job would try to see and reason with his God.

During the Diaspora, personal anguish can be even greater: there is still the feeling of special dedication to God, but the experience of living in alien lands seems to stress sharply the mythic pattern that each individual who is born is somehow dispossessed.

> My heart is in the East, and I in the uttermost West—
> My food has no taste, there is no sweetness in it

are the words of Judah Halevi in the section "The Poets of Moorish Spain." Job's defiant quarrel with God becomes in Abraham Ibn Ezra's poem a resigned protest against the inevitability of bad fortune, its wit, a defense against total despair:

> If I decided to sell lamps,
> It wouldn't get dark till the day I died.
>
> Some stars. Whatever I do,
> I'm a failure before I begin.
> If I suddenly decided to sell shrouds,
> People would suddenly stop dying.

It is understandable that many Jews in the Diaspora dreamed of Eden, a return to the promised land where one might live in harmony with nature and family. "Man is nothing but the soil of a small country, / nothing but the shape of his native landscape," writes Tchernichovsky. But the return does not miraculously resolve all conflicts—that would make dull poetry indeed. There are, as before, poems that defiantly praise present life against postponed hope; poems that shout their outrage at genocide. In their own land, at last, the Hebrews celebrate the will to live, now triumphant over despair against all odds. And still there is a sense of apartness and special dedication, if not to God, then to man and to life itself. The present dilemmas, best represented in the poetry of Yehuda Amichai, are remarkably similar to old ones. A German by birth, with European sensibilities, Amichai writes of the experiences of one who has become an "insider" but can never lose the perspective of the "outsider." Belonging to the history of his people whether he wants to or not, he finds the landscape of Israel strange—even savage—as in the poem "Mayor." In "National Thoughts" he describes what it is like to be "trapped in the homeland of the Chosen People," and how

> The language which described God and the Miracles,
> Says:
> Motor car, bomb, God.

As well as acquainting children with good translations of Hebrew poetry, this volume can speak to them with particular vividness about their own emotions and dilemmas. Adolescents are especially sensitive to feelings of exile and belonging. They know what it is like to be an exile in one's own place. And they know how to preserve—even if only through histrionics or deadpan wit—the sense of being special.

—William Rosen

ROUSSEAU'S ÉMILE AND EARLY CHILDREN'S LITERATURE

Sylvia W. Patterson. (Metuchen, New Jersey: Scarecrow Press, 1971).

Histories of children's literature usually hop through the eighteenth century in a single chapter. Newbery, Day, Edgeworth and a few others are leapfrogged in an impatient effort to get on to that "golden" nineteenth century. To see Patterson pause to search out some of the rarer stuff from the 1700's is pleasurable. That Patterson, limiting herself to the influence of one philosopher on ten English writers in the last twenty years of the century, can come up with a 177-page book demonstrates how rich the period can be. After lengthy summary of Émile, the author painstakingly scrutinizes for Rousseau's influence twenty-one works from: Anna Barbauld and John Aikin, Thomas Day, Maria Edgeworth, Eleanor Fenn, Dorothy and Mary Jane Kilner, Hannah More, Sarah Trimmer, and Mary Wollstonecraft.

Influence is too strong a word. Patterson acknowledges that her intent is to show what Rousseau's ideas were, that major authors knew them, and that some of the ideas crop up in the juvenile works covered. Where direct influence cannot be posited, Patterson wisely suggests that Rousseau's ideas coincide with a given author. Mostly, Patterson demonstrates such parallelism abundantly and credibly. Thus, when she points out that Rousseau felt the same way that Mary Wollstonecraft did about breast feeding, the reader cannot carp. A few pages later (p. 109) Patterson converts this to "Mary Wollstonecraft follows Rousseau in the idea of the mother nursing her own child." Such overreaching does not clarify but clouds the extent of Rousseau's influence. On Wollstonecraft there is also some omission. Only internal evidence is cited by Patterson to show that Original Stories (1788) exhibits Wollstonecraft's use of Rousseau, yet at least one biographer of Wollstonecraft gives the year and month when she read Émile— and her favorable reaction to it (G. R. Stirling Taylor, Mary Wollstonecraft: a Study in Economics and Romance, London: Martin Secker, 1911, p. 74).

In summarizing Émile and in illustrating the central irony of Rousseau's disciples writing any books for children, Patterson is admirable. I would fault only the selective vision. What about some apostles of Rousseau who, though French, had a wide English audience? Maria Edgeworth saw Arnaud Berquin's The Children's Friend (England, 1783) as universally popular. She also translated a work of Madame de Genlis to whom one critic attributes more influence in England than Émile.

Even accepting the restriction to English authors, one finds the works chosen with a restricted field of vision. Granted that three works by Lady Eleanor Fenn can epitomize the fourteen or so she wrote, why not include Fables in Monosyllables (c. 1783), which Patterson mentions but does not cite even though it contains the first direct quotation from Rousseau in an English children's book? Why omit that and then hunt for parallels to Émile in her other works? One suspects that Fenn's Fables were not accessible to the author. Only eight of the major works traced by Patterson are used in eighteenth-century versions; of the eight only four are first editions. Such versions are admittedly hard to come by, but later editions are likely to be brutally revised the way even Goody Two-Shoes was butchered by nineteenth-century editors.

To focus on major authors is a sound way of explicating Rousseau. It might be difficult to grant even nodding attention to what Percy Muir calls the "monstrous regiment" of anonymous and lesser known female writers of the period. One can dispense with Harriet English or Lucy Peacock, but Lucy Pinchard in The Two Cousins (1794) and H. S. 's Anecdotes of Mary (1795) both contain direct quotations from Rousseau. There may be more among the hack writers.

Under minor lapses in biography, the reader should know that the Kilners, Mary Jane and Dorothy, were not sisters, as Patterson has them, but sisters-in-law.

The notion of Rousseau's influence on juvenile literature which has often been skeletally treated elsewhere has been fleshed out by Patterson. But grateful as the reader might be for the finished product, he might prefer a little more meat on those bones.

—Robert J. Bator

OPPOSITES

Richard Wilbur. Illustrated by the author. (New York: Harcourt Brace Jovanovich, 1973. $3.75).

Everyone knows what opposites are, but how many know what opposites is? According to the publishers, "Richard Wilbur, his wife, and his four children used to play a rather unusual game around the dinner table. One member of the family would suggest a word, and then everyone would join in a lively quarrel about its proper opposite." Out of that game came this book. Although, given its origins, there is less word-play and more attribute-play than one might have expected: one of the opposites of squash is bean, because one's a yellow vegetable and the other is green, and the opposite of fox is ox, because one's clever and the other's dull. Yet this is neither here nor there because Opposites, whatever it is, is disappointing. Wilbur's letters are willing but his spirit, in this case, is wooden. Which again is hardly what anyone would have expected.

What would be the opposite of Opposites? Biting elegance, perhaps, instead of bourgeois fastidiousness:

> I don't think I should care to know
> Those hairless dogs of Mexico
> Who ramble naked out of doors
> And must be patted on their pores.   (# 23)

> What is the opposite of hat?
> It isn't hard to answer that.
> It's shoes, for shoes and hat together
> Protect our two extremes from weather.   (# 20)

> The opposite of spit, I'd say,
> Would be a narrow cove or bay.
> (There is another sense of spit,
> But I refuse to think of it.
> It stands opposed to all refined
> And decent instincts of mankind!)   (# 34)

I'd like to believe that this pose is a mock one, but throughout the book there's too much evidence that his culture-bound perspective is truly what it seems to be. Even if it weren't what it seems, there'd be something questionable about it. I've a notion that, in children's books especially, mockingly posed values are in effect values posed for real. And if one playfully confuses mental health with fine-print etiquette, one perpetrates a real confusion nonetheless.

> What is the opposite of nuts?
> It's soup! Let's have no ifs or buts.
> In any suitable repast
> The soup comes first, the nuts come last.
> Or that is what sane folk advise;
> You're nuts if you think otherwise.   (# 1)

All in fun? Maybe. Though I wouldn't care to be caught bolting my food in this here dining stanza here. If the tenor of the book is any indication, next we'll be using hair styles as indices to morality. Again. As the short and long hairs used to do. And I once heard the wife of an Air Force sergeant accuse the French of being immoral because they didn't put toilet paper around the seats before they sat on them. Wilbur, of course, doesn't go nearly as far. Nor is he about to. Still, his class-bound perspective leaves the verses with remarkable blind spots.

> The opposite of junk is stuff
> Which someone thinks is good enough,
> Or any vessel on the seas
> That isn't in the least Chinese.   (# 5)

The opposite of junk is booze, silly. The opposites is, stew in your juice or blow your fuse. Ask any twelve-year-old: junk, in every sense except Chinese, is what you learn about at school.

Or, the opposite of Opposites might be thoroughly pointless verses—at least, ones that wouldn't hobnob with reactionary innuendo.

> What is the opposite of riot?
> It's lots of people keeping quiet.   (# 8)

A couplet caught in the act of turning its back to the world. And on the other side, in the opposite corner . . . What's the opposite of riot? No, not race. It's oppressed people keeping in their place.

This could and should have been a spirited, liberating little book. Wilbur has an extraordinary wit that can play with things and ideas as well as with words, and what's more he can make concerted play of them. Yet here, somehow, the going gets more and more pinched and graceless, like an old cracked shoe.

> What is the opposite of Cupid?
> If you don't know, you're pretty stupid.
> It's someone with a crossbow who
> Delights in shooting darts at you,
> Not with the kind intention of
> Persuading you to fall in love,
> But to be mean, and make you shout,
> "I hate you," "Ouch," and "Cut it out."   (# 24)

So much for the verses, of which there are thirty-nine pages for $3.75. As for the drawings—they're unimaginative, crude and lucid. They make their points in an unpretentious way, which is all they need do. Occasionally, and this is welcome, they go against the grain of the verses they accompany.

Children are more deserving of Things Of This World than of Opposites, which is a kind of shell game with the middle term (the term that gives it body and life) missing. Next time around I hope Wilbur gives the children a demonic book or a loving gracious one. Either would do, as either would rise to the occasion of its audience. In any event he might write for them in earnest, with the freshness and verve he's capable of.

—James Scully

THEY NAMED ME GERTRUDE STEIN

Ellen Wilson. With 16 photographs. Ages 12 and up. (Farrar, Straus, and Giroux, $5.50).

Through reading biographies at an early age, I soon learned that being was not, in itself, enough: you had to make something of yourself in order to leave your mark. A biography of Gertrude Stein, geared to readers six or eight years too young to read Stein straight, is not quite the anomaly it sounds: it presents a fascinating personality for its own sake, without the usual emphasis on tangible success. The book's format is enticingly "adult"; well-printed on quality paper, with a number of photographs. But there are disappointments.

"There may have been times in her life that Gertrude Stein wished that she weren't so large." It gets off to an auspiciously Steinian start, distinctly along the order of "Rose Herbert made it very hard to bring her baby to its birth''; unfortunately, the effect is not sustained. The writing is, in fact, rather erratic, and not without occasional jarring misjudgments and omissions.

What twelve year-old would not feel daunted on being told that The Autobiography of Alice B. Toklas " . . . proved to be written in a way that was not cryptic, esoteric, repetitious, or tangential?" (p. 105). Several clarifications which would have been useful to young readers are not forthcoming: Ms. Wilson gives no inkling of what "automatic writing" might be, nor does she explain why proper Parisians found "The Rites of Spring" and the 1905 Salon d'Automne so shocking, although she stresses that they did. And although one thread of the narrative deals with the intricacies of Stein's stylistic innovations, it is only in the last ten pages that the reader makes any sort of contact with the writing itself, when Ms. Wilson offers Stein's own explication of "a rose is a rose is a rose."

But Ms. Wilson's most annoying habit is the old primer trick of ending her chapters with a falsely "climactic" exclamation or rhetorical question, presumably designed to maintain the reader's attention from chapter to chapter. The final sentence I find particularly condescending: "Yes, no matter what the answer or what the question, life had always been interesting to Gertrude Stein."

Still, in all, it's not a bad book; not by a long shot. There is much that should be stimulating to sensitive readers; for example, an excellent exploration of the analogous elements in painting and writing, and a concisely subtle passage on death:

It wasn't so much that she was afraid of dying as that she was

frightened by the idea of dissolving into nothingness, of not existing after death.

(p. 19)

And a moment of supreme delicacy:

> And so throughout the year, with a growing affection between these
> two, Gertrude was drawn into the realm of emotional involvement
> with one of her own sex . . . . Her first doubt was an old one,
> since she had always assumed that the only acceptable kind of deep
> attachment was that between a woman and a man. But here was a
> woman who was offering her more love and devotion than any man
> had ever shown her.

(p. 53)

The spirit of homoemotionality has seldom been expressed more simply and mov-
ingly.

And this is the book's true value: Ms. Wilson has a gift for expressing abstract emotional and aesthetic matters in a manner both simple and thought-pro-
voking. It's an unusual gift which, to my mind, transcends the book's stylistic
flaws.

—Susan E. Bittker

EDUCATIONAL SURVIVAL KIT:
LEARNING, BASIC HUMAN INTERESTS, AND
   THE TEACHING OF CHILDREN'S LITERATURE

Francelia Butler, J. Bruce W. McWilliams, Robert G. Miner, Jr.

   The teaching of children's literature in the Humanities is of necessity innovative at this time because it is still not generally accepted or taught as part of the
traditional curriculum. As a result of this state of affairs, and after consistent
experimentation, we have happened upon a way of teaching children's literature
which we think might eventually lead to a whole new way of structuring learning.
What we suggest is to rearrange material in accordance with basic human interests instead of the traditional subjects.

   Some recent theories of learning seem to reinforce our own findings. The
Biological Boundaries of Learning, by Martin Seligman and Joanne Hager (New
York: Appleton-Century Crofts, 1972), suggests that it is not so much condi-
tioning and environment but evolutionary (survival) value that determines the ef-
ficiency of learning. (Indeed, all human beings share certain basic needs and
interests that derive from them, and are preoccupied by these survival needs and
interests in one form or another all of their lives.) In Motivation and Personality, Abraham Maslow defines the basic needs as safety, love, esteem, self-actualization, and of course, the physiological ones. When these are satisfied,

> At once other and higher needs emerge and these, rather than
> physiological hungers, dominate the organism. And when these
> in turn are satisfied, again new (and still higher) needs emerge,
> and so on. This is what we mean by saying that the basic human
> needs are organized into a hierarchy of relative prepotency.

—Motivation and Personality,
Harper & Row: New York, 1970

   Beside Maslow's, many systems exist for determining basic human needs:
mythology, psychology, sociology, anthropology, philosophy, to name a few.
For the purposes of our course, we decided that the simplest way to arrive at a
working list was to go into the most fundamental substratum: the basic physiological activities necessary for survival, from which needs and interests derive
—respiration, ingestion, digestion, excretion, and reproduction. We are not
suggesting that a dignified university should have catalog offerings such as Excretion 101. What we are suggesting is that a curriculum structured around
these functions might produce a more interesting and productive learning experience than the usual one.

   Without attempting here to prove why learning is more efficient when structured this way (most probably because it is the ultimate kind of "relevance"), we

can only assert that we have tried the approach on classes of varying sizes and found it effective, at least if a consistently increasing enrollment is any indication.

Most literature for children assumes a quality of perception in its audience that literature for adults must strive to create: what T. S. Eliot, in speaking of the metaphysical poets, called "the direct sensuous apprehension of thought." Most non-children have lost this capacity, in part at least as a result of the enforced segregation of responses that modern education has deemed essential to its process. (See Children's Literature, I (1972), Appendix, for details.) Our experience has been that approaching children's literature through the basic functions helps adults escape that segregation and more fully respond to the literature.

Furthermore, as a way of structuring a course, the five functions offer interesting metaphorical perspectives. Thus respiration suggests a literature which enables smothered human beings to breathe freer. All learning is ingestion. Observations derived from this process parallel digestion. Reproduction, most tampered with by society, takes spiritual and other subliminal forms in literature. Excretion or the separation through digestion of unneeded products has its parallel in the many doubles in literature—the Doctor Jekylls and Mr. Hydes, where evil is separated and examined for any negative or positive values it may contain. The problem, then, is to determine which of the various symbols, metaphors, or literary works as a whole is most closely connected with which function. Most of them, of course, are involved in varying degrees in all literature.

Respiration and Children's Literature

One entire genre of literature—the pastoral—has to do with going back to a simpler form of existence, where one can "breathe free" both physically and psychologically. The criticism in this area is vast, and we can only suggest possible ways of applying it to children's literature. One way is to take up in turn the fables, folktales, fiction, fantasy, drama, and rhymes which seem to be concerned with the pastoral.

Skip-rope rhymes are the most basic of children's literary lore, one of the few forms of literature created by children themselves. Evident in these rhymes is the urge to breathe free, the urge for the pastoral, the awareness and fascination with the survival function of breathing. The rhymes may be related to ancient rites—the leaping up may be an attempt to set a corresponding pattern for crops, that they will grow up in the same way—or for children themselves. (See Francelia Butler, The Skip Rope Book, Dial Press: New York, 1963; and "Skip-Rope Rhymes: Some International Variations," Signal, volume 10, Weaver's, Amberly, Glos., England, January, 1973.)

There are little known skip-rope rhymes, such as this one from Greece:

Play is fun
    everywhere
But playing games is double fun
    in the open air.

And this one from Portugal:

Let's do like the olive trees
    Swing and sway in the breeze
When I put my knee on the ground
    Dust comes up all around.

Or this from Luxemburg:

Little rope, little rope, oh my little rope,
Unwind yourself from the round ball;
Twirl round and round and high.
Take me outdoors to the air and the sun,
Out of my room, out of the house, the narrow house;
Nobody can catch us!
Little rope, little rope, oh my little rope,
Unwind yourself from the ball.

From Iran comes a rhyme (for leaping, not necessarily for rope jumping) for the
Noruz (New Year's) celebration, March 21, the first day of spring:

Bright fire of Noruz
    As I leap to and fro
Take away my paleness
    Give me your golden glow.

From Woo Kyung Ho of Seoul, Korea:

Cucumbers are ripening in the fields
    Twelve brothers are hanging on a tendril
Rope, rope, let's jump over the rope and over the moon
    Let's play as friends, as affectionate friends.

And a well-known, subtle, and extremely rhythmic rhyme from England:

The high skip
 The sly skip
  The skip like a feather,
   The long skip
    The strong skip
     The skip all together,
      The slow skip
       The toe skip
        The skip double double,

> The fast skip
> The last skip
> The skip against trouble!

In fiction, Heidi and Robinson Crusoe can be studied. The latter is part of the "island" literature which suggests all stories in which children exist on their own, breathe free through their independence of the parent figures.

In drama, students can act out the pastoral scenes in As You Like It or The Winter's Tale (after all, children were acting in Shakespeare's plays in Shakespeare's day). Or they can express themselves through creative dramatics. Unfortunately, there are few good children's plays. According to the needs listed in Writer's Market, publishers demand plays simultaneously suitable for "church groups, women's clubs, or children," with such additional requirements as "snappy dialogue." One scholar, in attempting to find a good children's play to produce, read over 800 plays published in accordance with these demands, and could not find a single play of real literary quality. (This fact alone might be a comment on how unbasic, or rather, unrelated to children's needs, most children's literature is.)

Ingestion and Children's Literature

The quests in literature have to do with the ingestion of experience (Maslow would label them "self-actualization" needs). Through quests, all human beings can vicariously experience their own struggle, present and future. Perhaps for this reason, one distinguished professor teaches Spenser's Faerie Queene and Pilgrim's Progress as children's literature. Besides these older fantasies, there is the quest of Tolkien's Hobbit, the quest of Winnie-the-Pooh for the North Pole, the quest for self understanding of Toad in the Wind-in-the-Willows, Dorothy's quest in The Wizard of Oz, and Huck's quest on the river—to name but a few. Henry Miller's beautiful story, The Smile at the Foot of the Ladder, has to do with a clown's ingestion of experience.

In folktales, there are all the quests of younger sons—the wonderful quest of Prince Ivan in "The Firebird" story and the quest of the young maiden in "East of the Sun and West of the Moon." In myth, we cite the stories of Ulysses and Aeneas, and Hercules, a hero to whom Shakespeare makes frequent reference. Then there is the legend of Roland, who shows us, symbolically, at least, a way of meeting death head-on: blowing a horn in its face. Irish and Scandinavian cultures are particularly rich in such tales.

Digestion and Children's Literature

Fables—those of Aesop and LaFontaine are particularly well known, and the Hindu and Buddhistic tales deserve to be better known—record a series of brief experiences and then note the lessons digested from these experiences. Fables are told all over the world and can form a fascinating study in comparative children's literature—the direction in which the field is moving, anyway. They are far more influential in human society than has been generally recognized and deserve far more study than they have received.

Fable-like folktales, such as the international story, "The Blanket," allow children and other people to learn tenderness by experiencing vicariously what it is like to be old. (The tale is that of a husband, who, at his neurotic wife's insistence, asks his helpless old father to leave the household. The husband sends his son out to the barn to get a horse-blanket for the old man to take along with him. After a long time, the boy returns with the blanket, jaggedly cut in half. When the father remonstrates, the boy explains, "Daddy, I am saving half of it for you when you get old.") An equally moving fable-like story for children and adults, on another theme—what constitutes true success—is Solzenhitsyn's "Matryona's House."

Fantasy, too, offers lessons. The fate of Hans, Schwarz, and Gluck in The King of the Golden River shows what happens to those who exploit nature and their fellow man, and emphasizes the point of the story—the nature of true wealth. Students can follow along with Dorothy of The Wizard of Oz and digest her experiences—that selfish, capitalist exploitation, such as that of the Wicked Witch of the East, eventually boomerangs, and that many people who are awe-inspiring at a distance—a President in a White House—may turn out on closer inspection to be like the Wizard of Oz—a bit of a fraud. Readers can identify with Beatrix Potter's Peter Rabbit, disregard loving and wise counsel, enter danger zones, and, if very lucky, escape and learn to handle future experiences a little more intelligently.

Excretion and Children's Literature

In Jungian psychology, the shadow—the negative qualities in a human being—can be recognized and creatively used to reinforce the whole personality. Robert Louis Stevenson recognizes the indispensability of the shadow and at the same time, human puzzlement about it in his rhyme:

I have a little shadow that goes in and out with me
    And what can be the use of him is more than I can see.

The shadow is important in American Indian tales. In his book, Indian Tales, Jaime de Angulo beautifully describes the importance of the shadow:

"Mother, what was he singing?"
"Oh, he was singing about his shadow. That song is what the shadow sings. Your shadow, also. You must make him sing that way in the morning. Everybody's shadow comes home in the dawn, singing like that."
"And if he gets lost, what happens then?"
"Then you get sick and you die. You can't keep on living without your shadow."

In Biblical stories, one can discuss those who are twinned in narratives as possible projections of one personality: Cain and Abel, Jacob and Esau. Mirror images in legend can also be seen as shadows: Perseus destroying Medusa by looking at her image reflected in his shield; Narcissus reflected in the water; in folktales, the possible interrelationship between beautiful Snow White and the beautiful, but vain and wicked Queen, looking in the mirror.

Stories such as Thomas Day's Sandford and Merton, Poe's schoolboy, "William Wilson," Stevenson's Dr. Jekyll and Mr. Hyde, Thomas Y. Hughes' Tom Brown and his snobbish enemy are examples of the good-versus-bad personality in fiction. There is Tolstoy's great tale written for children in his last years about Esarhaddon, King of Assyria, who can only see the evil in his own nature objectively when his head is ducked under water.

In fantasy, there is Oscar Wilde's "Selfish Giant"—and the little lame boy, and most pertinent of all, possibly, C. S. Lewis' Last Battle, in which the children on earth are seen as Platonic—imperfect—shadows of their perfect real selves in heaven:

> "The Eagle is right," said Lord Digory. "Listen, Peter. When
> Aslan said you could never go back to Narnia, he meant the Narnia
> you were thinking of. But that was not the real Narnia. That had a
> beginning and an end. It was only a shadow or a copy of the real
> Narnia, which has always been here and always will be here: just as
> our world, England and all, is only a shadow or copy of something
> in Aslan's real world. You need not mourn over Narnia, Lucy. All
> the old Narnia that mattered, all the dear creatures, have been drawn
> into the real Narnia through the Door. And of course it is different;
> as different as a real thing is from a shadow or as waking life is from
> a dream." His voice stirred everyone like a trumpet as he spoke
> these words: but when he added under his breath "It's all in Plato,
> all in Plato: bless me, what do they teach them at these schools!"
> the older ones laughed. It was so exactly like the sort of thing they
> had heard him say long ago in that other world where his beard was
> grey instead of golden.

Reproduction and Children's Literature

It is interesting to relate the many folktales of life beneath the sea to the idea of emergence from and return to the womb. In one such tale, a little boy is running along a sandy shore. He sees a penny, but kicks it aside as too small in value to be worth picking up. Shortly thereafter a beautiful city rises from the sea and he runs across a little bridge and enters it. Along the main street merchants offer him fabulous textiles woven of gold and silver, and silk, and beautiful jewels in exotic settings. Any of these things or all of them he can have for a penny. But he does not have a penny. Then someone explains to him that the city is under a spell, that it rises from the sea once every five hundred years or so and can only remain above water if someone from the world of the living with real money makes a purchase. Sadly the boy goes back on shore and sees the city again sink under the waves, as bells faintly chime from the turrets.

The seminal nature of life as existing in a watery base and the need to form some kind of union with it is also suggested in the New England Indian tale of the boy who stands by the shore and sees a tiny Indian approaching in a canoe. The Indian offers to trade his miniature bow and arrows for the boy's and the boy refuses. Then the boy's grandmother advises him to make the trade—and when the boy follows her advice, the Indian imparts knowledge—that cooked bean-pods are good food. The boy thus learns that sometimes there is knowledge beyond the actual experience—the trade—and he initiates, to commemorate this understanding, the Indians' string-bean festival. (This story is told as it was related by Princess Redwing, a member of the Narragansett tribe in Hope Valley, Rhode Island.)

Among ballads, there is "Sir Patrick Spens." In poetry, Arnold's "Forsaken Merman." In fantasy, Andersen's "Little Mermaid." The choice in all literature is vast. There are also the folktales about frog princes and legends of gods beneath the sea.

Another approach to reproduction as a theme in children's literature can be through the cyclical movement in music—the folk "rounds" such as "Row, row, row your boat," "Ring around the Roses," "Round and Round the Mulberry Bush." There are all the folktales about magic rings, and stories that have a cyclical movement, structurally, with the quest ending and the hero returning, mission fulfilled. In fiction there is Robert H. Charles' story, A Roundabout Turn: a toad who wants to see the world accidentally gets on a merry-go-round and decides that the world makes him sick. And Gertrude Stein's The World is Round: "she would carve on the tree Rose is a Rose is a Rose is a Rose is a Rose until it went all the way round."

In fantasy, one can take up the cyclical nature of the stories of immortality— of being reunited with a loved person, as Antoine de St. Exupèry's Little Prince is reunited, through death, with his rose. Immortality exists in a circular well in a strange Vietnamese folktale. God stations himself at the bottom and calls up for those who believe in him to make the leap of faith down into his arms. But people are afraid: they tentatively dip their fingertips and their hair in the water —and this is all the immortality they ever have: their nails and their hair continue to grow after death.

Poetry with a circular motion includes Blake's "Spring," "The Lamb," and "The Echoing Green"—favorites of many children and adults. Often rhymes, including limericks, go in a circle. Edward Lear's limericks are brief dramatic tales of sad experiences with society and the way it smothers and confines the individual from beginning to end:

There was an old person of Bar
That passed all her life in a jar
Which was painted pea green
To appear more serene,
That placid old person of Bar.

Similarly, there is the plight of the "old man who when little / Fell casually into a kettle," and "the old man of Hongkong / Who never did anything wrong," and "the young person in green / Who seldom was fit to be seen."

Perhaps the neglect until recently of children's literature by scholars in the Humanities may turn out to be a blessing in disguise. With as yet no status quo in the field, methods of teaching the subject can be flexible—as various, unorthodox, and unpredictable as children's books themselves. It is in this spirit that we offer our own approach.

Marilyn Apseloff, an assistant professor of English at Kent State University, teaches children's literature.

Daniel L. Ater is head of the Storymime Theatre in Storrs, Connecticut. He completed his dramatic training at the Asolo Theatre in Sarasota, Florida.

Jan Bakker teaches in the English Department at the University of Tennessee, Knoxville. While teaching in the Far Eastern branch of the University of Maryland, he made a study of children's literature in Taiwan, Korea, and Japan.

Robert J. Bator, Ph. D., Loyola University, is an associate professor at Olive-Harvey College of the City Colleges of Chicago.

Susan E. Bittker is an Honors Student at the University of Connecticut. One of her special interests is Gertrude Stein and her circle.

Marcella Spann Booth, Ph. D., University of Texas, is a specialist in modern poetry. She prepared, in collaboration with Ezra Pound, From Confucius to Cummings An Anthology of Poetry (New Directions).

Bennett A. Brockman, Ph. D., Vanderbilt University, is a specialist in medieval literature at the University of Connecticut.

Francelia Butler, Ph. D. English, University of Virginia, teaches children's literature and Shakespeare in the English Department of the University of Connecticut.

Annabelle Simon Cahn is a visiting lecturer in art history at Yale University.

Glauco Cambon, Ph. D., University of Pavia, subsequently studied at Columbia on a Fulbright-Hays Fellowship. He is widely known for his criticism of Dante and modern American and British poetry and for his work in comparative literature.

Joseph Cary is the author of Three Modern Italian Poets: Saba, Ungaretti, Montale (New York University Press, 1969). He is contemplating a critical edition of Lewis Carroll's Sylvie and Bruno.

Nancy Chambers is editor of Signal Approaches to Children's Books (Weaver's, Amberley, Glos. GL 5 5BA, England, published three times a year). She is also the managing editor of Young Drama (P. O. Box 2, Stroud, Glos. GL 5 5BE, England, published three times a year by the Thimble Press in association with Heinemann Educational Books).

Charity Chang is head of the Serials Department, Wilbur Cross Library, University of Connecticut.

Leslie A. Fiedler, Samuel L. Clemens Professor at the State University of New York at Buffalo, is a critic and author of The Stranger in Shakespeare (1972) and many other works.

Rachel Fordyce specialized in children's theater at Northwestern University before receiving her doctorate in English from the University of Pittsburgh. She is an assistant professor at Virginia Polytechnic and State University, Blacksburg, Virginia.

J. C. Furnas, prolific writer of volumes and articles on social history, is best known to those in children's literature for his Voyage to Windward: The Life of Robert Louis Stevenson.

Laurence Gagnon, a former Woodrow Wilson Fellow, teaches in the Department of Philosophy and Religion, Colgate University.

Martin Gardner, author of over one-hundred scientific and critical works, is perhaps best known to those in the field of children's literature for his Annotated Alice and his introductions to several "Oz" books by L. Frank Baum. He also wrote eighty short stories for Humpty-Dumpty.

Donald Gibson, Ph. D., Brown University, is the author of The Fiction of Stephen Crane (Southern Illinois Press, 1969); co-editor with Carol Anselment, Black and White Stories of American Life (Washington Square Press, 1971); editor, Five Black Writers (New York University Press, 1970); and editor, Modern Black Poetry (Prentice-Hall, 1973).

John Graham, Ph. D., Johns Hopkins University, is assistant dean of the College of Arts and Sciences of the University of Virginia. He has written for The Massachusetts Review, Journal of the History of Ideas, Modern Fiction Studies, and is the editor of several volumes in his field.

David L. Greene, head of the English Department of Piedmont College, Demorest, Georgia, is completing his doctoral dissertation at the University of Pennsylvania. He is editor of The Baum Bugle.

Jacequeline Guéron, Ph. D., Harvard University, taught at Rutgers University and Barbard College before joing the staff of the Département of d'Anglo-Américajn of the Faculté de Vincennes, Paris, where she teaches English linguistics.

Joan Joffe Hall, Ph. D., Stanford University, is a prolific reviewer for newspapers and magazines. She is very active in the Women's Liberation Movement and teaches courses in women in literature.

Bernard Horn is a poet and an assistant professor of English at North Essex Community College, Haverhill, Massachusetts.

Lee Jacobus, Ph. D., Claremont Graduate School, is especially interested in Milton and the English literature of the seventeenth century.

Anne Jordan teaches children's literature at Western Michigan University, Kalamazoo. She is executive secretary of the Children's Literature Association.

Marcia R. Lieberman, Ph. D., Brandeis University, is a specialist in feminist criticism, including the feminine in fairy tales.

Alison Lurie, novelist and critic, teaches, among other subjects, children's literature at Cornell University.

James H. Matthews, Ph.D., Vanderbilt University, teaches at Eckerd College, St. Petersburg, Florida. His field is Irish literature. He recently returned from a year in Ireland, where he held a National Endowment for the Humanities fellowship.

William Robert McMunn, Ph.D., Indiana University, specializes in linguistics and the medieval period.

J. Bruce W. McWilliams is a graduate student in English at Georgetown University, Washington, D.C.

Milton Meltzer, chairman of the Children's Book Committee of the Author's Guild, New York City, has long been known for his books on civil rights, including those he co-authored with Langston Hughes, and the series on women's rights, which he edits for Thomas Y. Crowell.

Leonard R. Mendelsohn, Ph.D., University of Wisconsin, is an associate professor of English at Sir George Williams University, Montreal, and teaches in the Rabbinical College of Canada.

Michael Michanczyk is a professional puppeteer from Plantsville, Connecticut.

Robert G. Miner, Jr. is the first student of liberal arts at the University of Connecticut to write a doctoral dissertation ("Aesop in England") in the field of children's literature. He has taught children's literature and has conducted MLA seminars in the field.

Francis J. Molson, Ph.D., University of Notre Dame, teaches children's literature in the English Department of Central Michigan University, Mount Pleasant, Michigan.

John S. Morris is Colgate Professor of Humanities and Director of University Studies at Colgate University, Hamilton, New York.

Ruth B. Moynihan is a student of history in the doctoral program at Yale University. She is the mother of seven children.

William T. Moynihan is head of the English Department, the University of Connecticut.

Kenneth Muir, King Alfred Professor of Literature at the University of Liverpool, is an actor, director, critic, playwright, and editor of Shakespeare Survey.

Russel B. Nye, distinguished professor of English at Michigan State University, received a Pulitzer Prize for biography. He is interested in American cultural history and is a former president of the Popular Culture Association.

J. Donald O'Hara, Ph.D., Harvard University, has made a special study of modern and romantic literature. He has published in Book World, Saturday Review, New Yorker, and elsewhere.

254